LANDSCAPE DETAILING

Volume 3 STRUCTURES

LANDSCAPE DETAILING

Volume 3   STRUCTURES

Third Edition   Michael Littlewood

Architectural Press

Architectural Press
An imprint of Butterworth-Heinemann
Linacre House, Jordan Hill, Oxford OX2 8DP
225 Wildwood Avenue, Woburn, MA 01801-2041
A division of Reed Educational and Professional Publishing Ltd

A member of the Reed Elsevier plc group

OXFORD   BOSTON   JOHANNESBURG
MELBOURNE   NEW DELHI   SINGAPORE

Third edition 1997
Reprinted 1998

British Library Cataloguing in Publication Data
A catalogue record for this book is available from
the British Library

Library of Congress Cataloguing in Publication Data
A catalogue record for this book is available from
the Library of Congress

ISBN 0 7506 2320 9

Composition by Scribe Design, Gillingham, Kent
Printed and bound in Great Britian

CONTENTS

Volume 3   STRUCTURES

FOREWORD

It has always been the intention to produce a third book of *Landscape Detailing* dealing with Structures. The success of the first two – Surfaces and Enclosures in the third edition – has prompted this publication.

In case the reader has not seen the previous publications some parts of the text are repeated to ensure clarification for the purpose of the book.

Many landscape architects, architects, other professionals and students responsible for the production of drawn details and specifications for landscape construction works have a need for ready reference. This book has been produced to meet that need and it can be extended by additional sheets. It has been arranged for ease of copying of sheets and it is sufficiently flexible for designers to use the details for their specific requirements.

The range of materials for external works and their possible combinations for structures would make it impossible to provide a definitive book of details.

It is not the intention of this book to supplant the designer's own skill and experience, which is vital to the success of any project. This is still essential in evaluating the site conditions, assessing the character of the environment and creating sensitive design solutions.

It is hoped that the book, if used correctly, will allow the designer to spend more time on design details, avoiding the need to produce repetitive drawings for basic construction elements. It has been found that the details can be very useful for costing purposes and to support the preliminary design when presented to a client. To assist the designer and to save further time in writing specifications, simple check lists for these have been included, where appropriate, in this edition along with technical guidance notes and tables.

The compilation of specifications for Structures is much more arduous than for Surfaces and Enclosures, particularly where reclaimed materials and/or basic methods of construction are used.

Design information has been excluded; many other publications deal with this subject much more adequately than could be achieved in this book. General comments on appearance have been given only where it was felt appropriate.

ACKNOWLEDGEMENTS

I must give particular thanks to many people who have supported me in some way – no matter how small – and who have encouraged me to complete this third edition, which has been greatly enlarged to include structures.

My particular thanks must go to Butterworth-Heinemann – my publishers – who have supported my work and put up with so many frustrating delayed publishing dates. Thank you for being so patient. Also to landscape architects Andrew Clegg, Donna Young and many staff members of my former private practice in Bristol. A very special thanks must go to Paul Brian, Landscape Architect, for his valued assistance on the sketches; to Mike Bird, Architectural Draughtsman, for drawing many detail sheets; and to Mark Bailey and Jack Cunningham, students at Southampton Institute for the CAD drawings.

My appreciation must also go to Barrie Evans of the *Architect's Journal* for allowing the reproduction of the details on roofs, and to the Editor *L.D.* for allowing the article by James Hitchmough to be included. A very sincere and special thanks to the publishers of 'Time Saver Standards for Landscape Architecture' and also to the Countryside Commission for Scotland, both for their permission to use material on Decks and Bridges. A very special thanks to Mary Coles for typing the text and correcting it so many times.

I am also very grateful to Paul Brian and Fiona Hopes for checking the final manuscript and making helpful comments.

All of the above have contributed to this book to ensure that it eventually reaches the publishers, after such a long time.

INTRODUCTION

The landscape detail sheets have been produced in an effort to eliminate needless repetition in detailing landscape works covering hard elements. It is possible to use them without alteration, but in some cases minor modifications and additions to dimensions or specifications may be necessary. Lettering has been standardised by the use of a stencil (italic 3.5 mm). When a detail is required which is not available on a detail sheet, the new detail can be drawn by the designer using the standardised format, which will enable it to be added to the original collection of details and to be easily re-used on other projects. Readers are invited to send the publishers copies of their own details which they think would merit inclusion in future editions of this book. Appropriate acknowledgement will be made.

Each sheet portrays a detail without reference to its surroundings. This approach has been adopted because it affords to each detail the maximum number of possibilities for re-use. No attempt has been made to recommend a particular detail for a particular situation. This remains the responsibility of the landscape architect, architect or designer.

There are, of course, a great many other details which might be included on specific projects or in specific situations. In some cases, the detailing of site elements and site structures can be coordinated very carefully with the architect or building designer in order to ensure a uniformity of form and material. In yet other instances, various agencies and organisations may have standard details which must be used on their particular projects.

Notes

The notes which precede each section are intended to give only the briefest outline of main points. For more detailed guidance, the publications listed in Appendices A and B should be consulted.

Specifications

Specifications should not be written without a knowledge of the content of the relevant British Standards in Appendix C. Some British Standards contain alternative specifications which may prove more suitable in a particular case.

The task in writing specifications has now been made very much easier by the use of the word processor. Nevertheless, if a specification is to serve its purpose efficiently it must be concise and accurate, otherwise it could be misunderstood by all the people involved in the project.

To assist the designer and to ensure that he or she makes the minimum of omissions, a simple check list has been provided after the notes for each chapter or section. Ease of access to a particular section will encourage a contractor to read the specification and to conform with its requirements. So many contractors ignore the specifications and use only the bills of quantities. Probably the best way to ensure that the completed specification is satisfactory is for the designer to read it as if he or she were the contractor and could complete the project accordingly. Reference should be made to two main sources for specifications, namely the NBS of Newcastle-upon-Tyne and the publication *Specification*. Full details of their services are given in the Appendices.

Use of the detail sheets

The collection of detail sheets, as purchased, may, if users wish, be photocopied, punched and stored in a ring binder. The detail sheets have been laid out in such a way as to facilitate this operation. In the form of individual leaves the details can easily be traced or copy negatives can be made.

The sheets must be used in conjunction with a site layout drawing, preferably at

1:200. These may be more than one sheet, depending upon the size of the project. The layout drawings will convey all information on levels, directions of falls and setting-out dimensions. They also indicate the location of the elected details and the deployment of structural finishes. (See Figure 1.)

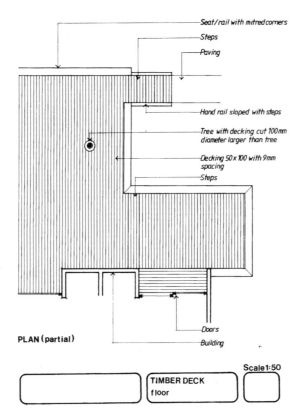

PLAN (partial)

Seat/rail with mitred corners
Steps
Paving
Hand rail sloped with steps
Tree with decking cut 100mm diameter larger than tree
Decking 50 x 100 with 9mm spacing
Steps
Doors
Building

Scale 1:50

TIMBER DECK
floor

Simple conjunction of details (for example, a deck with steps and a handrail) can be indicated on section and elevation drawings quite easily. (See Figure 2.)

Standards

British Standards and Codes of Practice are referred to where necessary. Users of this book living in countries where British Standards are not used should delete the reference to the British Standard and, if they feel it necessary, either insert a reference to an equivalent national standard or describe what is required in empirical terms.

Production of new detail sheets

Where the use of a detail not included in the original collection of detail sheets is required, the new detail can be produced on A4 tracing paper using a standard format. This will enable it to be added to the original collection and to be easily re-used. New details will be assigned a reference number by the design office, using their own reference system. The title of the new detail, as shown in the centre label at the foot of the drawing, can then be added to the contents list prefacing each section.

Issue of detail sheets

Detail sheets can be used in two ways. A set of photocopies can be issued to the contractor of the selected details, after completion of the title panel reference, and number-stamping each detail with the office stamp. The second method is to trace or copy a batch of details, grouped according to type and identified with key numbers, onto an A1 sheet of tracing paper and include the drawing with the contract set in the normal way.

Design detailing

The creation of good design can only come from the designer, and no amount of drawn details can be a substitute for this fact. The principles must be followed as Frazer Reekie has stated in his book *Design in the Built Environment:*

To make an objective assessment of a design, or to set about the process of designing, consideration has to be given to the three aspects which may be summarised as:

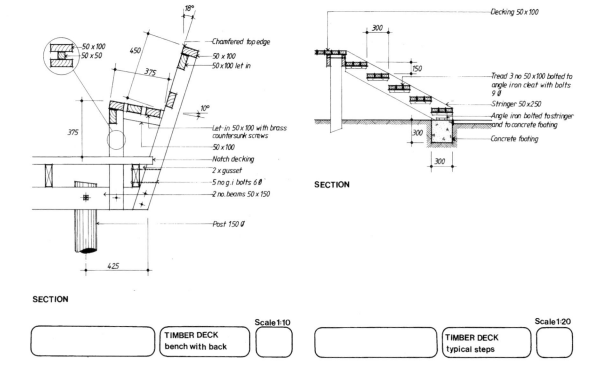

SECTION

Scale 1:10

TIMBER DECK
bench with back

SECTION

Scale 1:20

TIMBER DECK
typical steps

1. Function: The satisfying of requirements of use or purpose;
2. Structure: The physical implementation of function by the best available material(s), construction, manufacture and skills as conditions permit.
3. Appearance: The obtaining of satisfactory visual effects (sometimes referred to as 'aesthetic values').

Other words can be used to describe these three aspects but, on analysis, whatever words are used it will be found that almost every writer on building design, which may be extended to cover the built environment, is dealing with the same three fundamentals.

These three constituent parts of design are closely interrelated and each, to a greater or lesser extent, according to the nature of the subject, influences the others. An urban composition or a building or a detail that is truly well designed is one in the creation of which all three aspects have been fully considered and integrated. Integration may well be the key-word in good design. Not only does it mean the correct combining of parts into a whole but it implies, by association with integrity, soundness and honesty.

PERGOLAS, ARBOURS, ARCHES AND LYCH GATES

Definition

A *Pergola* is more often than not a directional structure that is leading from one space to another, drawing the eye down its length to a focal point, an entrance or for a framed view. They are often free-standing, long and tunnel shaped.

An *Arbour* (Arbor) is a static place, providing shelter to sit beneath a shady alcove. Usually it is connected to a building although it could be free-standing.

An *Arch* is usually a curved structure to an opening in a wall, fence or hedge, or it could be free-standing. A series of arches supporting or set along a wall becomes an arcade.

All three structures usually have open or semi-solid roofs.

A *Lych gate* (Lich gate) is a roofed gateway to a churchyard where traditionally the coffin awaited the clergyman's arrival under cover from the elements. Therefore its depth is determined by the average length of the coffin although modern church landscapes appear not to have this facility.

Pergola

The design of a pergola should reflect the mood and period of the buildings near it and echo the style and architectural features. The structure should look integrated by echoing the use of the materials in its construction.

The proportions of the pergola need to be considered carefully, particularly the horizontal to width relationship against the structure's overall dimension and the human form. The height of the verticals should be at least 2.50 m, but this will vary according to their spacing and the dimension of the materials as well as the type of vines selected which will eventually provide the bulk of plant growth.

Pergolas being linear are logical structures for walkways where they can provide cool fragrant shade or even edible fruits.

The shape of the structure can be rectangular or square, positioned over hard or soft surfacing. It can be designed to follow the line of a path or fit into a corner against a boundary wall or fence. More elaborate designs are feasible such as changes in overall height in order to transverse a slope or cover a flight of steps, or even building it on a stepped base.

The appearance of a pergola can vary by using stone or brick piers with timber beams. Variations in the height of the beams can provide a more interesting effect. Round columns or posts with round beams can provide a more natural look, the size of materials can determine a heavy (telegraph type poles) or light (bamboo poles) structure.

When the piers or columns are of masonry it is very important to provide a substantial roof structure. If it is too flimsy it will look out of scale.

Entrances to pergolas can be emphasised by using architectural type plants in containers (of good design) or a pair of urns or vases, or even create a small shaped wing wall. It is also possible to construct a roughly circular pergola, using short roof timbers to connect the posts, arranged around a central feature.

A free-standing structure such as a pergola can, because of its height, appear to loom over surrounding features. Equally if it is sited in a large open grass area it could look marooned or it may even block views from a building.

It is essential to site a pergola where it can blend with its surroundings or be part of the overall framework of the design. Because the structure is essentially angular it is essential to align it with straight sided features such as walls, fences or buildings to avoid it looking disjointed.

A sunny aspect is important if vines or fruit trees are to be trained against the pergola, and one of its long sides should face a southerly or easterly direction where it will receive sun for most of the day. It should not be sited in a location that is predominantly shaded by tall trees or buildings, or near a wall where it will receive little or no sunlight.

If the pergola is to be erected on a sloping or terraced site, the top of the structure must be stepped to follow the gradient; otherwise it will appear too lofty.

Pleached trees could also create pergolas, some like laburnum have yellow flowers in springtime while hornbeam or lime can provide dense shade even on the hottest day.

Arbours

There is usually no sharp break between the interior of the building and the exterior of the garden/landscape. The two tend to overlap in the area immediately around the building. This is where the need for the extension of the building roof for overhead protection is required and to provide protection from climatic extremes.

The arbour can supplement the building extending it into the landscape, making it feel larger, easing and strengthening the connection.

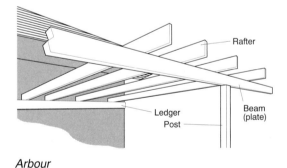

Arbour

The design should reflect the architectural character of the building and if possible it should be considered with the initial construction so that it does not look added on as so many do today. However, where this is not possible and the arbour is added on long after the construction of the building, greater architectural importance is necessary. It can be built as an independent structure but more often than not it then becomes a gazebo.

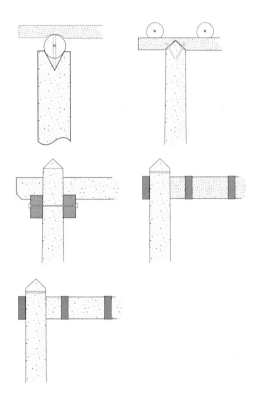

Typical pergola post and beam

Arbours should be structurally sound, and they also should look sound. The smallest post for any structure of this type would be 100 × 100, 100 × 150 is much better. If metal posts are used, the size is still important. Steel posts used for this purpose are usually square or rectangular tubes. These posts will need to be set on a frost-free concrete footing. The footing needs to rise above the soil line in order to keep the base of the post dry and so help slow rust. Many times, it is better to build a column out of 25 × 250 boards to give both a good scale for outdoors and plenty of strength. If this type of column is constructed then it must be capped or covered with copper or aluminium flashing to shed water and to stop birds from nesting inside the post.

The overlap of the architectural and landscape space is obvious and requires careful design treatment specific to the site and the needs of the users.

Typical arbour layouts

ARCHES AND LYCH GATES

Arches have played a very important part in the celebration of major events in towns and cities throughout the world. Likewise they are equally important at the smaller scale in landscape and garden projects particularly at the entrance to an area.

Arches can be elegant and intricate with or without a covering of plants. They can be made from a wide range of materials such as brick, stone, metal, plastic and timber. Arches can be a single depth structure that is part of a fence with a gateway feature or be much more substantial to include a small seat or mail/milk/parcel box depending upon its location.

The arch has for far too long not been given the attention it deserves by designers particularly where the site offers excellent opportunities for it to be constructed. Scale is the most important aspect to consider and it would be easy to make the mistake of making an arch without thinking about its proportions especially if purchasing a ready made structure.

Lych gates are an extension of the archway because they usually have a solid roof. There appears to be no reason why such a structure should not be used in contemporary landscapes where small groups of people could gather on their way to or from a building other than a church, especially prior to entering a parking area for cars and coaches. Lych gates should be built of materials that link to the main building on a site unless the structure requires it to be an obvious focal point in the landscape.

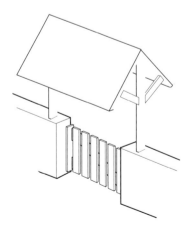

Lych gate

CONSTRUCTION

Basic Structure

Pergolas, arbours and arches are basically built of strong timber posts or metal columns with an arrangement of cross pieces of timber or metal which form an open roof. The sides are usually left open although they can be clad with trellis panels, fence panels or translucent plastic sheeting depending upon the degree of protection required.

Timber

Most structures are of post and beam design. Posts, properly spaced to provide adequate support, are set in the ground or securely connected to a firm foundation. The posts support horizontal beams (plates) which in turn support the roof rafters at right angles to the beams. Some structures are attached to existing buildings and a modification of the basic post and beam construction is used. A ledger strip is attached to the existing building. The building performs the function of the posts, and the rafters rest directly on the ledger strip.

Setting posts for support

Post Sizes – For most garden shelters, 100 × 100 posts are sufficiently large in size. On larger structures, bigger posts are sometimes necessary to support heavier roof loads and still maintain wide post spacing. 50 × 100 or 50 × 150 are sometimes used in tandem with a spacer block between them to form a column instead of a solid post.

Posts in the Ground – The simplest method of anchoring the post is to set it directly in the ground. For most structures, firmly tamped earth around the post will give sufficient rigidity. If the soil is sandy or unstable, a concrete collar should be poured around the post after it has been placed in the hole and earth tamped around the base.

The depth to which posts should be set depends on the soil conditions and wind load. 900 is adequate for most 2.40–3.0 m high structures, but it may be necessary to

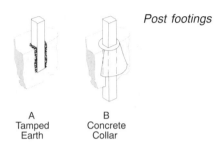

Post footings

A
Tamped
Earth

B
Concrete
Collar

set the posts deeper for higher shelters. When posts are set in the ground, the floor of the structure may be a wood deck, gravel, paving blocks, grass or earth. If a concrete slab is to be poured as the shelter floor, the posts are anchored to the slab rather than set in the ground.

Posts on Concrete – Three common methods are illustrated here. Patented post anchors of many types, available at most local building supply dealers, may be embedded in concrete. These provide positive anchorage of the post to the concrete. The nailing block method is where the post is toenailed to a wood block set in concrete. The nailing block is usually less secure, however, than a metal anchor bolted through the post.

When a concealed anchorage is desired, the drift pin is often used. A small space should be left between the bottom of the post and the concrete surface to avoid the accumulation of moisture and dirt.

Where the shelter is to be built above an existing wood deck, the posts may be placed over the existing support members of the deck. The posts should be firmly anchored with angle fasteners.

All metal parts used in connection with wood must be corrosion resistant to avoid staining.

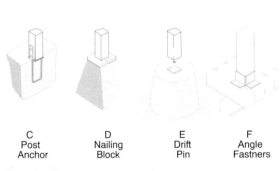

C
Post
Anchor

D
Nailing
Block

E
Drift
Pin

F
Angle
Fastners

Post footings

Connecting posts and beams

The beams support the roof rafters and tie the posts together, giving rigidity to the structure. To perform these functions properly, the beams must be adequately connected to the posts. Where design permits, the best bearing is achieved when the beam is placed directly on top of the post.

Several methods of connection are possible. A patented post cap is useful where the beam is the same width as the post. A wood cleat can also be used in connecting beams to posts. When the beam is smaller than the width of the post, it may be bolted to the post singly or in pairs. When 50 mm wood is used in tandem with a wood spacer block to form a column, a 50 mm thick horizontal member may be bolted between the two parts of the column.

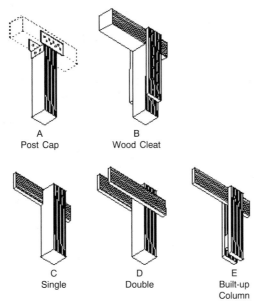

A
Post Cap

B
Wood Cleat

C
Single

D
Double

E
Built-up
Column

Beam connections

Installing the rafters

Rafters support the finished roof or may be used alone without further elements to create a roof pattern.
The method of installing rafters varies with the manner in which they meet the beam.

Most common is to have the rafters resting on top of the supporting member and toenailed or anchored to it by some other conventional method. Rafters may also be notched to lower roof height.
Rafters for either a flat or sloping roof which are to be flush with the top of the beam may be attached in one of several ways: a patented metal rafter hanger; a wood ledger strip nailed under the rafter for support, or the rafter can be toenailed and nailed from reverse side of beam.
When rafters extend from an existing building, they may be attached either flush or on top of a ledger strip fastened to the building. It is important that the ledger strip be bolted or securely fastened to the existing structure if it is to give the necessary support to the rafters.

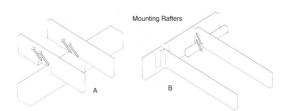

Mounting Rafters

A

B

Rafter details

Some roofing materials or methods require cross supports between rafters. This may be achieved by nailing blocking between the members.

Roofing possibilities

A wide variety of materials can be used for the roof. Shingles or shakes, reed fencing, bamboo, window screening, lath, louvres, canvas, glass or plastic can be used for covering. In most instances, only nailing is required for installation. The roofing material should harmonise with the nearby structures. A lath or slat roof creates shadows while letting light penetrate and breaks the wind without stopping vertical air circulation. The lath members might be anything from a slim 12 × 75 mm batten to a 50 mm thick piece. Generally widths more than 150 mm are not used as roof slats.

The roof slats are usually spaced at a distance equal to the width of one of the slats. Sometimes 50 mm thick material is used as slatting, allowing greater spans between rafters but requiring stronger rafters due to the greater weight on each rafter.

It may be desirable to make the roof slats removable. In such a situation they can be attached to a framework which fastens to the rafters in sections.

One very popular type of overhead shelter is the eggcrate. The eggcrate is composed of horizontal roof supports at right angles to one another, with equal spacing in both directions. Normally the rafters in each direction are the same depth and thickness and are flush on the underside. Two methods of constructing the eggcrate are shown.

In the first method rafters are placed in one direction and blocking nailed between them to form a straight line. Blocking can be secured by toenailing or nailing through the ends of the block from the other side of the rafters. Mortising is another method for constructing an eggcrate. This is used where the span is not large or the members are of sufficient size. Members in one direction are notched to fit complementary notches in the cross-members. The resulting joints should be flush on both planes.

Both the eggcrate and lath overheads may be covered over with another material, such as canvas, plastic or matting for more shade or protection from the elements. Some landscaping situations suggest a trellis or colonnade instead of a rectangular shelter. Posts are placed in a single line, either straight or curved, and crossbars to support the trellis are fastened to the posts at right angles in the same manner as beams. In this type of construction it is highly recommended that the posts be set in the ground for the stability which this method of anchoring offers. Diagonal bracing of the crossbars to the posts is recommended for added stability. The connecting rafters or trellis are nailed to the crossbars parallel to a line between the posts. Additional layers of lath or treillage may be added as desired.

The roof is usually fitted with additional supports for climbers, in the form of cane poles, trellis, mesh or line wires stretched between eyebolts. It is important that the main roof beams are made of strong timber so it can support a person's weight. Snow, especially when combined with a climber, can be very heavy and the structure must be able to withstand this loading.

Walls

Most structures have at least one wall, either solid or louvered, for privacy and protection against weather and insects. The climate will determine whether or not to completely enclose it.

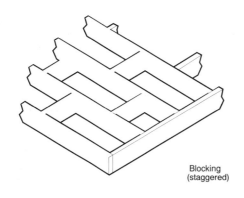

Blocking
(staggered)

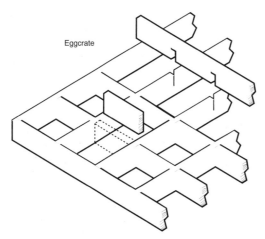

Eggcrate

Rafter details

In areas where winds are strong, walls in a structure will provide strength against racking, and diagonal bracing may not be needed. If walls are not desired in spite of prevalent winds, diagonal bracing or shear panels should be used at corners.

Floor

The type of flooring will depend on its location. If the structure is adjacent to an existing outdoor building or feature, it is often practical and attractive to make the floor similar to it, taking into account the weather.

A wood deck makes a fast-draining, easily maintained floor and can extend beyond the limits of a structure. Posts can also serve as supports for the deck framing. And on a site that is not level, a wood deck eliminates the necessity of grading. See Chapter 3 – Decks, Boardwalks.

The information for the construction has been supplied by the California Redwood Association Data Sheet 3C2-3 which is gratefully acknowledged.

MATERIALS

The two main materials used in the construction of pergolas, arbours and arches are timber and metal, although stone and brick is often included for columns.

Brick, stone, block

Where the pergola, arbour, arch or lych gate is to have its supports built of brick, stone or block then reference should be made to Landscape Detailing 1 Enclosures for construction details.

It is important to consider the fixings of the roof members to the columns which can be metal fasteners connected to both elements. Keep the roof members off the columns to allow free drainage of rainwater, ensuring a fall on the top of the columns.

Timber – Posts should be set solidly in the ground or on footings for simple bracing. It is essential that they are substantial and of adequate size for the loads and spans that they must carry. Beams should be horizontal and accurate.

Metal – Metal, in all its many structural forms can be used for frames, which are lighter and stronger than wood.

The techniques are primarily those of plumbing and welding. The parts are usually best made up completely in the workshop, which means that they must be more carefully designed beforehand. Metal is not so flexible as wood on the job. Iron and steel must be finished very carefully with paint or galvanising to avoid rusting. Frameworks of both wood and metal must be designed both for their own appearance, and for the lath, siding, plywood, or other panel material, or glass, plastic, wire screen, or netting which may be added to them. Metal will cost more than wood, therefore it is used only where extra strength or thinner members are required. Stone and brick columns must be carefully built with accurate levels and joints, as these are far more noticeable to the observer.

Nails and hardware

It is important to use corrosion resistant nails and other fastenings in the construction. Use only stainless steel, aluminium or quality hot-dipped galvanised fastenings. Common iron and steel fastenings or those galvanised by some other process are likely to corrode on exposure to weather, causing unattractive stains and loss of strength and holding power.

Plant supports

Several options are available:
Trellis Panels – These can be used both on the sides and on the roof by fixing them to the main framework.
Line Wires – Galvanised wire, coated with plastic, can be fixed between the posts and the existing top and additional bottom rails to form a vertical, horizontal or criss-crossing form of support for plants. The line

wires should be secured with staples or nails. Alternatively, use screw-in vine eyes to attach the wires.

Mesh – Plastic-coated chain link mesh fencing can be stretched to fit across the pergola framework and secured with staples. Alternatively, choose a lightweight geotextile mesh which can be fixed in the same way.

It is important to design structures to suit specific vines, select vines to suit specific structures, or design both together to solve specific problems. For instance, wisteria will cover as much as an acre of ground, and is very long-lived; therefore it should be planted only on large strong structures which are expected to remain in place for many years. Star jasmine, on the other

Galvanised Chain Link-
or plastic mesh stapled
to the pergola posts and
cross-rails.

Line Wires-
stretched vertically, horizontally
or in criss-cross fasion from
eyes fixed to the pergola.

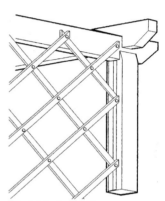

Prefabricated Trellis-
in diamond or square pattern
cut to fit across the posts
and nailed on.

Plant supports

When the climbers have become established, support their heavy stems by tying them to lead or plastic-headed wall nails, driven into the main supporting timbers of the structure.

Strength of construction is important if plants are to be used on a structure especially as they have more weight than other plants of equal size because they support none of their own weight.

If the structure is in an open windy location the wind causes the foliage of the plant to act as a sail and causes constant movement that will gradually work the structure's joints loose.

It is better to bolt the major joints with strap metal or galvanised fasteners. Posts should be set in concrete below the frost line, for best results.

hand, will not climb much above 3.0 m, and is suited to modest structures and intimate scale.

Vines are very apt to be messy in tight spots, to build up mounds of dead wood which are very difficult to clear out, to rot, distort, or undermine construction and cause leaks in a roof.

PLANNING AND BUILDING REGULATIONS

The Local Authority should be consulted before structures are designed, if they are being added after construction of the main buildings. Often there are special rules about when an additional structure is considered to be attached to the main building, when a part of it, and when not.

Or there may be special ways of determining whether or not a structure comes under the provisions of regulations. Again, there may be special rules governing how far such elements may project into front, side, or rear areas or what proportion such structures may occupy.

For example, in some areas one may build an open frame arbour without permit, setting the posts in the ground as for a fence. If one should then decide to place any sort of solid roofing over the top of this arbour it becomes a roofed structure in the eyes of the Planning Department. It then comes under building regulations, and may have to have its posts cut off and separated from the ground by concrete. Immediately, of course, the structure will lose its rigidity and will have to have an entirely new bracing system, and so on. Such problems are best avoided by foresight.

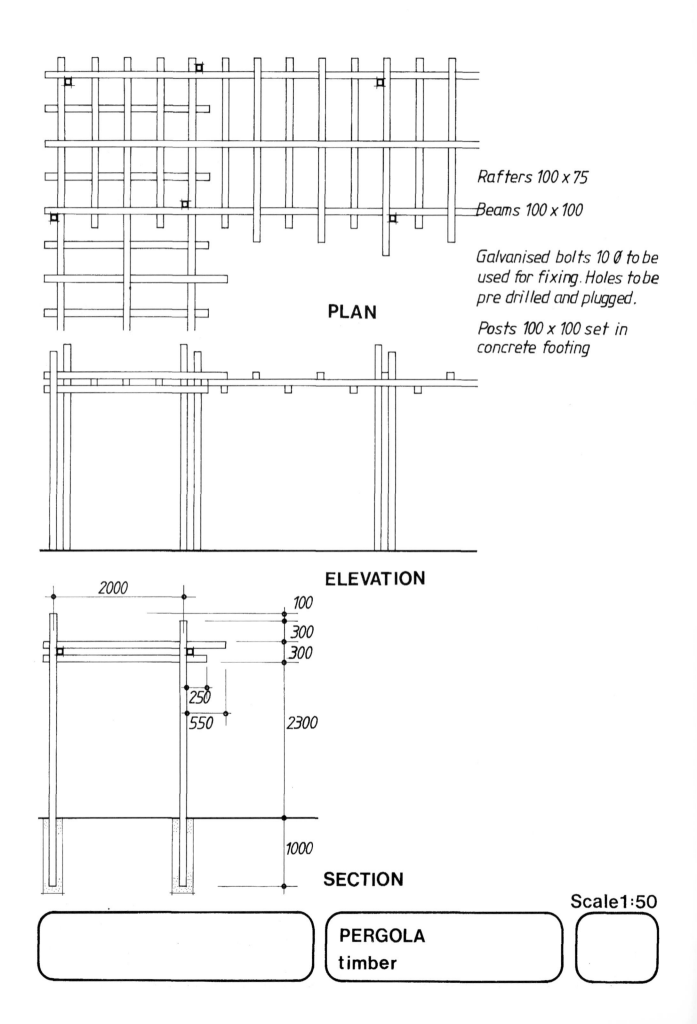

PLAN

Rafters 100 x 75

Beams 100 x 100

Galvanised bolts 10 Ø to be
used for fixing. Holes to be
pre drilled and plugged.

Posts 100 x 100 set in
concrete footing

ELEVATION

2000

100

300

300

250

550

2300

1000

SECTION

PERGOLA
timber

Scale 1:50

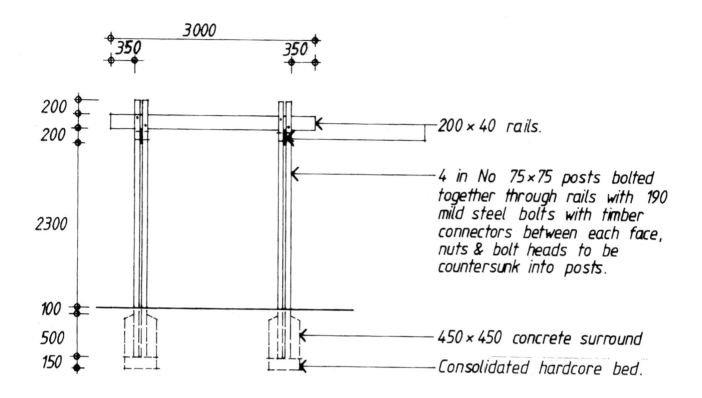

ELEVATION

- 200 × 40 rails.

- 4 in No 75×75 posts bolted together through rails with 190 mild steel bolts with timber connectors between each face, nuts & bolt heads to be countersunk into posts.

- 450 × 450 concrete surround

- Consolidated hardcore bed.

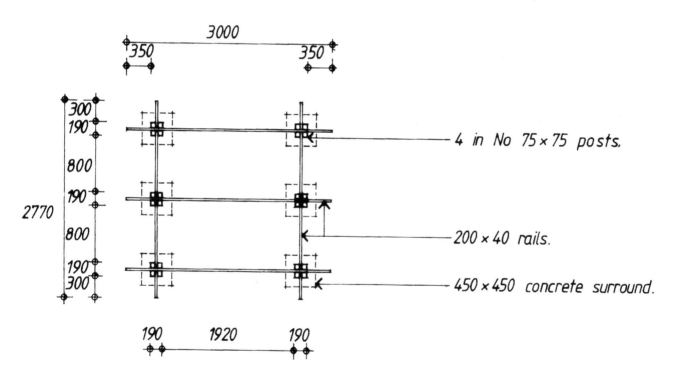

PLAN

- 4 in No 75 × 75 posts.

- 200 × 40 rails.

- 450 × 450 concrete surround.

Scale 1:50

PERGOLA
timber

11

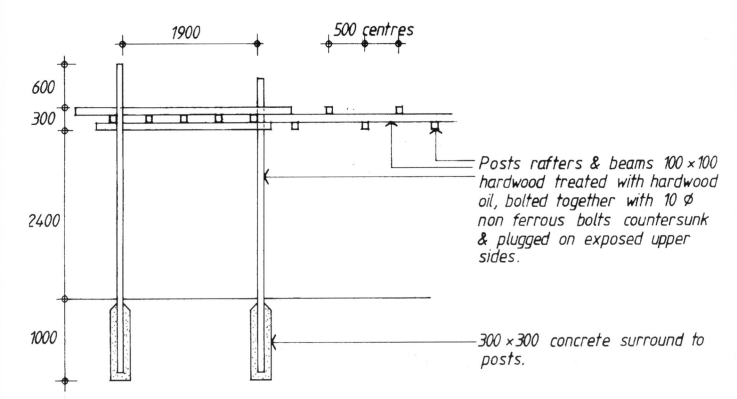

1900   500 centres

600

300

2400

1000

Posts rafters & beams 100 × 100
hardwood treated with hardwood
oil, bolted together with 10 Ø
non ferrous bolts countersunk
& plugged on exposed upper
sides.

300 × 300 concrete surround to
posts.

SECTION

500
200

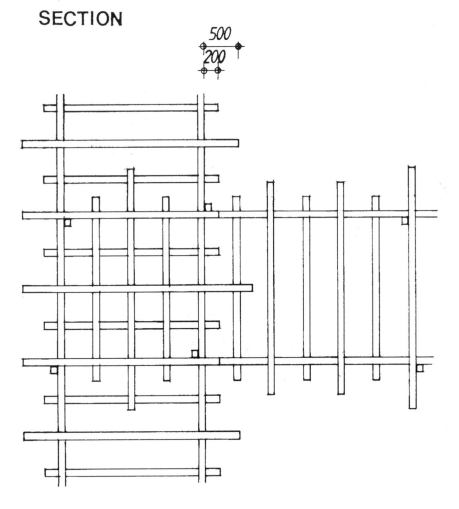

PLAN

Scale 1:50

PERGOLA
timber

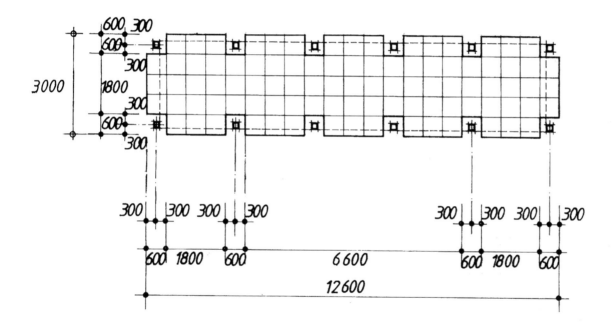

FLOOR PLAN

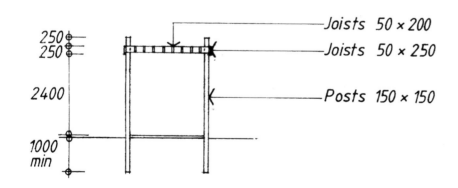

Joists 50 × 200
Joists 50 × 250
Posts 150 × 150

SECTION

PERGOLA
timber

Scale1:100

1/2

13

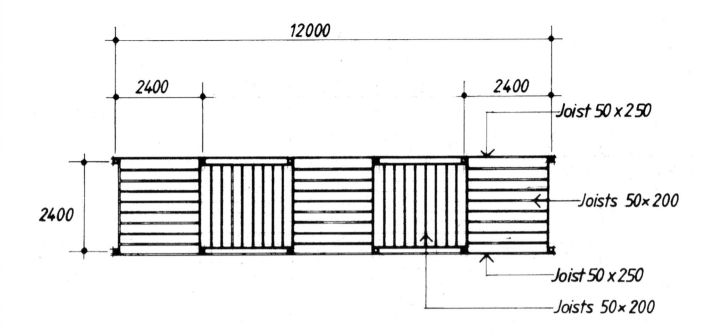

ROOF PLAN

Joist 50 x 250

Joists 50 × 200

Joist 50 x 250

Joists 50 × 200

12000

2400

2400

2400

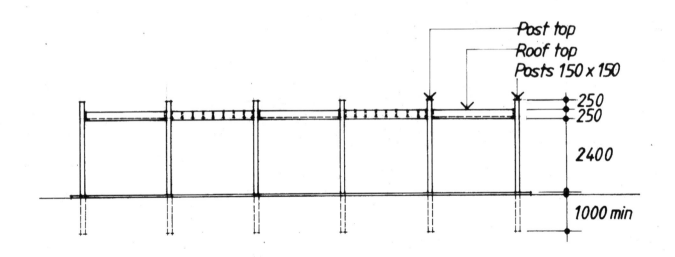

Post top
Roof top
Posts 150 x 150

250
250

2400

1000 min

ELEVATION

Scale 1:100

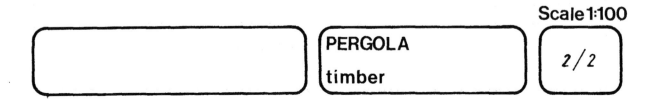

PERGOLA

timber

2/2

14

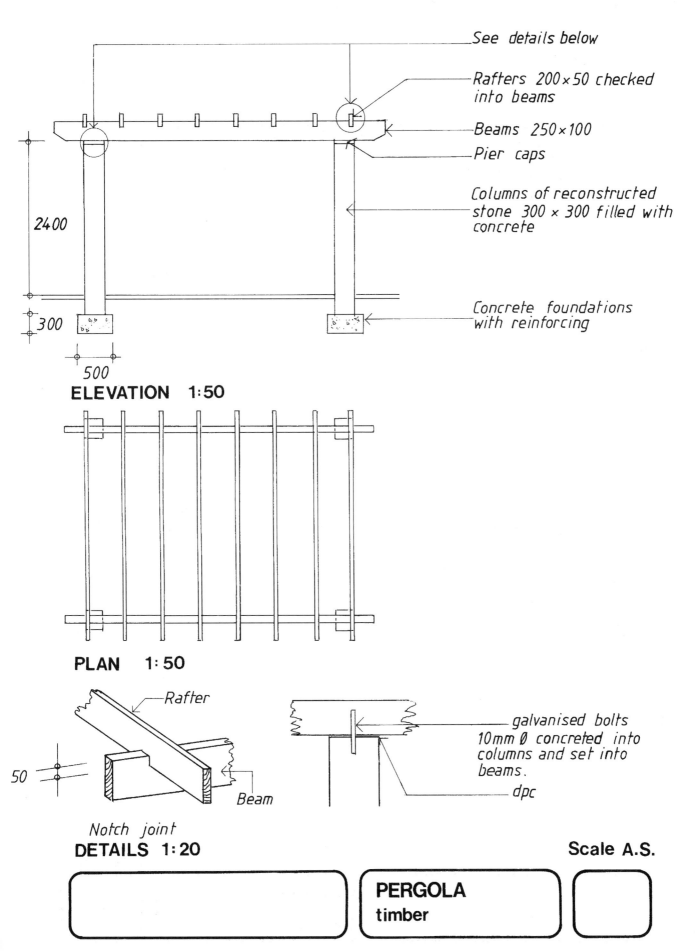

See details below

Rafters 200 × 50 checked into beams

Beams 250 × 100

Pier caps

Columns of reconstructed stone 300 × 300 filled with concrete

Concrete foundations with reinforcing

2400

300

500

ELEVATION 1:50

PLAN 1:50

Rafter

Beam

50

Notch joint

galvanised bolts 10mm Ø concreted into columns and set into beams.

dpc

DETAILS 1:20

Scale A.S.

PERGOLA
timber

15

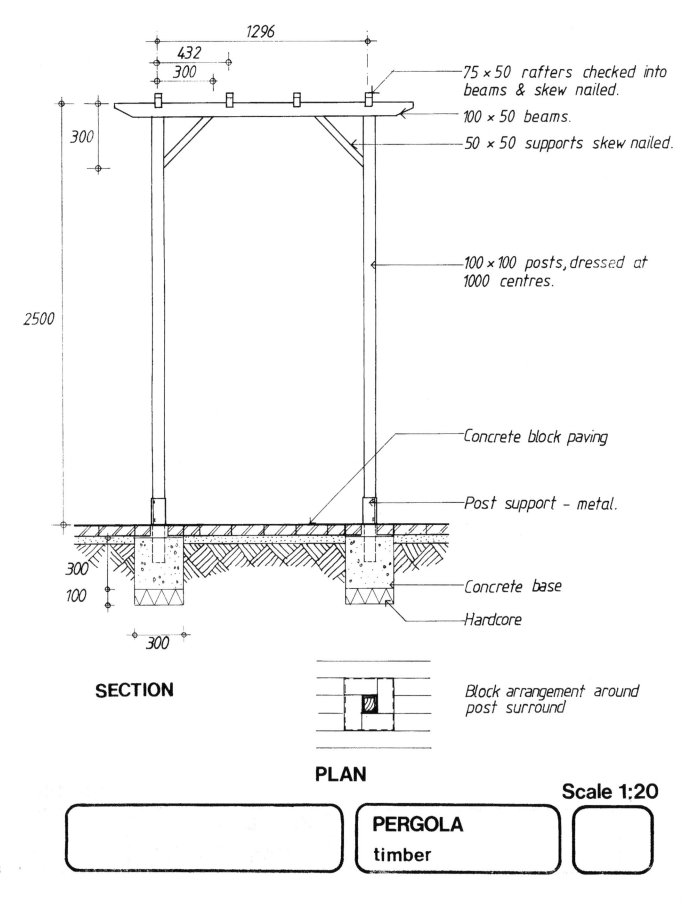

1296

432

300

75 × 50 rafters checked into beams & skew nailed.

100 × 50 beams.

50 × 50 supports skew nailed.

300

100 × 100 posts, dressed at 1000 centres.

2500

Concrete block paving

Post support - metal.

300

100

Concrete base

Hardcore

300

SECTION

PLAN

Block arrangement around post surround

PERGOLA

timber

Scale 1:20

16

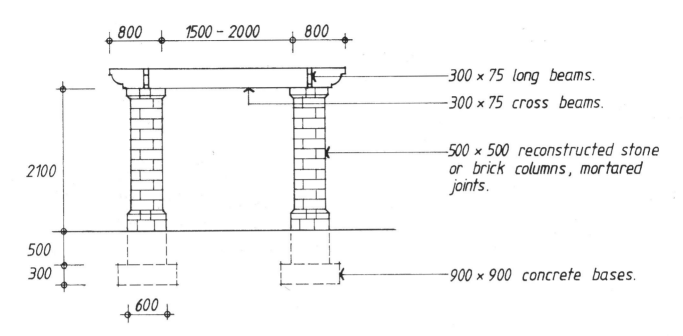

800 | 1500 – 2000 | 800

———300 × 75 long beams.

———300 × 75 cross beams.

———500 × 500 reconstructed stone
or brick columns, mortared
joints.

2100

500
300

———900 × 900 concrete bases.

600

ELEVATION

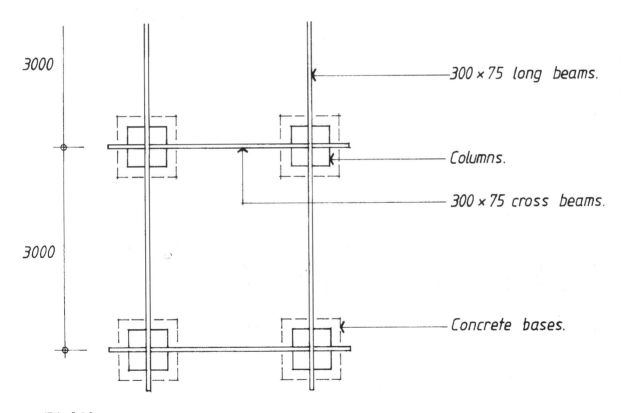

3000

———300 × 75 long beams.

———Columns.

———300 × 75 cross beams.

3000

———Concrete bases.

PLAN

Scale 1:50

**PERGOLA
timber, brick/block**

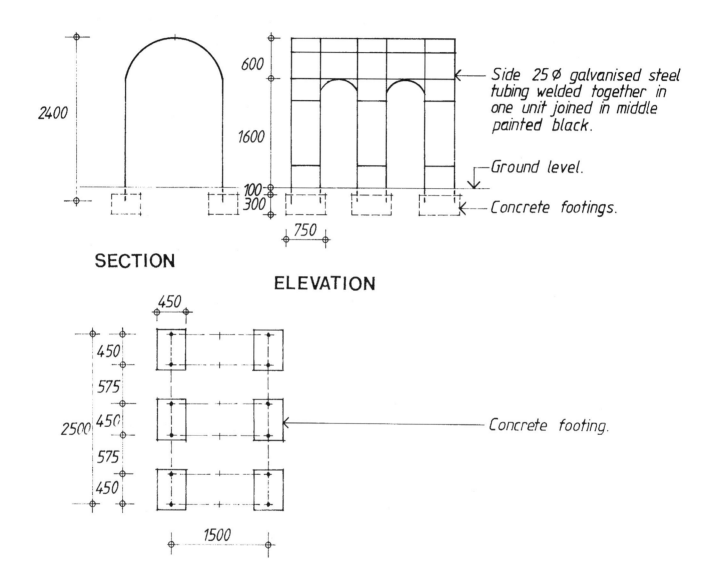

SECTION

2400

600

1600

100
300

750

Side 25 ∅ galvanised steel
tubing welded together in
one unit joined in middle
painted black.

—Ground level.

—Concrete footings.

ELEVATION

450

450

575

2500   450

575

450

1500

Concrete footing.

PLAN

Scale 1:50

PERGOLA
metal

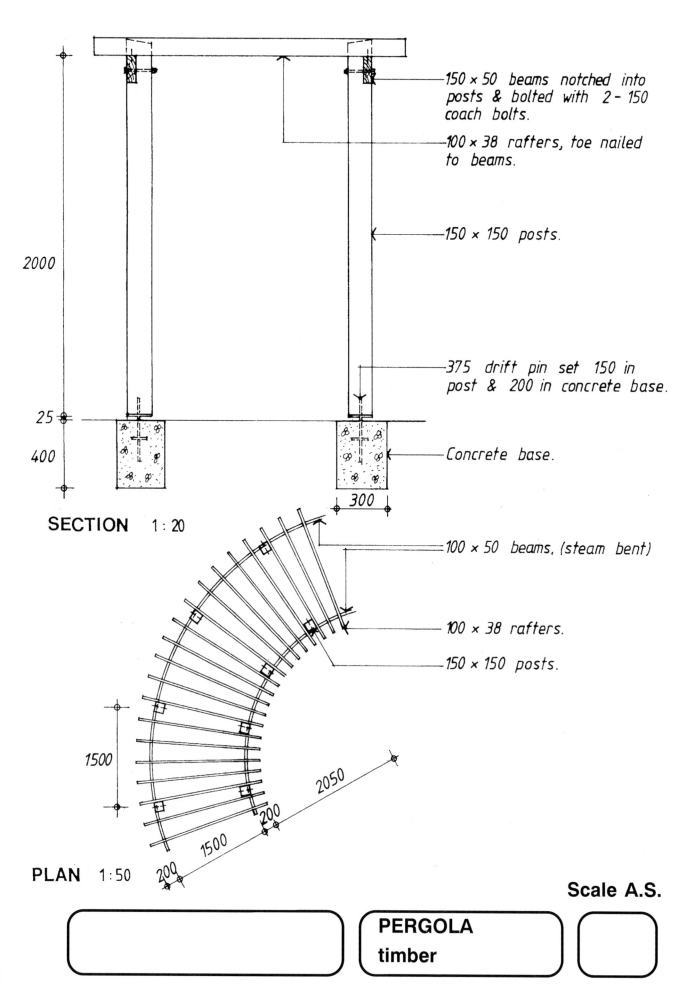

150 × 50 beams notched into posts & bolted with 2 – 150 coach bolts.

100 × 38 rafters, toe nailed to beams.

150 × 150 posts.

375 drift pin set 150 in post & 200 in concrete base.

Concrete base.

2000

25

400

300

SECTION 1 : 20

100 × 50 beams, (steam bent)

100 × 38 rafters.

150 × 150 posts.

1500

2050

200

1500

200

PLAN 1:50

Scale A.S.

PERGOLA

timber

19

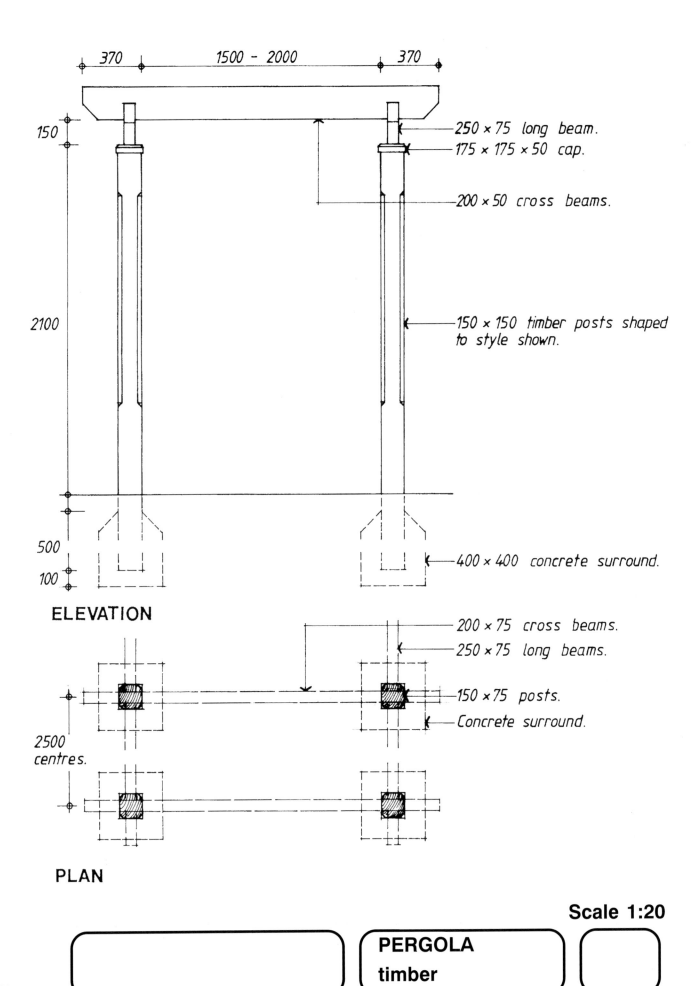

370   1500 – 2000   370

150

2100

500

100

ELEVATION

250 × 75 long beam.

175 × 175 × 50 cap.

200 × 50 cross beams.

150 × 150 timber posts shaped to style shown.

400 × 400 concrete surround.

200 × 75 cross beams.

250 × 75 long beams.

150 × 75 posts.

Concrete surround.

2500 centres.

PLAN

Scale 1:20

PERGOLA

timber

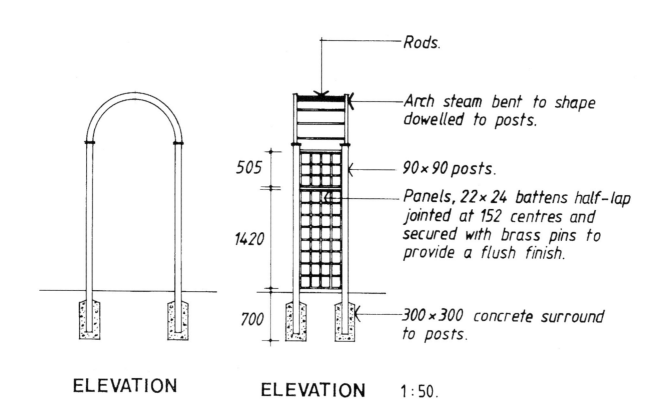

Rods.

Arch steam bent to shape dowelled to posts.

90 × 90 posts.

Panels, 22 × 24 battens half-lap jointed at 152 centres and secured with brass pins to provide a flush finish.

300 × 300 concrete surround to posts.

505

1420

700

ELEVATION

ELEVATION 1:50.

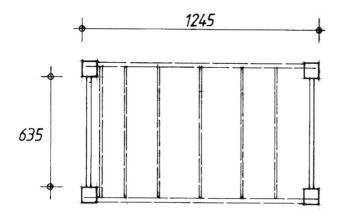

1245

635

PLAN 1 : 20

ARCH
timber

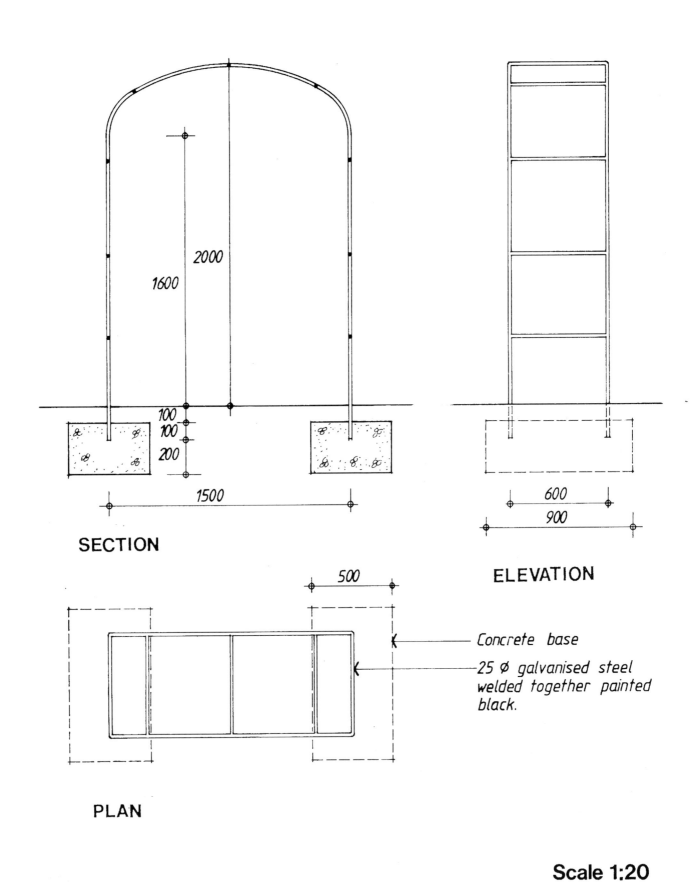

SECTION

2000

1600

100
100
200

1500

500

PLAN

ELEVATION

600
900

Concrete base

25 ⌀ galvanised steel welded together painted black.

Scale 1:20

ARCH
metal

22

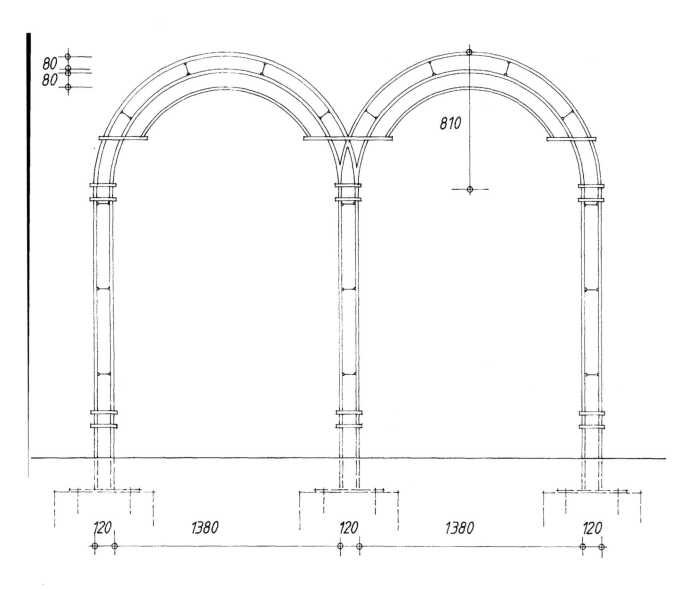

ELEVATION

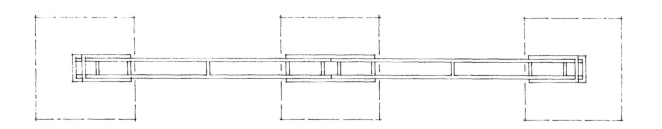

PLAN

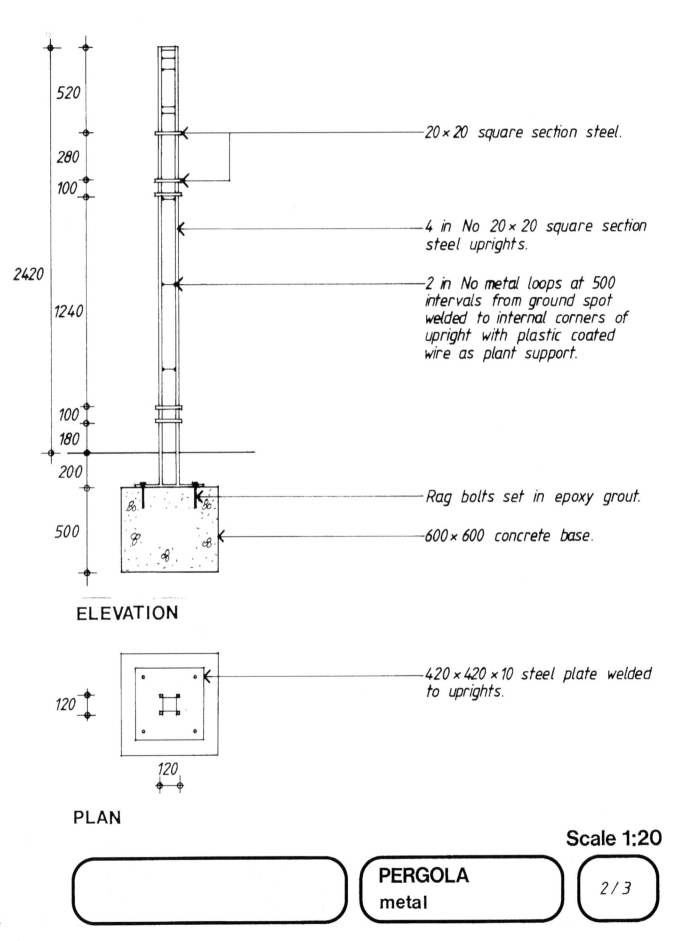

520

280

100

2420

1240

100

180

200

500

ELEVATION

20 × 20 square section steel.

4 in No 20 × 20 square section steel uprights.

2 in No metal loops at 500 intervals from ground spot welded to internal corners of upright with plastic coated wire as plant support.

Rag bolts set in epoxy grout.

600 × 600 concrete base.

120

120

PLAN

420 × 420 × 10 steel plate welded to uprights.

Scale 1:20

PERGOLA
metal

2 / 3

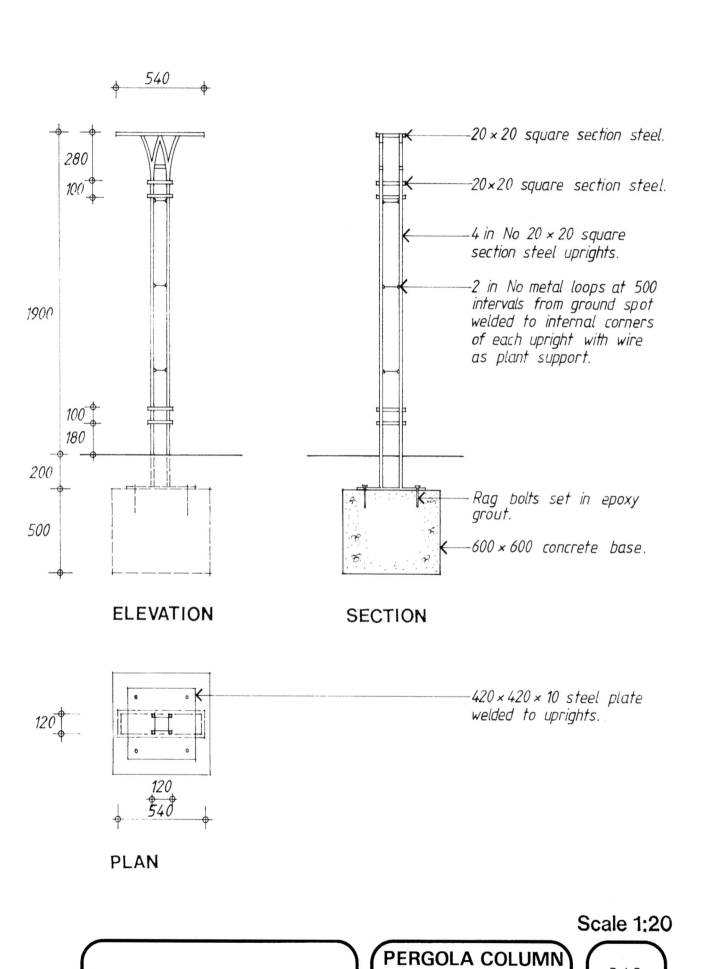

540

280
100

1900

100
180

200

500

ELEVATION

20 × 20 square section steel.

20×20 square section steel.

4 in No 20 × 20 square section steel uprights.

2 in No metal loops at 500 intervals from ground spot welded to internal corners of each upright with wire as plant support.

Rag bolts set in epoxy grout.

600 × 600 concrete base.

SECTION

120

120
540

PLAN

420 × 420 × 10 steel plate welded to uprights.

Scale 1:20

PERGOLA COLUMN
metal

3 / 3

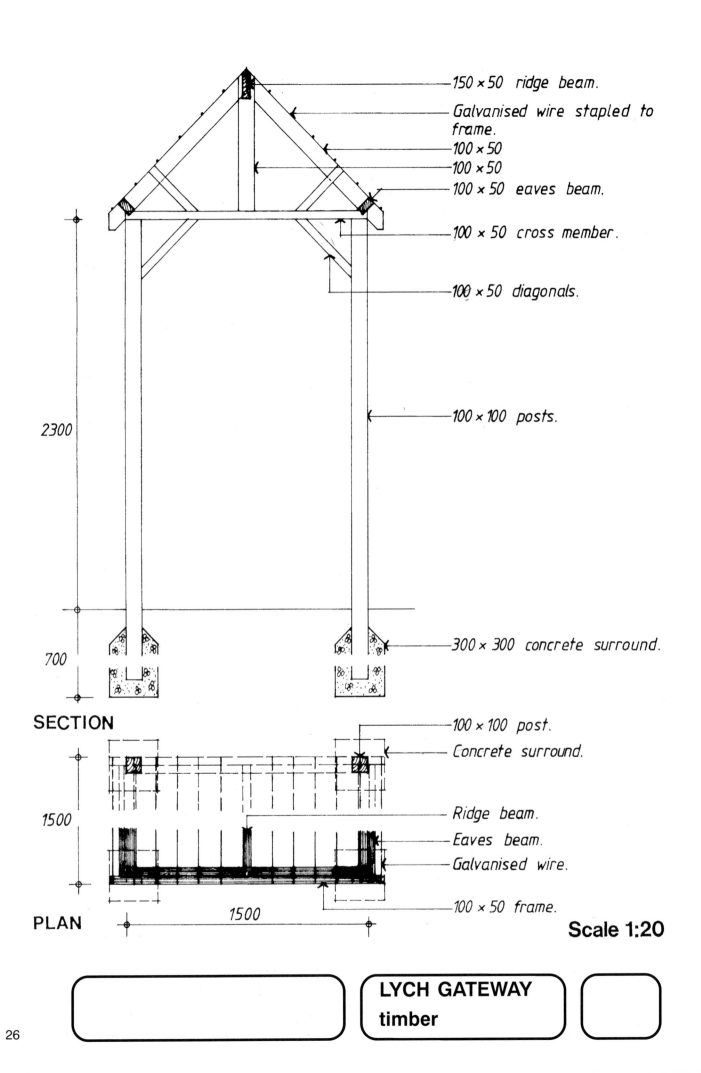

150 × 50 ridge beam.

Galvanised wire stapled to frame.

100 × 50

100 × 50

100 × 50 eaves beam.

100 × 50 cross member.

100 × 50 diagonals.

100 × 100 posts.

2300

700

300 × 300 concrete surround.

SECTION

100 × 100 post.

Concrete surround.

1500

Ridge beam.

Eaves beam.

Galvanised wire.

100 × 50 frame.

PLAN

1500

Scale 1:20

**LYCH GATEWAY
timber**

26

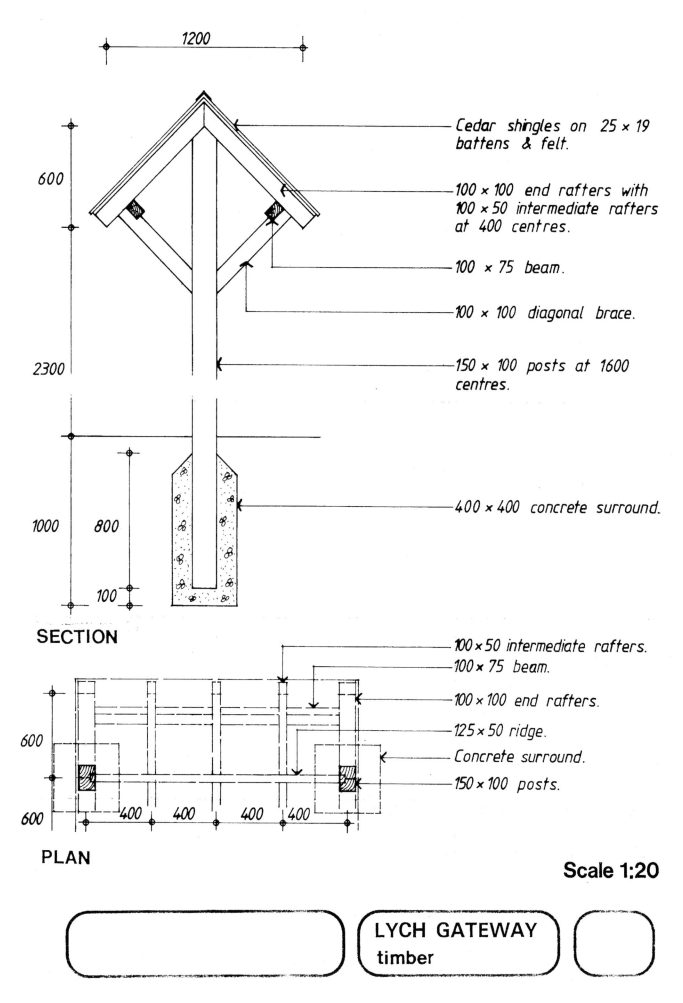

1200

600

2300

SECTION

1000   800

100

Cedar shingles on 25 × 19 battens & felt.

100 × 100 end rafters with 100 × 50 intermediate rafters at 400 centres.

100 × 75 beam.

100 × 100 diagonal brace.

150 × 100 posts at 1600 centres.

400 × 400 concrete surround.

100 × 50 intermediate rafters.
100 × 75 beam.
100 × 100 end rafters.
125 × 50 ridge.
Concrete surround.
150 × 100 posts.

PLAN

600

600

400   400   400   400

Scale 1:20

LYCH GATEWAY
timber

27

SHELTERS, GAZEBOS AND SHEDS

This chapter deals only with small buildings such as summerhouses, gazebos, loggias, sheds, pavilions, bus shelters and kiosks, which require more architectural input into their design. While there are now a vast amount of ready-made designs it is still very often necessary for the landscape architect and garden designer to be able to design a structure that is much more suitable to the 'genus-loci'.

Small structures usually demand choice locations and they are objects to be observed as well as to use. They need detailing with considerable care.

SUMMERHOUSES

Summerhouses have been the one building ubiquitous in the English garden for a very long time, along with the garden shed. The contrast in style, size and even function is considerable. It is unfortunate that the design of summerhouses has on the whole been rather mundane due to mass production. Where individual flair has revealed itself they are among the most whimsical of garden elements. They are gardeners' follies designed solely for pleasure.

Summerhouses are more serious structural buildings, but they can be ornate. The walls are likely to be solid, even built of masonry, and include insulation, heating and power with windows and doors. A second storey might feature a light, breezy room, with excellent views over the landscape or garden. Summerhouses are often planned with unusual architectural features and colour schemes, for their role as garden sculpture is as important as their value as shelters.

There are two basic types – the 'lookout' and the chalet.

The 'lookout' is a summerhouse from which the landscape or garden can be viewed

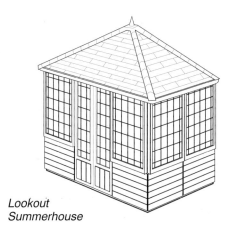

*Lookout
Summerhouse*

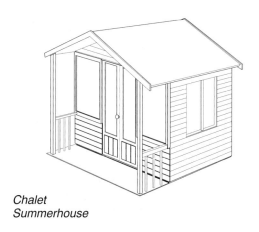

*Chalet
Summerhouse*

while the occupants can be protected from inclement weather. The walls are extensively glazed.

The chalet type is basically an extension of the house to provide more room for hobbies, work or leisure. There are fewer windows and there is often a veranda. They are often used as a 'sleep-out' for younger people or for temporary overnight accommodation for visitors.

They can be made in various shapes such as hexagon, octagon, square or rectangular. They are usually constructed of lightweight timber with cedar shingle roofs although overlap boarding is used occasionally.

GAZEBOS AND LOGGIAS

Gazebos and loggias have much in common and there is now very little difference between them although one way to differentiate would be to keep gazebos mainly open sided whereas loggias would have some sides closed in for protection. 'Initially, gazebos (thought to be derived from the Latin 'I will gaze') were similar smaller buildings designed to direct attention to a rather specific and spectacular view usually beyond the garden. They were consequently often set on mounds or walls and frequently located on the margin of gardens.'

Gazebos are structures built of wood or metal and in plan they are usually circular, hexagonal or octagonal with a raised floor edged by a decorative balustrade. They can range in style from the simple conical thatched roof on tree trunks of rough timber posts to the sophisticated ornate structure embellished with intricately detailed railings, brackets and cornices finished with a special finial or ornament marking the peak of the roof.

Loggias can be of any shape in plan and are built of a wide variety of materials. They often look like small pavilions.

SHELTERS

The use of a shelter in the landscape determines its design and location, for example a recreational shelter in a rural area should look quite different from one in an urban area both in the architectural style, colour and type of materials.

Planning must include decisions as to the need for sun and wind control, plumbing electricity and storage. Consideration should also be given to the relation of the shelter to other activity areas, buildings and natural objects present.

Most shelters, like houses, are essentially rectangular in plan. Many variations are possible involving the same basic construction elements.

Basic roof designs used in shelters include a flat roof, a sloping or shed roof, a gable (peaked) roof and a pyramid roof. The flat and shed roof are by far the most commonly employed because they are economical but the gable and pyramid are far more attractive but cost more.

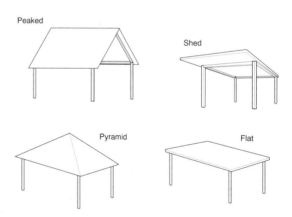

Basic roof designs

Although appearance is often the deciding factor in the design of the roof, if the roof is to be watertight it should be slightly sloped to allow for moisture run-off. The flat and shed roofs may be cantilevered beyond their normal overhangs.

The minimum height of any shelter should be 2400 mm. No matter what type of roof, the ceiling should be high enough to allow for head clearance in all areas. The height of the shelter should not interfere with surrounding objects such as utility poles or wires.

Shelters can be built of timber, brick, stone or concrete block for walls with either solid or timber floors and roofs of timber (shingles or felt), slate or corrugated iron. One shelter that has been utilitarian and around for a long time is the bus shelter. Various styles have evolved more noticeably in urban areas using materials such as glass and polycarbonate sheeting. It is unfortunate that no bus shelter emerged which became as 'friendly' to the public as the red telephone kiosk.

Many shelters are small buildings and have been used for a wide variety of activities such as cricket pavilions, stables, garages, sports changing rooms and storage for equipment and machinery and even educational and craft uses. Many styles have evolved but again it is very important that these structures are designed for the site's architecture and not on the whim of a catalogue illustration.

Regulations

Check with local building authorities before starting construction to find out the local building requirements and restrictions placed on garden structures, both free-standing and attached to dwellings.

SHEDS

These utilitarian buildings are not the most inspiring in terms of architectural style yet they offer the opportunity to be integrated with other structures and made attractive by the garden/landscape designer. Size is often determined by the area available rather than the requirements for the various uses, tools and equipment. Sheds are usually located at the bottom of a garden rather than near a house due to the shed being regarded as an eyesore. The doorway should be close to ground level to allow easy access for lawn mower or wheeled equipment.

There are three basic types – the Apex, Pent and Dual Purpose.

The Apex – has a pitched roof with a central ridge and is considered to be the more attractive style.

The Pent – has a flat roof which slopes gently backwards. Check that sufficient headroom has been allowed. This style if it has full glazing on one long side makes an excellent potting shed.

The Dual Purpose – this is a shed with a greenhouse which reduces the need for more buildings on a site.

While the majority of sheds are made from timber other longer lasting materials such as bricks and concrete blocks can be used. The cost is probably the same as cedar timber. Roofs are usually of felt which again makes the building utilitarian and cheap. Using corrugated metal sheeting (which can be painted) is preferable as this will allow mosses and lichens to grow on it. If costs permit, timber battens or shingles could also be used to make the building more attractive.

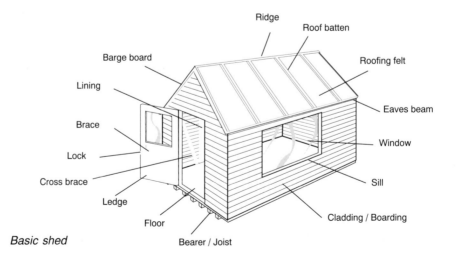

Basic shed

Construction

Most small buildings constructed today utilise one of three principal construction methods: stud, post and beam or pole framing.

1. Stud framing
Stud framing consists of two styles, platform or balloon, and the former is the most common modern method. It uses dimensional timber, ranging in size from 50 × 100 to 50 × 300, regularly spaced to frame walls, floors and roofs.
Platform framing is the most widely-used method of wood construction for small barns, sheds and shelters because it requires less labour and materials than post-and-beam framing and its construction details are simpler. As the individual framing members are relatively light and small, one person can erect an entire building alone.
Although seldom used as much these days, balloon framing is one method of framing a two-storey structure. The primary difference is the studs run continuously from the foundation to the rafter plate.
The floors are supported on ribbons or supports fastened to the studs.

2. Post and beam framing
Post and beam framing is an older, traditional method of barn construction dating back to medieval times. With this

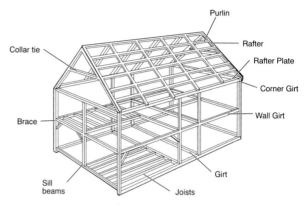

Post and beam framing

method large beams and posts, such as 150 × 150 and 200 × 200, form the frame. Post and beam framing requires more skill and materials than the other methods but nevertheless has certain advantages such as being:
• strong and durable
• more fire resistant
• flexible for allowing larger doors and windows
• easily erected in a short time

3. Pole framing
Pole framing is actually the oldest method, dating back to the Stone Age.
Pole barn framing, however, has fast become popular due to the increasing availability of pressure-treated poles, the

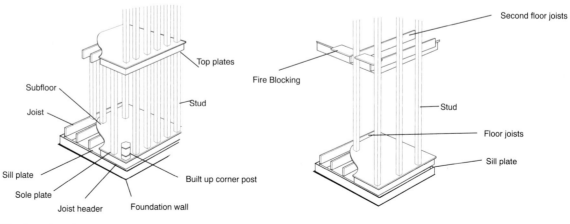

Platform framing

Balloon framing

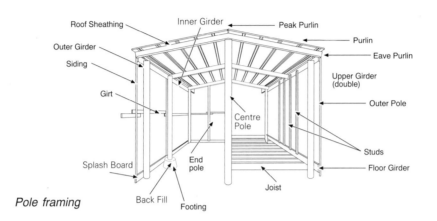

Pole framing

Labels: Roof Sheathing, Inner Girder, Peak Purlin, Outer Girder, Purlin, Siding, Eave Purlin, Girt, Upper Girder (double), Outer Pole, Centre Pole, Studs, Splash Board, End pole, Floor Girder, Back Fill, Footing, Joist

ease of construction and the relatively low cost. Pole building is simplified by machine-cut and pressure-treated poles or posts and it is usually combined with platform framing of doors, floors and roofs.

This method uses poles or posts either set into the ground or onto concrete piers or footings. The beams (in the post and beam method) are replaced by nailed on or bolted girts and girders of dimensional timber, while the floors and roofs are framed either on site or they can be purchased ready made. Examples of pole connections and fixings are given below.

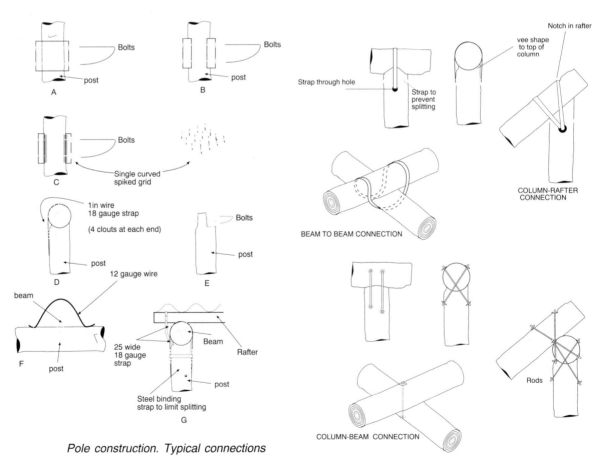

Pole construction. Typical connections

Foundations

Unless a building is portable it must be anchored to the ground and sit on a solid support. This depends on the use and type of building, the soil upon which it sits, and the desired cost of the building.

For example a simple shelter for animals with an open side is often constructed using pole barn methods because they are economical, fast, and easy. On the other hand a garage or small workshop is often constructed on a poured concrete slab because this simplifies construction and provides better protection against insects, rodents and weather.

Construction guidelines

The following guidelines apply to all small timber buildings in this chapter:

- **Floor**. Sound construction is essential. If timber, both sides should be treated with a preservative – tongued-and-grooved boards are much better than plywood or hardboard.
- **Bearers**. These should be heavy-duty timbers, pressure-treated.
- **Framework**. The upright frames should be no more than 600 mm apart and there should be stout cross braces between them.
- **Door**. Make sure it is wide enough for ready access by the mower,

wheelbarrow, etc. It should be soundly constructed with at least 3 ledges and 2 braces. A strong lock with key is essential. Hinges and all other metal parts should be rust-proof.
- **Eaves** There should be sufficient overhang to make sure that rainwater from the roof is kept well away from the walls.
- **Gutters**. These should be used to convey water to butts or barrels.
- **Roof**. Use shingles or tongued-and-grooved boards rather than plywood. Alternatively use corrugated metal sheeting. Roofing felt should be thick and it should cover the eaves beams completely. Make sure that the headroom is high enough. Narrow gauge corrugated iron could also be used.
- **Cladding**. The boards must be weatherproof and rot-proof – softwood should have been pressure-treated with a preservative. Feather-edged and waney-edged weather-boarding is the cheapest, but it is the least weatherproof. It is better to choose tongued-and-grooved or shiplap cladding.

Regular maintenance such as staining timbers and painting metalwork is essential to prolong the life of any building.

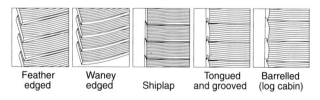

Feather edged   Waney edged   Shiplap   Tongued and grooved   Barrelled (log cabin)

Cladding

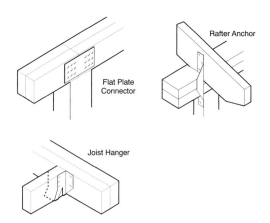

Rafter Anchor

Flat Plate
Connector

Joist Hanger

Typical examples

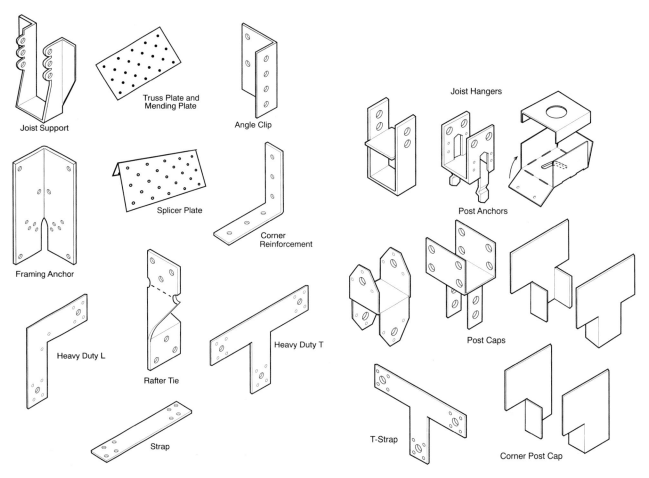

Joist Support

Truss Plate and
Mending Plate

Angle Clip

Framing Anchor

Splicer Plate

Corner
Reinforcement

Heavy Duty L

Rafter Tie

Heavy Duty T

Strap

Joist Hangers

Post Anchors

Post Caps

T-Strap

Corner Post Cap

Typical steel supports

Typical steel fasteners

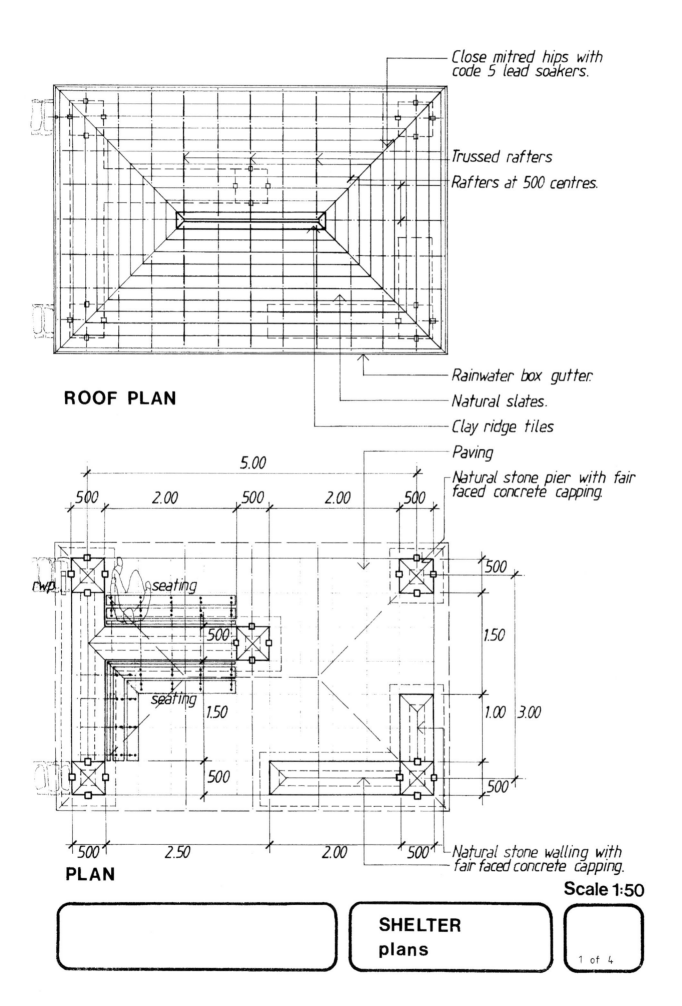

ROOF PLAN

Close mitred hips with code 5 lead soakers.

Trussed rafters

Rafters at 500 centres.

Rainwater box gutter.

Natural slates.

Clay ridge tiles

Paving

Natural stone pier with fair faced concrete capping.

5.00

500 2.00 500 2.00 500

500

rwp.

seating

500

1.50

seating

1.50

1.00 3.00

500

500

500 2.50 2.00 500

Natural stone walling with fair faced concrete capping.

PLAN

Scale 1:50

SHELTER
plans

1 of 4

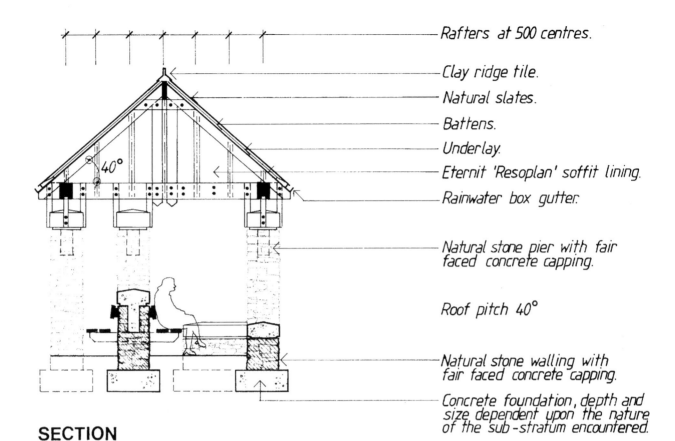

Rafters at 500 centres.

Clay ridge tile.

Natural slates.

Battens.

Underlay.

Eternit 'Resoplan' soffit lining.

Rainwater box gutter.

Natural stone pier with fair faced concrete capping.

Roof pitch 40°

Natural stone walling with fair faced concrete capping.

Concrete foundation, depth and size dependent upon the nature of the sub-stratum encountered.

40°

SECTION

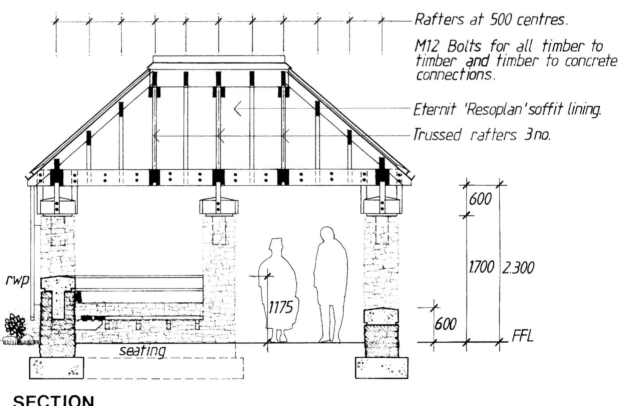

Rafters at 500 centres.

M12 Bolts for all timber to timber and timber to concrete connections.

Eternit 'Resoplan' soffit lining.

Trussed rafters 3no.

rwp

seating

1175

600

1.700 | 2.300

600

FFL

SECTION

Scale 1:50

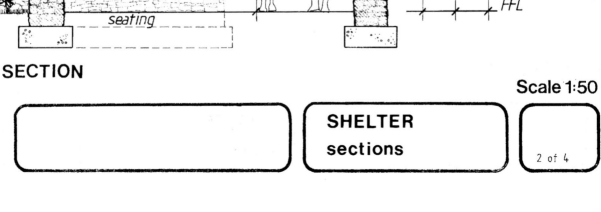

SHELTER
sections

2 of 4

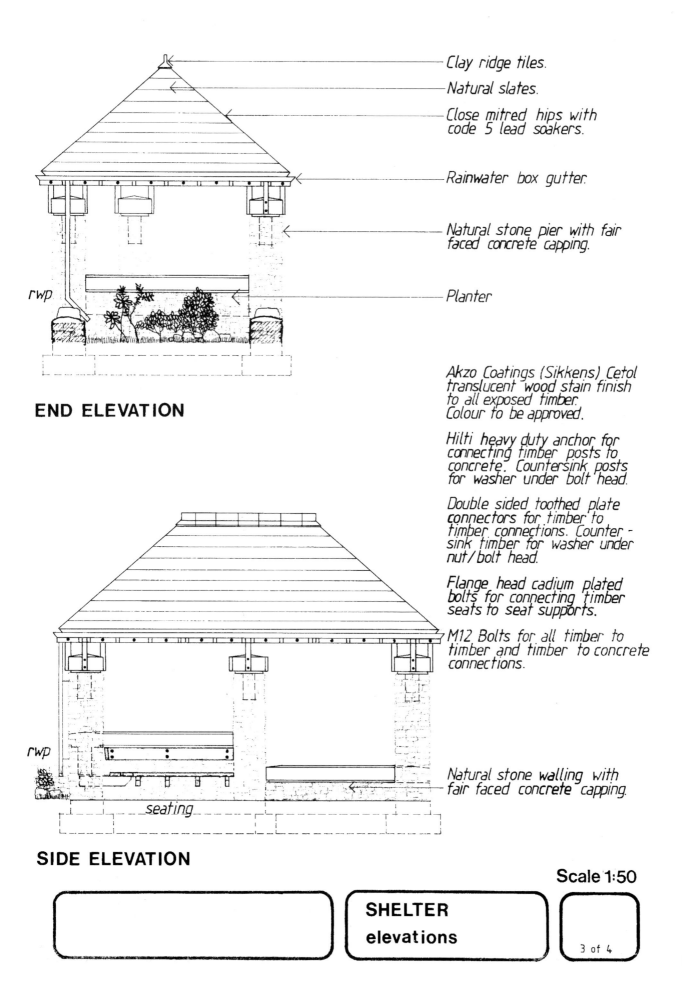

Clay ridge tiles.

Natural slates.

Close mitred hips with code 5 lead soakers.

Rainwater box gutter.

Natural stone pier with fair faced concrete capping.

Planter

END ELEVATION

rwp

Akzo Coatings (Sikkens) Cetol translucent wood stain finish to all exposed timber. Colour to be approved.

Hilti heavy duty anchor for connecting timber posts to concrete. Countersink posts for washer under bolt head.

Double sided toothed plate connectors for timber to timber connections. Counter-sink timber for washer under nut/bolt head.

Flange head cadium plated bolts for connecting timber seats to seat supports.

M12 Bolts for all timber to timber and timber to concrete connections.

Natural stone walling with fair faced concrete capping.

rwp

seating

SIDE ELEVATION

Scale 1:50

SHELTER

elevations

3 of 4

37

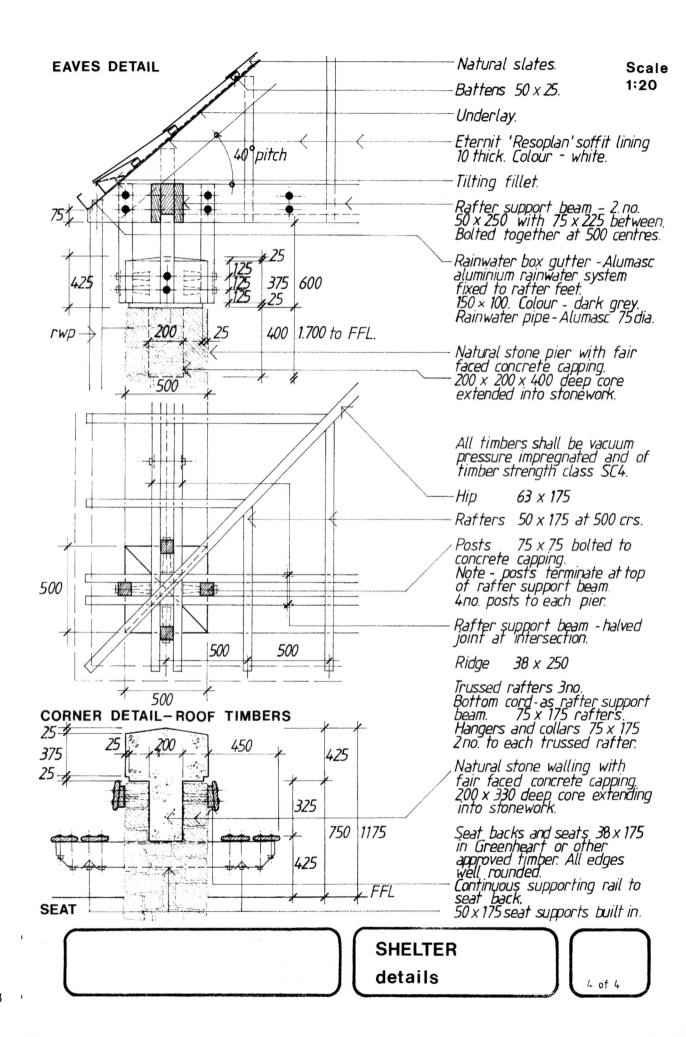

EAVES DETAIL

Natural slates.

Battens 50 x 25.

Underlay.

Eternit 'Resoplan' soffit lining 10 thick. Colour - white.

Tilting fillet.

Rafter support beam - 2. no. 50 x 250 with 75 x 225 between. Bolted together at 500 centres.

Rainwater box gutter - Alumasc aluminium rainwater system fixed to rafter feet. 150 x 100. Colour - dark grey. Rainwater pipe - Alumasc 75 dia.

Natural stone pier with fair faced concrete capping. 200 x 200 x 400 deep core extended into stonework.

All timbers shall be vacuum pressure impregnated and of timber strength class SC4.

Hip   63 x 175

Rafters 50 x 175 at 500 crs.

Posts   75 x 75 bolted to concrete capping. Note - posts terminate at top of rafter support beam. 4no. posts to each pier.

Rafter support beam - halved joint at intersection.

Ridge   38 x 250

Trussed rafters 3no. Bottom cord - as rafter support beam.   75 x 175 rafters. Hangers and collars 75 x 175 2no. to each trussed rafter.

Natural stone walling with fair faced concrete capping. 200 x 330 deep core extending into stonework.

Seat backs and seats 38 x 175 in Greenheart or other approved timber. All edges well rounded.

Continuous supporting rail to seat back. 50 x 175 seat supports built in.

CORNER DETAIL - ROOF TIMBERS

SEAT

40° pitch

75

425

rwp

200 25   400 1.700 to FFL.

500

125 25
125 375 600
125 25

500

500 500

500

25
375
25

25 200 450

425

325

750 1175

425

FFL

Scale 1:20

SHELTER

details

4 of 4

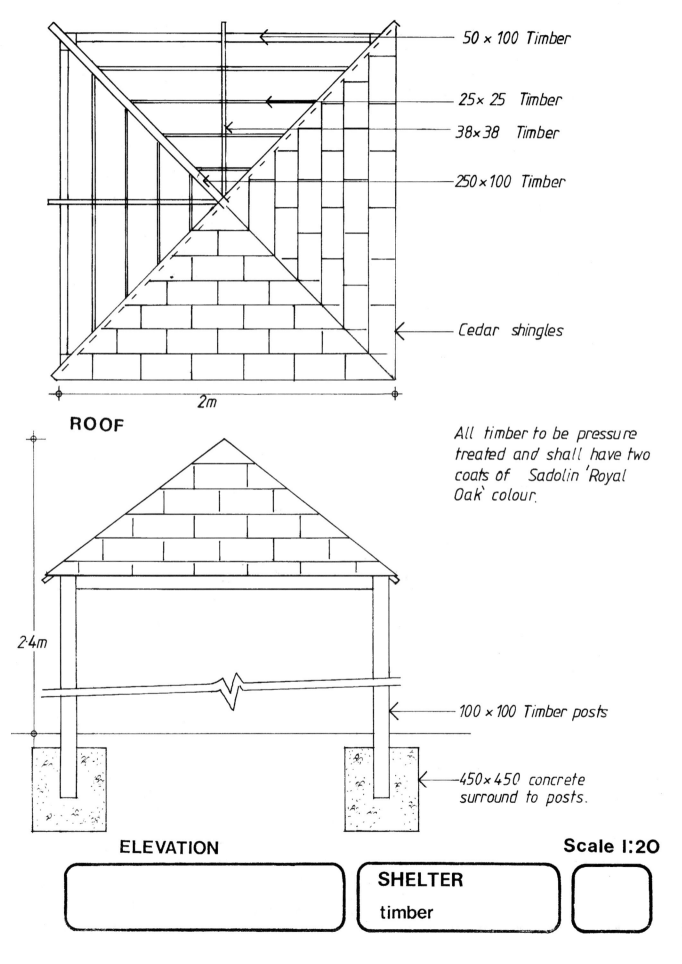

50 × 100 Timber

25× 25 Timber

38×38 Timber

250×100 Timber

Cedar shingles

ROOF

2m

All timber to be pressure
treated and shall have two
coats of Sadolin 'Royal
Oak' colour.

2·4m

100 × 100 Timber posts

450×450 concrete
surround to posts.

ELEVATION

Scale 1:20

SHELTER

timber

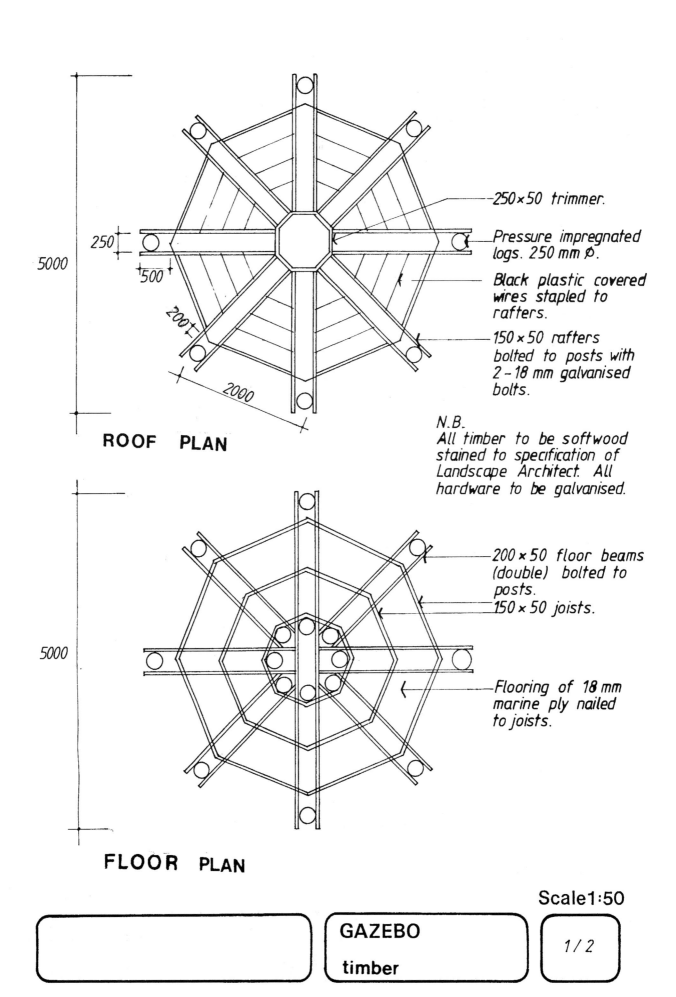

250×50 trimmer.

Pressure impregnated logs. 250 mm ⌀.

Black plastic covered wires stapled to rafters.

150×50 rafters bolted to posts with 2-18 mm galvanised bolts.

250

500

200

5000

2000

ROOF PLAN

N.B.
All timber to be softwood stained to specification of Landscape Architect. All hardware to be galvanised.

200×50 floor beams (double) bolted to posts.

150×50 joists.

Flooring of 18 mm marine ply nailed to joists.

5000

FLOOR PLAN

Scale 1:50

GAZEBO

timber

1/2

40

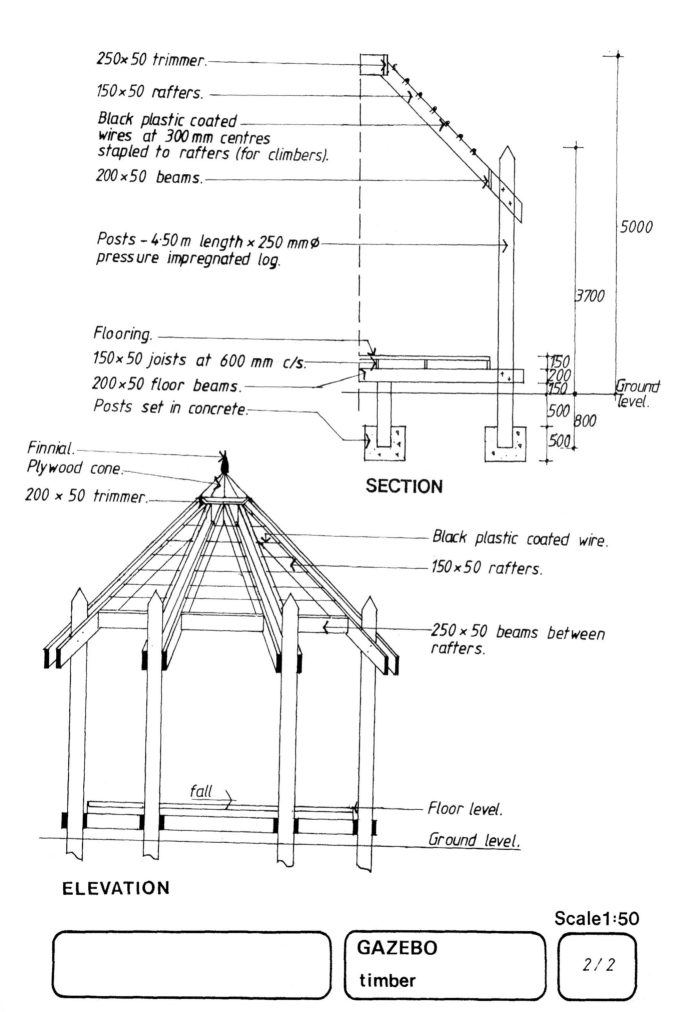

250×50 trimmer.

150×50 rafters.

Black plastic coated
wires at 300 mm centres
stapled to rafters (for climbers).

200×50 beams.

Posts - 4·50 m length × 250 mmø
pressure impregnated log.

Flooring.

150×50 joists at 600 mm c/s.

200×50 floor beams.

Posts set in concrete.

5000

3700

150
200
150

Ground
level.

500
800

500

SECTION

Finnial.
Plywood cone.
200 × 50 trimmer.

Black plastic coated wire.

150×50 rafters.

250 × 50 beams between
rafters.

fall

Floor level.

Ground level.

ELEVATION

Scale 1:50

GAZEBO

timber

2 / 2

41

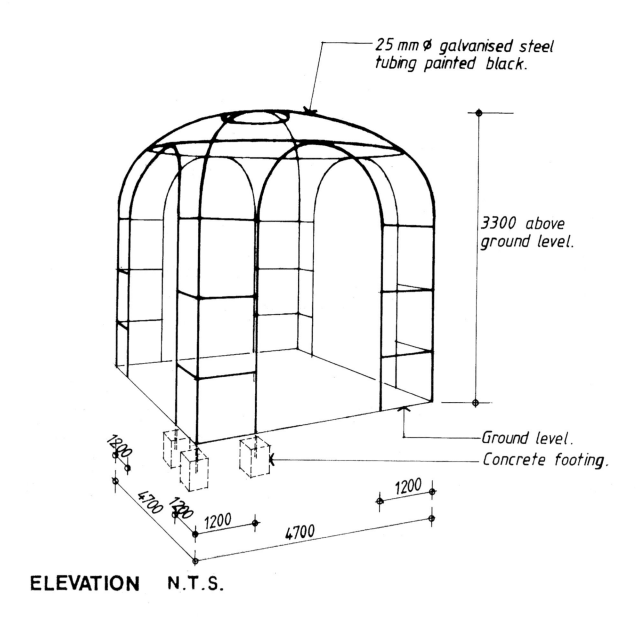

25 mm ø galvanised steel tubing painted black.

3300 above ground level.

Ground level.

Concrete footing.

1200

4700

1200

1200

4700

1200

ELEVATION   N.T.S.

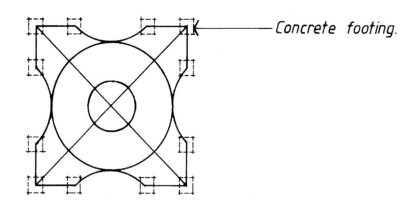

Concrete footing.

PLAN

Scale 1:100

| GAZEBO |
| metal |

42

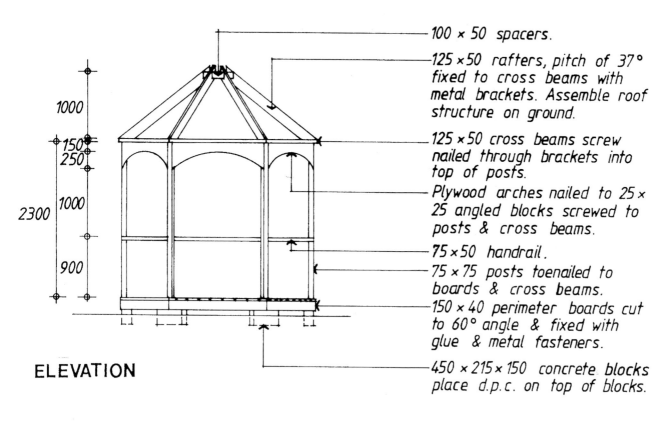

ELEVATION

100 × 50 spacers.

125 × 50 rafters, pitch of 37°
fixed to cross beams with
metal brackets. Assemble roof
structure on ground.

125 × 50 cross beams screw
nailed through brackets into
top of posts.

Plywood arches nailed to 25 ×
25 angled blocks screwed to
posts & cross beams.

75 × 50 handrail.

75 × 75 posts toenailed to
boards & cross beams.

150 × 40 perimeter boards cut
to 60° angle & fixed with
glue & metal fasteners.

450 × 215 × 150 concrete blocks
place d.p.c. on top of blocks.

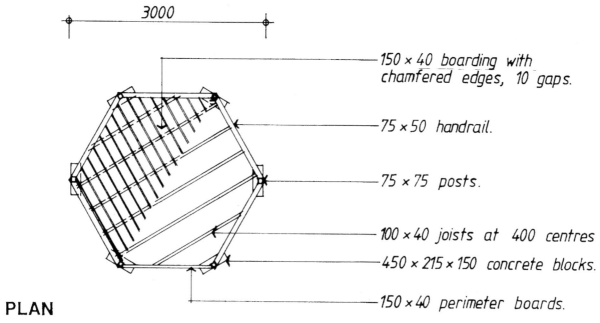

3000

150 × 40 boarding with
chamfered edges, 10 gaps.

75 × 50 handrail.

75 × 75 posts.

100 × 40 joists at 400 centres

450 × 215 × 150 concrete blocks.

150 × 40 perimeter boards.

PLAN

Scale 1:50

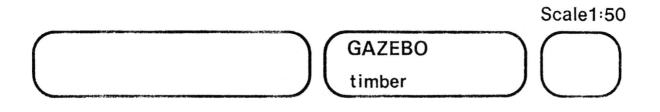

GAZEBO

timber

43

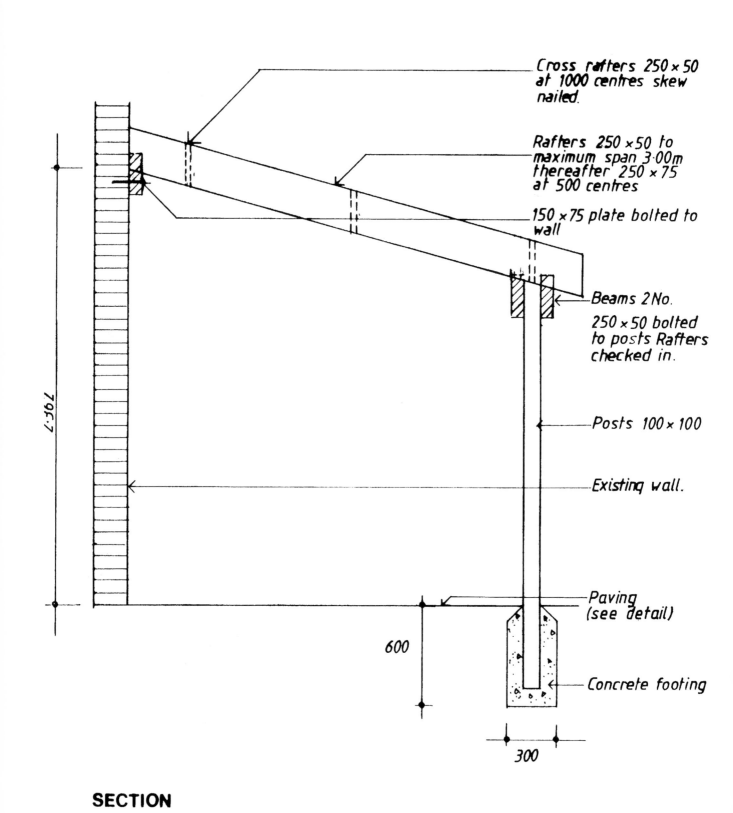

Cross rafters 250 × 50
at 1000 centres skew
nailed.

Rafters 250 × 50 to
maximum span 3·00m
thereafter 250 × 75
at 500 centres

150 × 75 plate bolted to
wall

Beams 2 No.

250 × 50 bolted
to posts Rafters
checked in.

Posts 100 × 100

Existing wall.

Paving
(see detail)

Concrete footing

7·961·7

600

300

SECTION

Scale 1:20

ARBOUR
timber

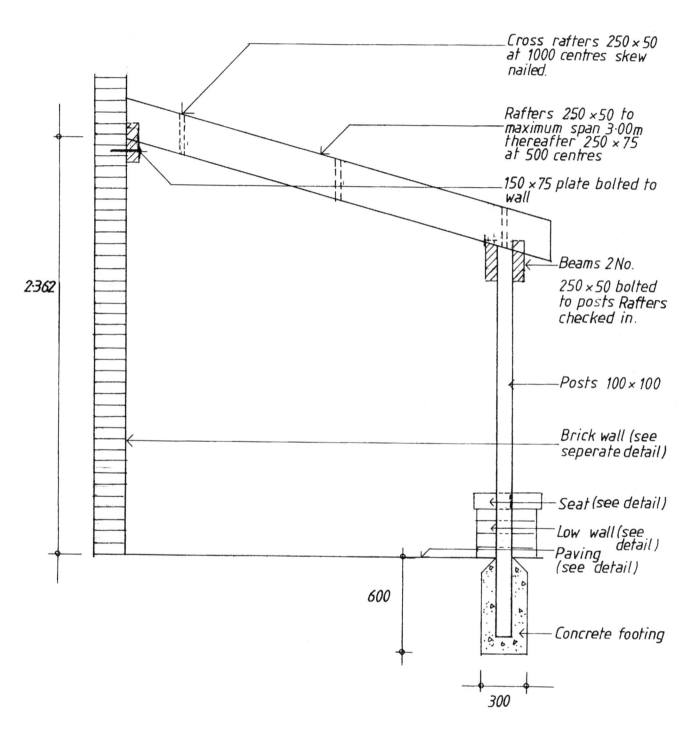

Cross rafters 250 × 50
at 1000 centres skew
nailed.

Rafters 250 × 50 to
maximum span 3·00m
thereafter 250 × 75
at 500 centres

150 × 75 plate bolted to
wall

Beams 2 No.

250 × 50 bolted
to posts Rafters
checked in.

Posts 100 × 100

Brick wall (see
seperate detail)

Seat (see detail)

Low wall (see
detail)

Paving
(see detail)

Concrete footing

2·362

600

300

SECTION

Scale 1:20

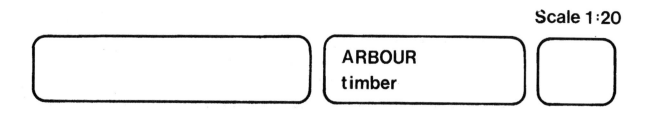

**ARBOUR
timber**

45

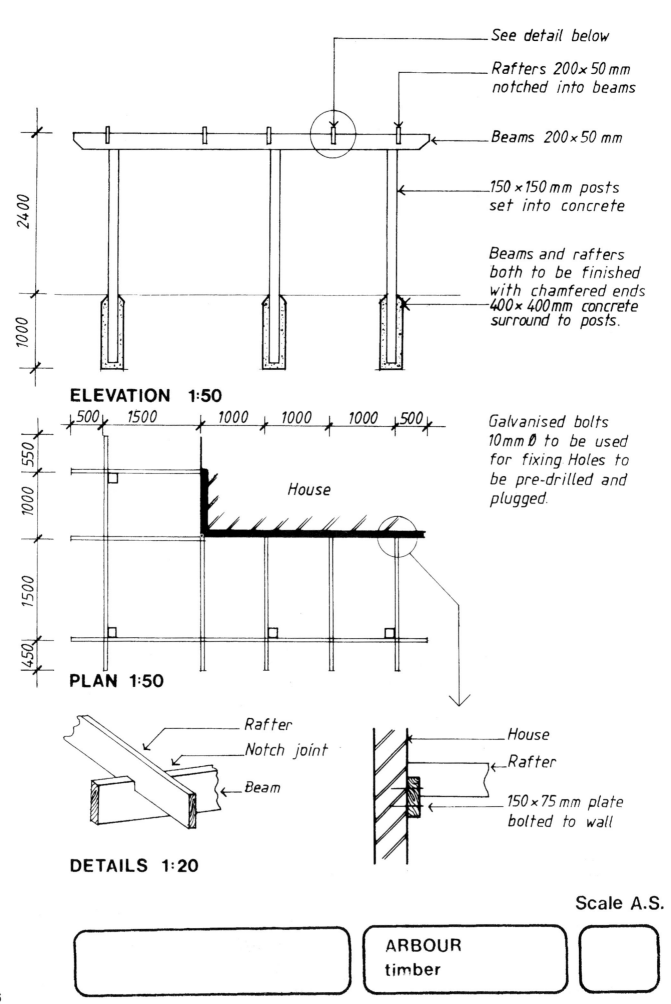

See detail below

Rafters 200 × 50 mm
notched into beams

Beams 200 × 50 mm

150 × 150 mm posts
set into concrete

Beams and rafters
both to be finished
with chamfered ends
400 × 400 mm concrete
surround to posts.

2400

1000

ELEVATION 1:50

500 1500 1000 1000 1000 500

550

1000

1500

450

Galvanised bolts
10 mm ∅ to be used
for fixing. Holes to
be pre-drilled and
plugged.

House

PLAN 1:50

Rafter
Notch joint
Beam

House
Rafter
150 × 75 mm plate
bolted to wall

DETAILS 1:20

Scale A.S.

ARBOUR
timber

46

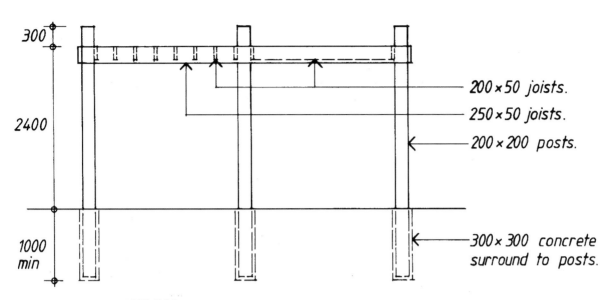

300

2400

1000
min

200 × 50 joists.

250 × 50 joists.

200 × 200 posts.

300 × 300 concrete
surround to posts.

ELEVATION

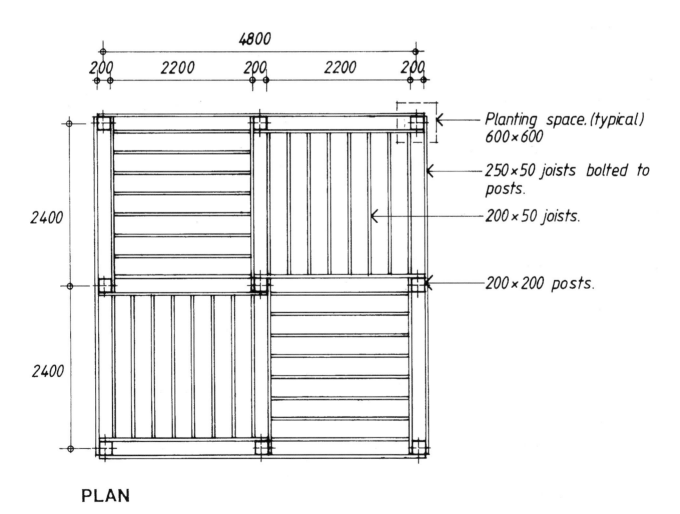

4800

200   2200   200   2200   200

2400

2400

Planting space. (typical)
600 × 600

250 × 50 joists bolted to
posts.

200 × 50 joists.

200 × 200 posts.

PLAN

Scale 1:50

ARBOUR
timber

DECKS AND BOARDWALKS

Design considerations

The design of a deck or boardwalk will be greatly influenced by the method of construction, the type and size of materials, costs and the method of maintenance.
A typical deck and its components is shown below.

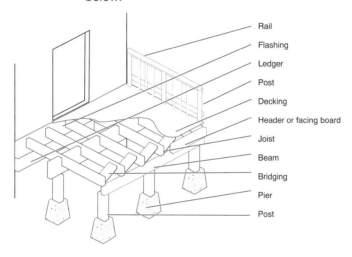

Rail
Flashing
Ledger
Post
Decking
Header or facing board
Joist
Beam
Bridging
Pier
Post

There are two methods of framing for a deck – platform framing and board and beam framing. Each has advantages and disadvantages and the choice of one over the other is influenced by the designer's aesthetic preferences, cost comparisons, the site location, the type and size of timber specified. Some timbers are resistant to decay and others will require preservation and the appearance can again be affected if the structure is stained. Metals will need to be hot-dipped galvanised cadmium plated or primed and painted to minimise corrosion. Rusting nails and metal components will stain the wood and eventually lose their strength and holding capacity. The design and construction must comply to local planning and building regulations. Checks should be made before commencing any

design. The appearance or finish of the decking, as well as the railings, benches, planters, etc., is usually far more important than other wood members because all are in clear view of the users of the deck. The type of wood used for decking is sometimes of better quality or appearance, than the type used for the underlying support members.

CONSTRUCTION

FRAMING

Platform framing

This is a beam and joint method of construction with few beams being required because the joists carry the load over a wide area and usually function as closely spaced beams.
The joist spacings are determined by the load carrying ability of the joists, by the maximum allowable decking spans and by the timber used. Because of the inclusion of the joists this type of framing results in a deeper profile of the deck.

Board and beam framing

In this method of framing no joists are used because the beams are spaced close together to function like joists. The decking should not be less than 50 mm.

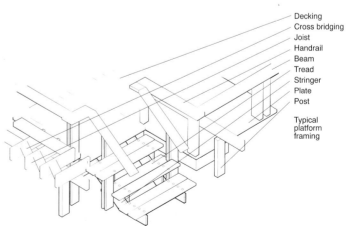

Decking
Cross bridging
Joist
Handrail
Beam
Tread
Stringer
Plate
Post

Typical platform framing

The beam spacings are determined by the maximum allowable decking spans, the cross-sectional dimensions of the beams and their allowable spans. A major advantage of this type of framing is its shallow profile. It is commonly used in the construction of boardwalks and ground level decks.

Basic components

Both methods of framing have the same basic components which are described in detail as follows:

Decking

This refers to the top surface which is used by pedestrians. It is supported directly by either joists or beams, depending on the framing method employed. The allowable span of the decking material determines the maximum spacing of the joists or, in the case of plank-and-beam framing, the maximum spacing of the beams.

Joist spacing directly related to maximum allowable span of decking

Beam spacing directly related to maximum allowable span of decking

Post spacing directly related to maximum allowable span of beams

Decking joist and beam span

- Decking is usually laid flat but can be laid on edge.
- Decking material should be greater than 25 mm (nominal thickness), but 50 mm (nominal) material is most common. Plank-and-beam framing typically requires 50 mm (nominal thickness) or greater decking material and wider planks than those used in platform framing.
- The use of square-edge planks with (5.0 to 6.5 mm) spacing between planks is

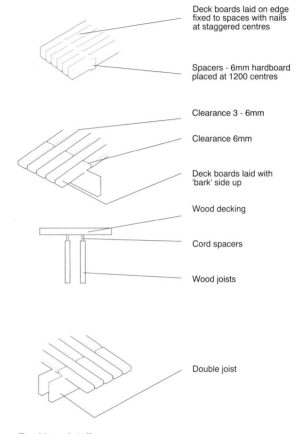

Deck boards laid on edge fixed to spaces with nails at staggered centres

Spacers - 6mm hardboard placed at 1200 centres

Clearance 3 - 6mm

Clearance 6mm

Deck boards laid with 'bark' side up

Wood decking

Cord spacers

Wood joists

Double joist

Decking details

preferable to tongued-and-grooved planks because of better drainage.
- Decking wider than 150 mm is not recommended because of its propensity to warp.
- Edges of decking timbers should have chamfered edges 5.0 to 6.5 mm. Sketch 3.4 shows various patterns.

Joists

Joists are used only in platform framing and their function is to provide support to short spans of decking boards and to distribute imposed loads over a wide area which is why they are spaced closely together (400–600 mm).
When fastening joists and beams, especially with bolts, care must be taken to prevent weakening of the member along the line of maximum shear.

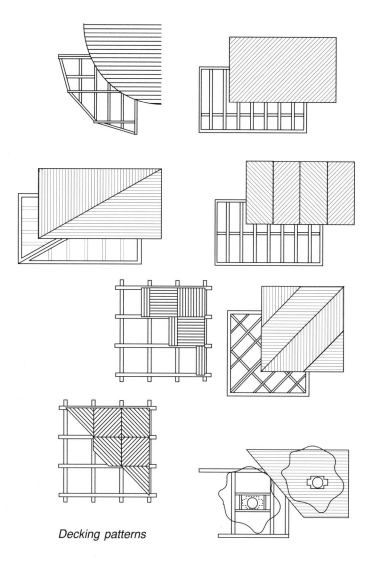

Decking patterns

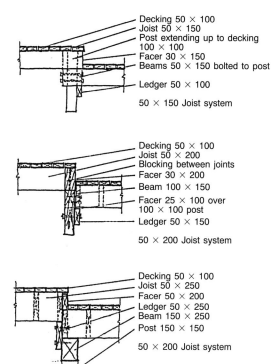

Decking 50 × 100
Joist 50 × 150
Post extending up to decking
100 × 100
Facer 30 × 150
Beams 50 × 150 bolted to post
Ledger 50 × 100

50 × 150 Joist system

Decking 50 × 100
Joist 50 × 200
Blocking between joints
Facer 30 × 200
Beam 100 × 150
Facer 25 × 100 over
100 × 100 post
Ledger 50 × 150

50 × 200 Joist system

Decking 50 × 100
Joist 50 × 250
Facer 50 × 200
Ledger 50 × 250
Beam 150 × 250
Post 150 × 150

50 × 200 Joist system

Level changes

- Joists must be so orientated that the cross section's longitudinal axis is vertical (i.e. narrow dimension up).
- Ideally, joists should be supported on each end by a beam, a ledger, or metal hangers, but nailing directly to a facer is sometimes adequate for small decks with light loading requirements.

Beams

The purpose of the beam is to support the weight of the joists, decking and other elements i.e. planters, seats, handrails, steps etc. This weight is then transferred to the posts or foundations with the beam

spacing depending upon the span of the joists or decking. Usually beams are spaced 1.80 to 2.40 m apart in plank and beam framing and 2.40 to 2.90 m apart in platform framing.

The common types of beams are:

1. *Simple beam:* rests on a support at each end.
2. *Cantilevered beam:* supported at one end only.
3. *Overhanging beam:* projects beyond one or both supports.
4. *Continuous beam:* rests on three or more supports.
5. *Fixed beam:* fixed at both ends.

Beams should be orientated so that the cross-section's longitudinal axis is vertical.

Posts

Posts carry all the weight of the structure to the foundation but if it is a ground level deck or a boardwalk then these vertical elements will not be necessary. Beams or joists can rest directly on the foundations.

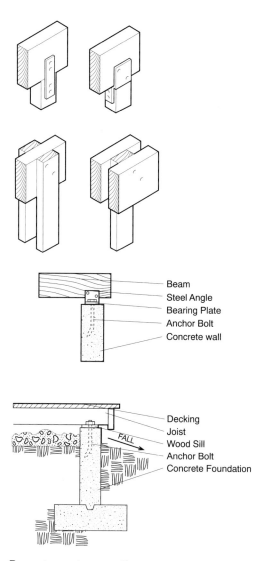

Beam to post connections

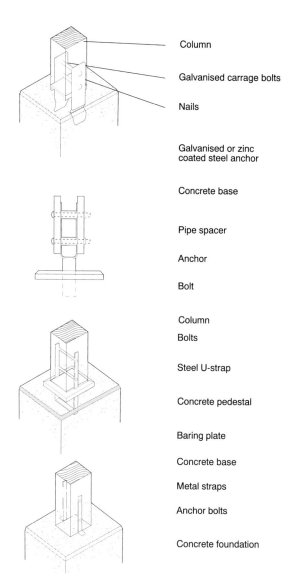

Column

Galvanised carrage bolts

Nails

Galvanised or zinc coated steel anchor

Concrete base

Pipe spacer

Anchor

Bolt

Column

Bolts

Steel U-strap

Concrete pedestal

Baring plate

Concrete base

Metal straps

Anchor bolts

Concrete foundation

Post to pier connections

Where posts are used their spacing must relate to the allowable span of the beams being supported. Square cross-section wooden posts have the least propensity to twist or warp.

- Posts extended up through the deck or boardwalk can also serve as a railing component. Size posts to resist buckling or crushing.
- Steel or masonry columns are usually not tested for bearing strength except under extremely heavy loading conditions.

- Minimise moisture infiltration at the exposed top end of wood posts by angle cutting, capping, or covering.

Footings

The purpose of the footing is to anchor the deck or boardwalk to the ground and at the same time carry its weight and loading. Footings must extend below the frost line to prevent movement caused by the processes of thawing and freezing. However, this is not necessary for light structures; should a deck be attached to a stabilised structure then it too must be made stable. See details at end of chapter.

• Pier-and-beam foundations are necessary on expansive clay soils, unstable organic soils, and deep fills.
• The size of the footing depends on the weight to be supported and on the load-bearing capacity of the soil.
• Reinforcing is necessary in larger footings and piers to prevent failure of the concrete, especially in colder climates.
• Humid climates require different footing types and post connections than arid

climates because of moisture trapping problems.
• Protect footings from the possibility of washouts, i.e. soil erosion around the footing.

Bracing and blocking

This is used to help stabilise the structure especially if it is free standing, by limiting lateral movement and should be considered on all vertical supportive elements exceeding 1500 mm in height and at corners.

Blocking is more common in platform framing than it is in plank-and-beam framing. It is less important for large decks, especially when long joist spans are used. When bracing ensure that moisture trapping is avoided in methods of fastening and that connections are not weakened by too many bolts and nails.

Consider the aesthetic factors when using bracing and blocking and make it an integral part of the whole design.

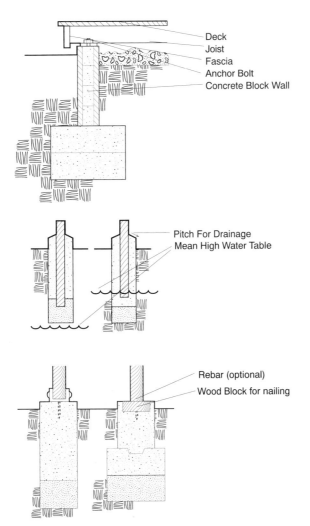

Footings and pier details

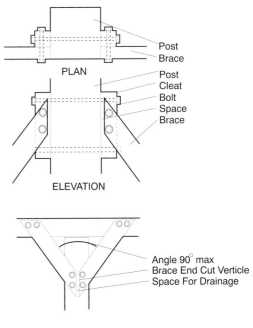

Bracing details

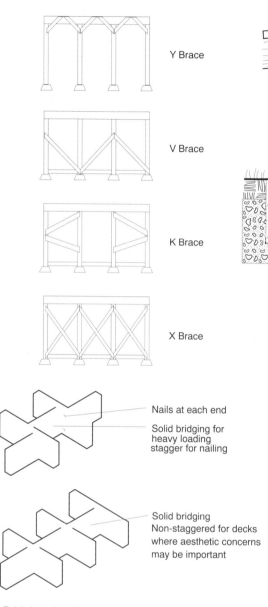

Y Brace

V Brace

K Brace

X Brace

Nails at each end

Solid bridging for heavy loading stagger for nailing

Solid bridging Non-staggered for decks where aesthetic concerns may be important

Bridging details

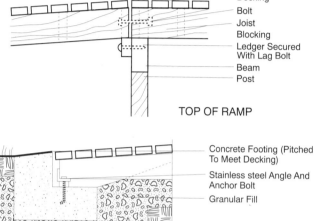

Decking
Bolt
Joist
Blocking
Ledger Secured With Lag Bolt
Beam
Post

TOP OF RAMP

Concrete Footing (Pitched To Meet Decking)

Stainless steel Angle And Anchor Bolt

Granular Fill

RAMP FOOTING

Ramp details

Stairs and railings

Depending on the height of the structure and its required space will determine the need for stairs or railings. A railing is not required when one or two steps are used for low decks but may be desirable for elderly and handicapped persons.

Changes of level can be achieved by other means such as regrading terraced decking or ramps. Boardwalks can follow the profile of the ground while low level decks may not require either steps or railings.

Stairs, ramps, railings and other such features contribute significantly (i.e. attractiveness) to the finished deck or boardwalk and therefore require careful attention to design detail.

Ensure that local building regulations are checked particularly with regards to access for the disabled.

Wood stairs generally utilise stringers and treads. Stringers can be 50 × 250 mm or 50 × 300 mm attached to the deck and to a firm base, probably concrete. Two stringers can support treads up to 1100 mm in width for average grade timber.

Stringers can be notched to hold treads, or cleats can be attached. The latter are stronger. Nails, by themselves, are not recommended as fasteners on stairs. The riser–tread relationship may be a little steeper than for other outdoor steps according to prevailing practice. Risers over are not recommended.

Construction techniques for stair and railing connections vary widely. The design is often determined by the extent of durability and safety necessary.

For information on tread/riser ratio see Landscape Detailing Book 1, Surfaces.

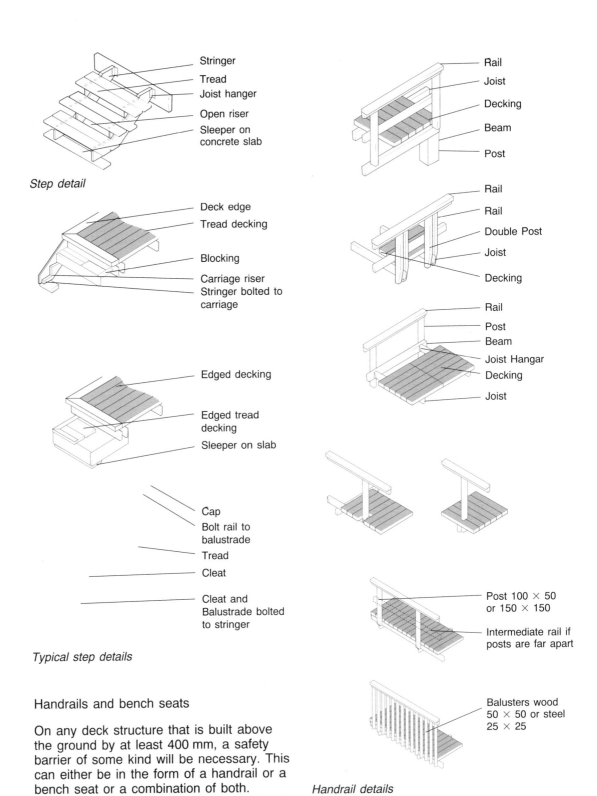

Step detail

- Stringer
- Tread
- Joist hanger
- Open riser
- Sleeper on concrete slab

- Deck edge
- Tread decking
- Blocking
- Carriage riser
- Stringer bolted to carriage

- Edged decking
- Edged tread decking
- Sleeper on slab

- Cap
- Bolt rail to balustrade
- Tread
- Cleat
- Cleat and Balustrade bolted to stringer

Typical step details

- Rail
- Joist
- Decking
- Beam
- Post

- Rail
- Rail
- Double Post
- Joist
- Decking

- Rail
- Post
- Beam
- Joist Hangar
- Decking
- Joist

- Post 100 × 50 or 150 × 150
- Intermediate rail if posts are far apart

- Balusters wood 50 × 50 or steel 25 × 25

Handrail details

Handrails and bench seats

On any deck structure that is built above the ground by at least 400 mm, a safety barrier of some kind will be necessary. This can either be in the form of a handrail or a bench seat or a combination of both. The posts for handrails should be rigid and can be either vertical or set at an angle, but they must be securely fixed to the frame of the structure. The height of the rail should be of a minimum height for people to lean on or against. Posts should not be more than 1800 mm apart to support a 50 × 100 mm rail.

Posts may be a part of the structure and extended through the deck boards or be attached to beams. Fasteners other than nails, except in small intermediate rails, are recommended.

Benches can be combined with railings for additional utility and function and can be integrally designed and constructed.

Support members can be wood bolted to joists extending up through the decking or

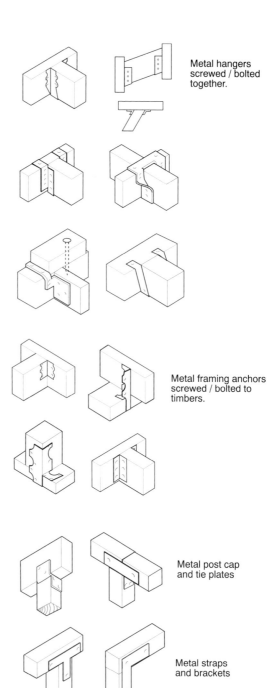

Metal hangers screwed / bolted together.

Metal framing anchors screwed / bolted to timbers.

Metal post cap and tie plates

Metal straps and brackets

Typical framing anchors

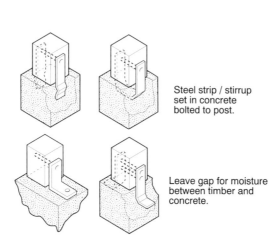

Steel strip / stirrup set in concrete bolted to post.

Leave gap for moisture between timber and concrete.

Typical post anchors

fabricated metal straps attached to the surface of the deck.

Materials

While careful attention to timber quality and grade is important the main factors to consider are:

    Hardness
    Warp resistance
    Ease of working
    Paint holding
    Stain acceptance
    Nail holding
    Heartwood decay resistance
    Proportion of heartwood

Bending strength
Stiffness
Strength as a post
Freedom from pitch

More information on this subject is available from TRADA. The various types of metal hardware require equal consideration as briefly described below.

Anchors, Hangers and Plates

Various types of anchors, hangers and plates are used to achieve easy and strong connections between various wood members and between wood members and concrete foundations. See Figure 3.12.

Nails

Those types of nails that are commonly used in wood deck and boardwalk construction are shown below.

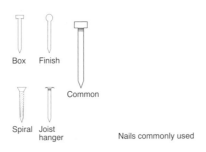

Nails commonly used

- The dimensions, shape, and surface of a nail affect its holding power. Normally, a nail 2½ times as long as the thickness of the board nailed should be used. Hot-dipped galvanised, zinc-coated, cement-coated, ring, and spiral nails also resist withdrawal.
- Nails with heads (e.g. common) should be used for structural framing. Finish nails are only used in non-structural situations where appearance is important. Driving the nail at a slight angle will improve its holding power.
- Nails may tend to pull out under heavy loading conditions. Bolts or lag bolts should be used in such instances.
- Aluminium, stainless-steel, and hot-dipped galvanised nails resist rusting and consequent staining of wood.

Wood screws

Those types of screws that are commonly used in wood deck and boardwalk construction are shown below.

Flathead Oval head Roundhead

Wood screws commonly used

- A screw should be long enough to embed more than one-half of its length into the base.
- Clearance and pilot holes help the installation of wood screws and will prevent splitting of the wood member.
- Flathead screws may be flush or countersunk. Washers under the head are recommended for roundheaded screws, especially with softer woods. These can also be countersunk.

Bolts

Those types of bolts that are commonly used in wood deck and boardwalk construction are shown below.

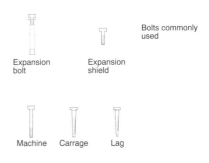

Expansion bolt

Expansion shield

Bolts commonly used

Machine Carrage Lag

- Bolts should be long enough to permit a washer under both the head and the nut and allow at least 5 mm to protrude beyond the nut. Carriage bolts are used with metal plates with a square hole to prevent the bolt from turning while being tightened.
- A hole 1 mm greater than the diameter of the bolt should be drilled for a snug fit.
- Lag bolts require a washer under the head. The threaded end of a lag bolt

should never be exposed. Pilot holes allow the installation of the lag bolt and will prevent splitting of the wood member.

Masonry

It should be noted that concrete, brick or stone can be used to build the supports for the deck structure. In certain climates they are far more durable and stronger and can offer many aesthetic advantages as well.

Metal

In addition to hardware, metal products such as tubing can be used for such structures as railings, foot rests, arbours, overhead canopies, planters, and the like. Members such as I-beams and metal columns can be substituted for wooden beams and posts, respectively.

Plastics

The wide variety of plastics available make this material ideal for railings, arbours, overhead canopies, tubs, planters, and the like. Plastics offer durability, light weight, and innumerable colours. As construction materials, plastics have yet to be used to their fullest potential.

Plants

Plant materials can be used with low decks and boardwalks to define edges and to help prevent users from accidentally walking or falling off the structure. Plant materials can also provide screening and windbreaks that might otherwise have to be constructed and maintained at much greater expense.

TABLES FOR TIMBER SIZES

There are several methods of determining the size and spacing of the components to be used. One is through complex mathematical formulae for determining reflection, bending moments, horizontal shear, allowable stresses, etc.

Another is through tables. These tables have been developed as a general guide for component selection in most situations, and they can be used to save time on calculations.

Most structures will begin with footings (down to the frost line or no less than 600 mm depth for stability), to which the posts are attached. The posts in turn support the beam. Whether or not joists are used depends upon the design. A low deck close to the ground may not have sufficient room available to use joists. More beams closer together will solve the problem, based on the chart for 'allowable spans of deck boards or planking' a 1500 mm average wood species.

TABLE 1. POST SIZES (MINIMUM)

Post size (mm)	Load area[1] Beam spacing × Post spacing (m²)									
	3.30	4.45	5.55	6.70	7.80	9.0	10.0	11.15	12.25	13.35
100 × 100	up to 3.60	up to 3.0 m heights		up to 2.40 m heights			up to 1.80 m heights			
100 × 150		up to 3.60 m heights		up to 3.0m heights			up to 2.40m heights			
150 × 150		up to 3.60 m heights								

Source: USDA Handbook No 432
Example: If the beam supports are spaced 2.50 m on centre and the posts are 3.50 m on centre then the load area is 8.75 – use the next larger area 9.0
[1]Based on 195 kg/m² deck live load plus 49 kg/m² dead load.

TABLE 2. MINIMUM BEAM SIZES AND SPANS[1]

Beam size	Spacing between beams								
	1200	1500	1800	2100	2400	2700	3000	3300	3600
100 × 150	Up to 1.80								
75 × 200	Up to 12.80	Up to 1.80							
100 × 200	Up to 12.40	Up to 2.10	Up to 1.80						
75 × 250	Up to 12.70	Up to 2.40	Up to 2.10	Up to 1.80					
100 × 250	Up to 3.0	Up to 2.70	Up to 2.40		Up to 2.10		Up to 1.80		
75 × 300	Up to 33	Up to 3.00	Up to 2.70	Up to 2.40	Up to 2.10			Up to 1.80	
100 × 300	Up to 3.60	Up to 3.30	Up to 3.00	Up to 2.70		Up to 2.40		Up to 2.10	
150 × 250		Up to 3.60	Up to 3.30	Up to 3.70	Up to 2.70		Up to 2.40		
150 × 300			Up to 3.60		Up to 3.30		Up to 3.00		Up to 2.40

Source: USDA Handbook No 432

[1]Beams are on edge. Spans are centre to centre distance between posts or supports. (Based on 195 kg/m² deck live load plus 49 kg/m² dead load.

[2]Example: If the beams are 2.80 m apart, use the 3.0 column 75 × 250 up to 1.80 spans, 100 × 250 or 75 × 300 up to 2.10 spans, 100 × 300 or 150 × 250 up to 2.70 spans, 150 × 300 up to 3.30 spans.

TABLE 3. MAXIMUM ALLOWABLE SPANS FOR DECK JOISTS[1]

Joist size (inches)	Joist spacing (inches)		
	400	600	800
50 × 150	2.40	1.90	1.50
50 × 200	3.00	2.40	2.00
50 × 250	3.90	3.10	2.50

[1]Joists are on edge. Spans are centre distances between beams or supports. Beamed on 195 kg/m² deck live loads plus 49 kg/m² dead load.

TABLE 4. MAXIMUM ALLOWABLE SPANS FOR SPACED DECK BOARDS[1]

	Maximum allowable span (mm)					
	Laid flat			Laid on edge		
50 × 100	50 × 50	50 × 75	50 × 100	50 × 75	50 × 100
300	1050	1050	1050	1650	2700

Source: USDA Handbook No 432

[1]These spans are based on the assumption that more than one floor board carries normal loads. If concentrated loads are a rule, spans should be reduced accordingly.

The publication 'Time Saver Standards for Landscape Architects' provides considerable technical information on this subject and is a very useful reference.

In situations involving upper level decks where use will be made of the space below, a minimum number of supporting beams and posts will probably be desirable. This will require larger beams and posts and the use of joists to distribute the load to the fewer number of beams.

Footings will generally be in concrete and sized to handle the load in relation to the bearing capacities of the soil. Consult a structural engineer if in any doubt. At a minimum a 400 × 400 square × 250 deep is recommended for footings.

BOARDWALKS

Boardwalks are often used to provide raised safe access across dunes, marsh or other sensitive and easily disturbed landscapes. They are usually built with a permanent rigid construction almost always of timber, although galvanised steel and concrete have been used.

A wood boardwalk has a foundation, framing, decking, sometimes a railing if over 750 mm above ground level and special features such as benches or view platforms. Depending upon location and design, the foundation is almost always a pier or wood post. If in contact with the ground or submerged in water the post of

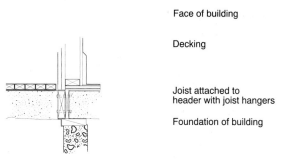

Face of building

Decking

Joist attached to header with joist hangers

Foundation of building

Bridging

150mm Well-graded gravel

Gravel edge

Parquet deck

75mm sand

75mm gravel

Planking

Concrete ties

Gravel

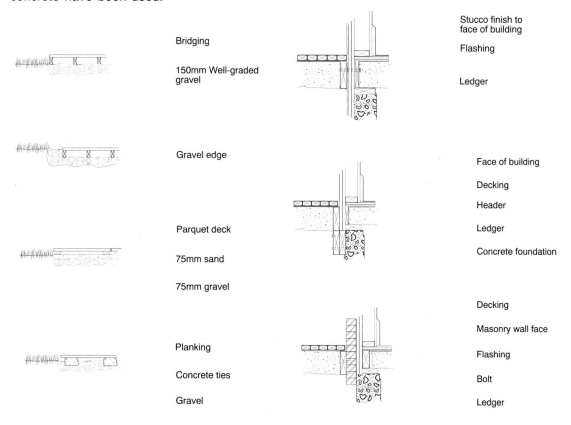

Stucco finish to face of building

Flashing

Ledger

Face of building

Decking

Header

Ledger

Concrete foundation

Decking

Masonry wall face

Flashing

Bolt

Ledger

Ground level decks

Typical anchorage to fixed structures

softwood must be treated with a preservative, preferably a non-toxic type. If hardwood is used it must be from a sustainable source. Softwood thinnings – half or full round – could be used if treated. For ground level boardwalks old railway sleepers or telephone/power poles could be used as these materials have already been treated and are substantial in size. Sleepers are normally 250 $\times$ 125 $\times$ 2.4 m long. Poles are usually 300/400 diameter, lengths vary from 6 to 10 m. For the construction of an above ground boardwalk the post serves the same function as the foundation for a bridge.

Construction is similar to footbridges and the decking plays the same important structural role. Where hand rails are used they should also be built to the same requirements as for foot-bridges.

Boardwalks can have platform framing or plank and beam framing. Platform framing involves a beam and joist system of structural support, while plank and beam framing means that only beams and wood decking are installed on top of the posts. The size, type and spacing between beams will determine design load capacity. The most effective plank and beam construction uses the least amount of material to achieve the strongest design load capacity.

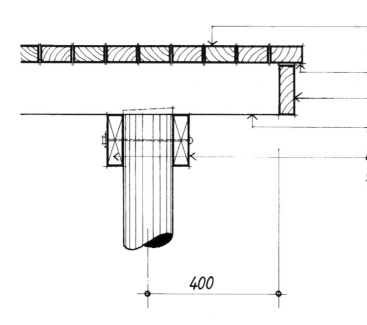

Deck 50 x 100 boards with
9mm spacing

Overhang 12mm

Trim 50 x 150

Joist 50 x 150 at 6000 centres

Beams 2 no. 50 x 150 with
galvanised iron carriage bolt
15Ø 250mm long with
washer

400

SECTION

TIMBER DECK
edge (with trim)

Scale 1:10

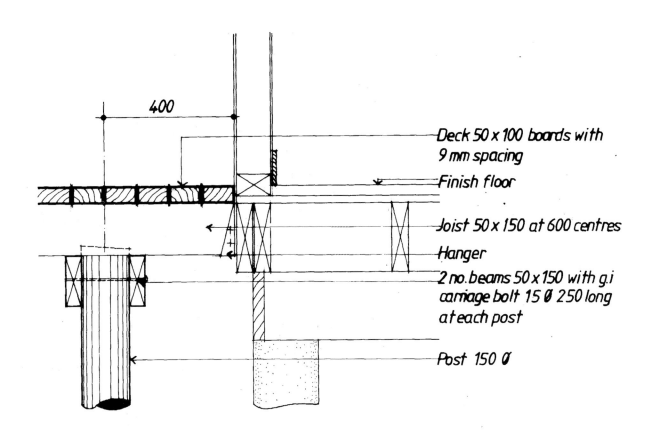

400

Deck 50 x 100 boards with
9 mm spacing

Finish floor

Joist 50 x 150 at 600 centres

Hanger

2 no. beams 50 x 150 with g.i
carriage bolt 15 Ø 250 long
at each post

Post 150 Ø

SECTION

TIMBER DECK
junction with building

Scale 1:10

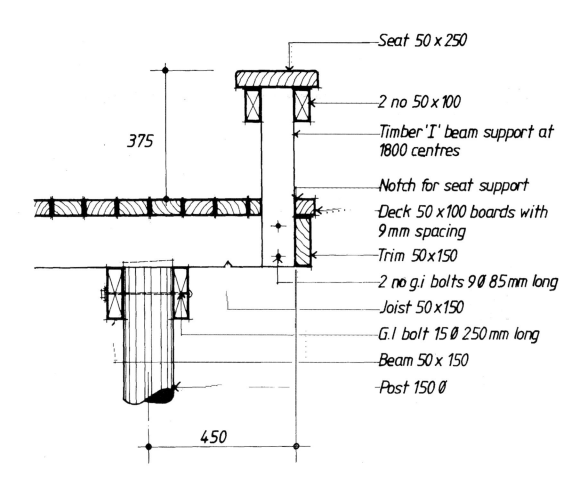

SECTION

Seat 50 x 250

2 no 50 x 100

Timber 'I' beam support at 1800 centres

Notch for seat support

Deck 50 x 100 boards with 9 mm spacing

Trim 50 x 150

2 no g.i bolts 9Ø 85 mm long

Joist 50 x 150

G.I bolt 15 Ø 250 mm long

Beam 50 x 150

Post 150 Ø

375

450

Scale 1:10

TIMBER DECK
seat/rail (with trim)

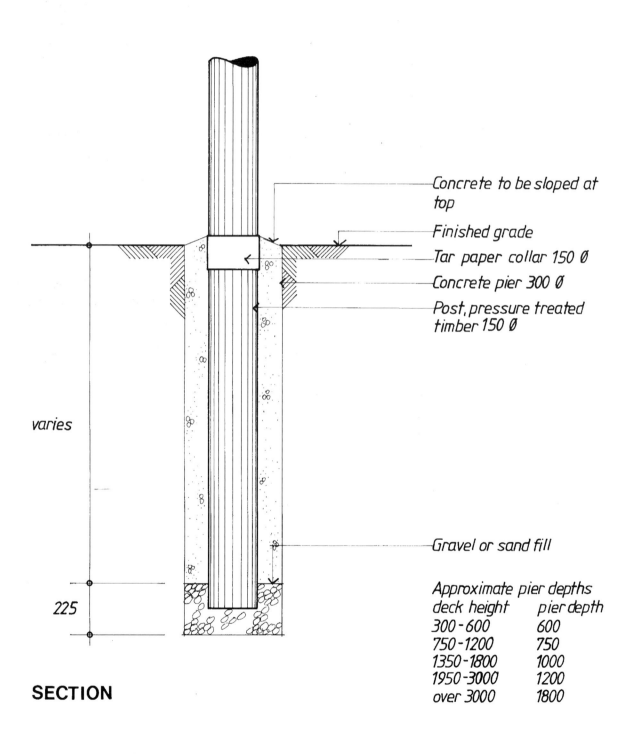

Concrete to be sloped at top

Finished grade

Tar paper collar 150 Ø

Concrete pier 300 Ø

Post, pressure treated timber 150 Ø

Gravel or sand fill

varies

225

SECTION

Approximate pier depths

deck height	pier depth
300 - 600	600
750 - 1200	750
1350 - 1800	1000
1950 - 3000	1200
over 3000	1800

Scale 1:10

TIMBER DECK
post detail (typical)

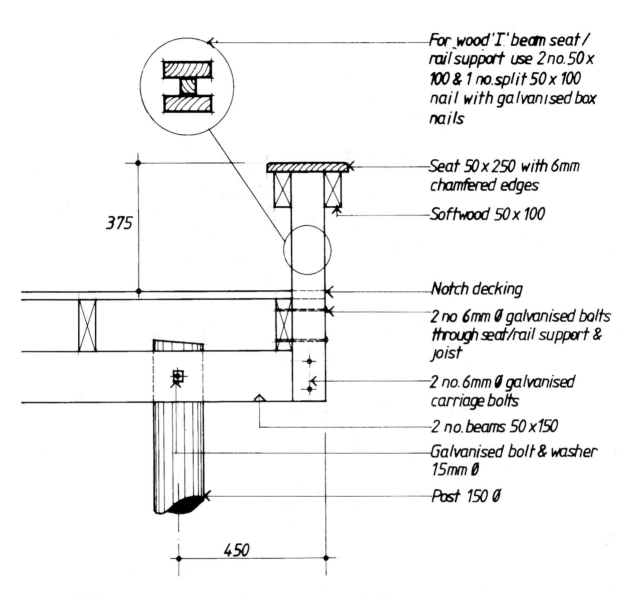

For wood 'I' beam seat / rail support use 2 no. 50 x 100 & 1 no. split 50 x 100 nail with galvanised box nails

Seat 50 x 250 with 6mm chamfered edges

Softwood 50 x 100

375

Notch decking

2 no 6mm Ø galvanised bolts through seat/rail support & joist

2 no. 6mm Ø galvanised carriage bolts

2 no. beams 50 x 150

Galvanised bolt & washer 15mm Ø

Post 150 Ø

450

SECTION

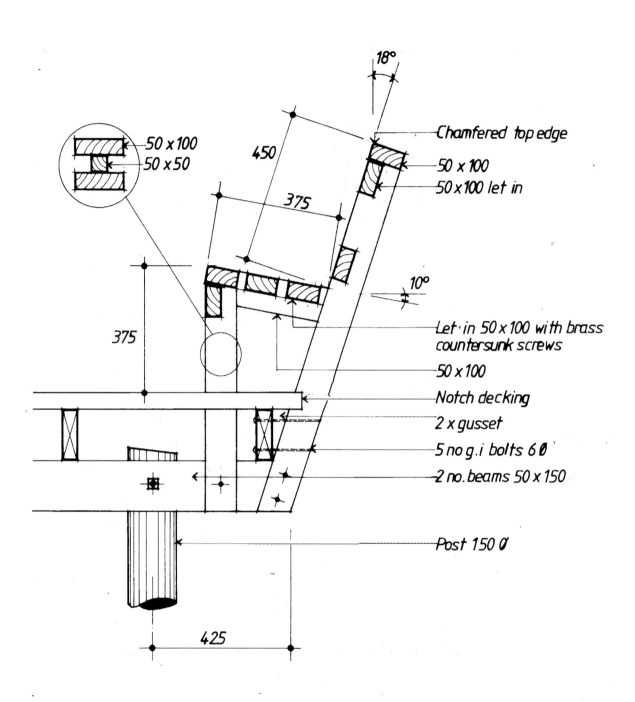

18°

50 x 100
50 x 50

Chamfered top edge

450

375

50 x 100

50 x 100 let in

10°

375

Let·in 50 x 100 with brass
countersunk screws

50 x 100

Notch decking

2 x gusset

5 no g.i bolts 60

2 no. beams 50 x 150

Post 150 ∅

425

SECTION

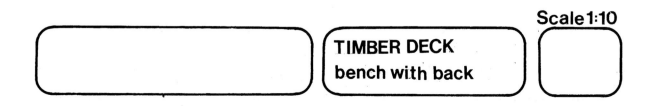

TIMBER DECK
bench with back

Scale 1:10

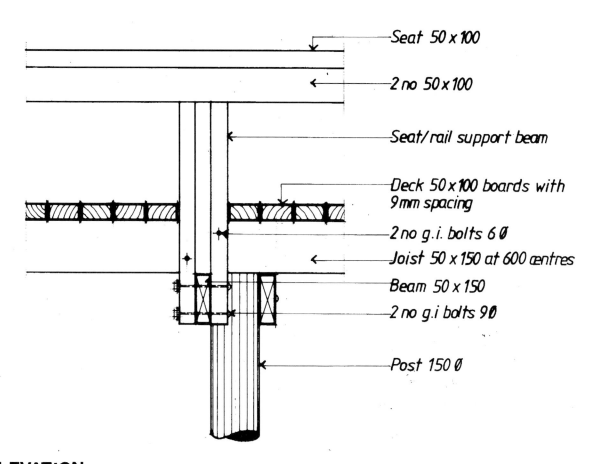

Seat 50 x 100

2 no 50 x 100

Seat/rail support beam

Deck 50 x 100 boards with 9mm spacing

2 no g.i. bolts 6 Ø

Joist 50 x 150 at 600 centres

Beam 50 x 150

2 no g.i bolts 9Ø

Post 150 Ø

ELEVATION

Scale 1:10

TIMBER DECK
seat/rail (with trim)

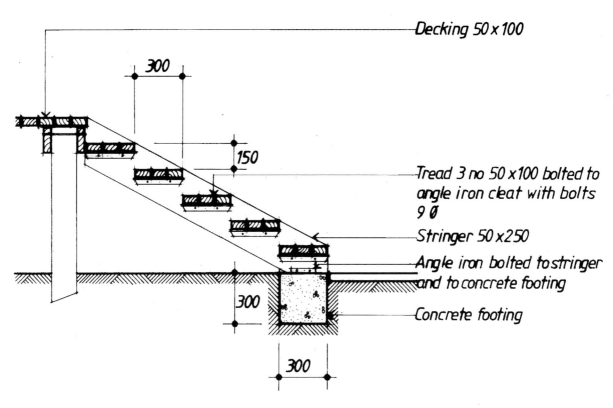

Decking 50 x 100

300

150

Tread 3 no 50 x 100 bolted to
angle iron cleat with bolts
9 ∅

Stringer 50 x 250

Angle iron bolted to stringer
and to concrete footing

Concrete footing

300

300

SECTION

TIMBER DECK
typical steps

Scale 1:20

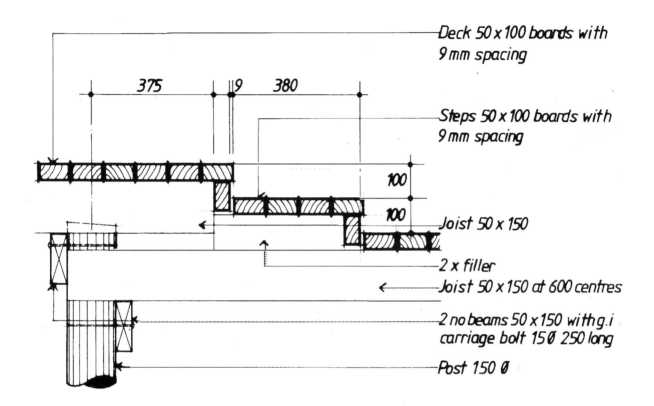

Deck 50 x 100 boards with 9 mm spacing

375   9   380

Steps 50 x 100 boards with 9 mm spacing

100

100

Joist 50 x 150

2 x filler

Joist 50 x 150 at 600 centres

2 no beams 50 x 150 with g.i carriage bolt 15 Ø 250 long

Post 150 Ø

SECTION

Scale 1:10

TIMBER DECK
lower level

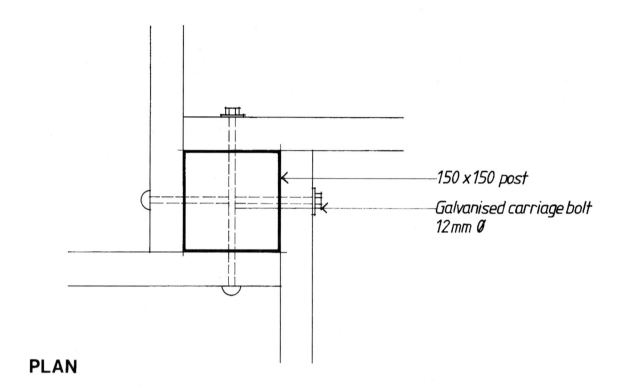

PLAN

150 x 150 post

Galvanised carriage bolt
12 mm ⌀

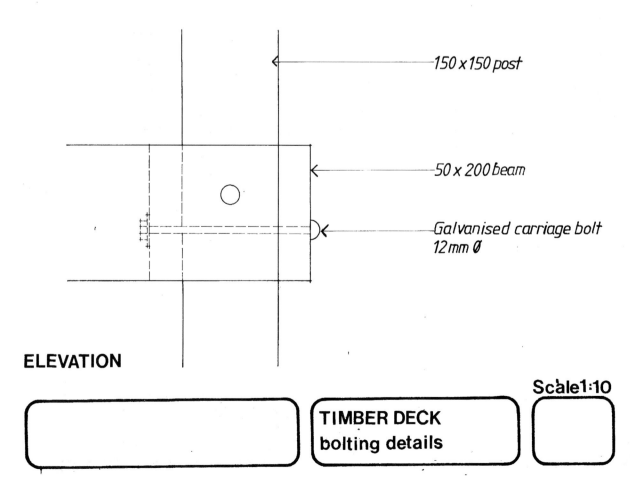

150 x 150 post

50 x 200 beam

Galvanised carriage bolt
12 mm ⌀

ELEVATION

Scale 1:10

TIMBER DECK
bolting details

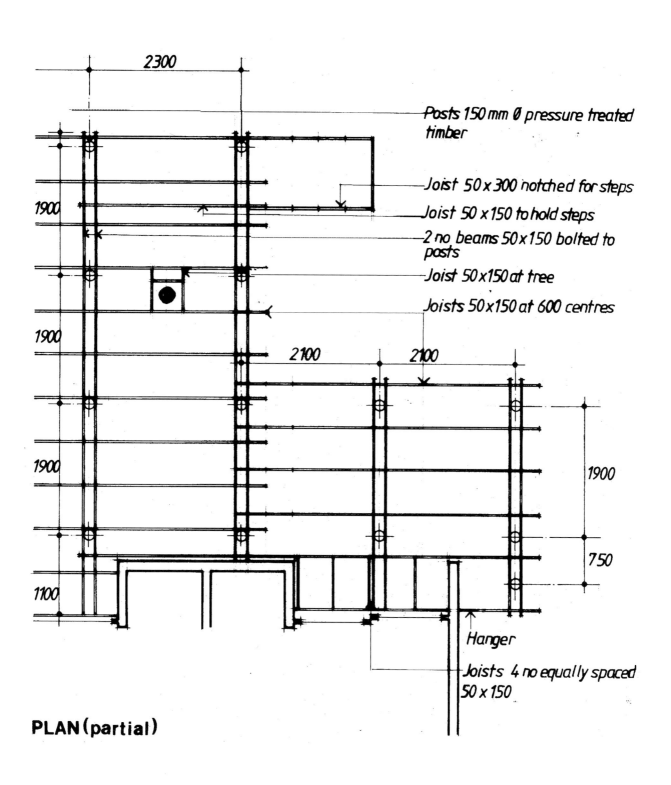

2300

Posts 150mm Ø pressure treated timber

Joist 50 x 300 notched for steps

Joist 50 x 150 to hold steps

2 no. beams 50 x 150 bolted to posts

Joist 50 x 150 at tree

Joists 50 x 150 at 600 centres

1900

1900

2100   2100

1900

1900

1900

750

1100

Hanger

Joists 4 no. equally spaced 50 x 150

PLAN (partial)

Scale 1:50

TIMBER DECK
framing

71

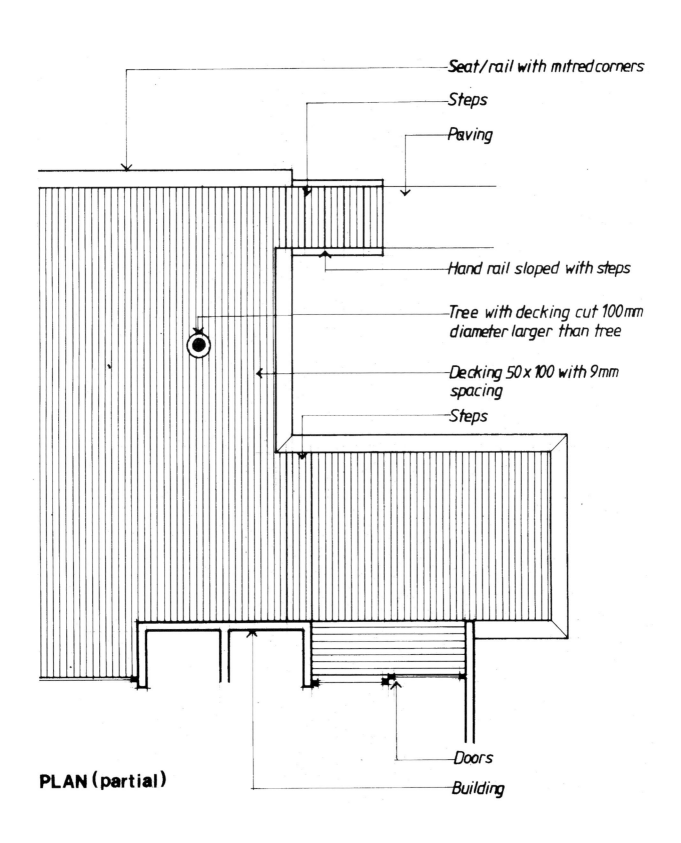

Seat/rail with mitred corners

Steps

Paving

Hand rail sloped with steps

Tree with decking cut 100mm diameter larger than tree

Decking 50 x 100 with 9mm spacing

Steps

Doors

Building

PLAN (partial)

TIMBER DECK
floor

Scale 1:50

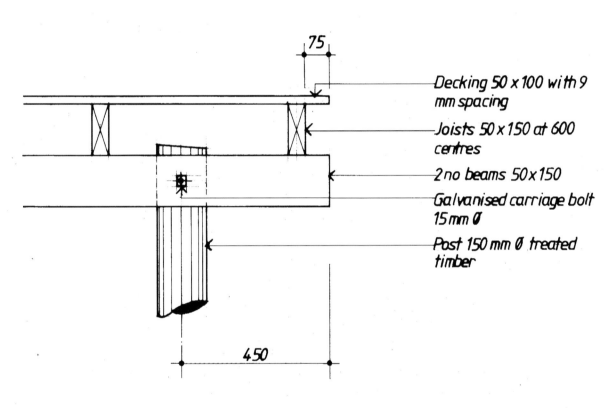

75

Decking 50 x 100 with 9 mm spacing

Joists 50 x 150 at 600 centres

2 no beams 50 x 150

Galvanised carriage bolt 15 mm Ø

Post 150 mm Ø treated timber

450

SECTION

Scale 1:10

TIMBER DECK
edge (without trim)

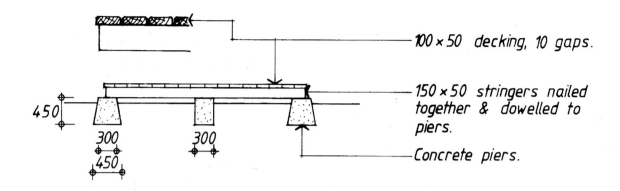

100 × 50 decking, 10 gaps.

150 × 50 stringers nailed together & dowelled to piers.

Concrete piers.

450

300   300

450

SECTION

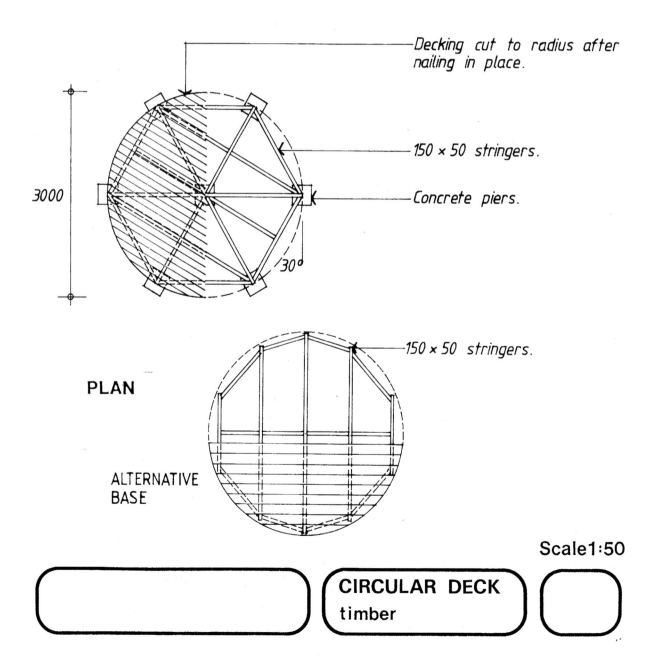

Decking cut to radius after nailing in place.

150 × 50 stringers.

Concrete piers.

3000

30°

150 × 50 stringers.

PLAN

ALTERNATIVE BASE

Scale 1:50

CIRCULAR DECK
timber

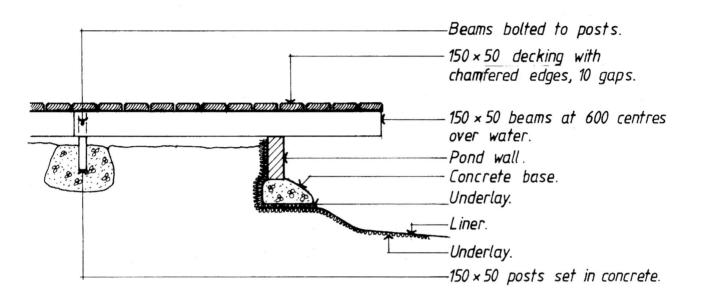

Beams bolted to posts.

150 × 50 decking with chamfered edges, 10 gaps.

150 × 50 beams at 600 centres over water.

Pond wall.

Concrete base.

Underlay.

Liner.

Underlay.

150 × 50 posts set in concrete.

SECTION

Scale 1:2O

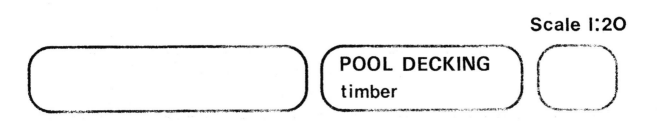

POOL DECKING
timber

75

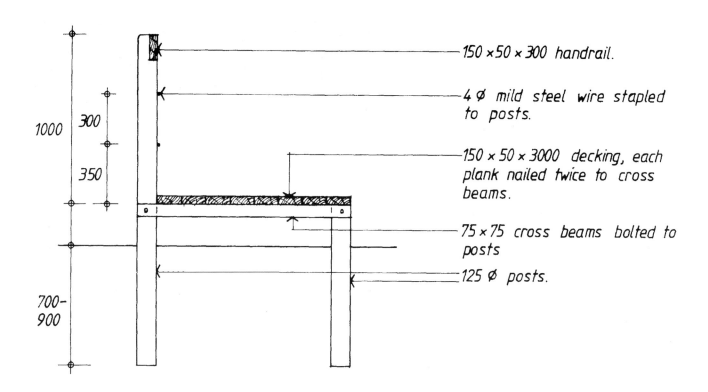

SECTION

150 × 50 × 300 handrail.

4 ∅ mild steel wire stapled to posts.

150 × 50 × 3000 decking, each plank nailed twice to cross beams.

75 × 75 cross beams bolted to posts

125 ∅ posts.

1000

300

350

700-900

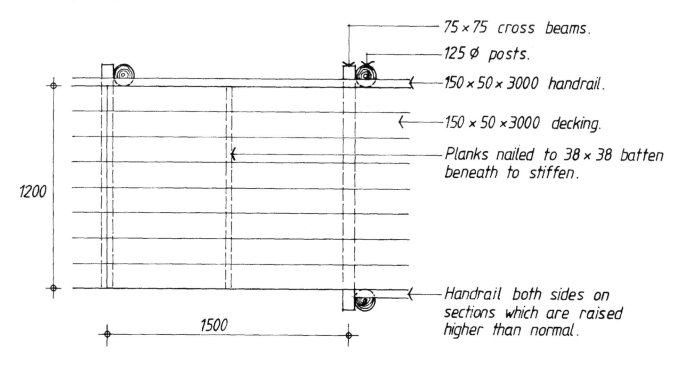

PLAN

75 × 75 cross beams.

125 ∅ posts.

150 × 50 × 3000 handrail.

150 × 50 × 3000 decking.

Planks nailed to 38 × 38 batten beneath to stiffen.

Handrail both sides on sections which are raised higher than normal.

1200

1500

Scale 1:20

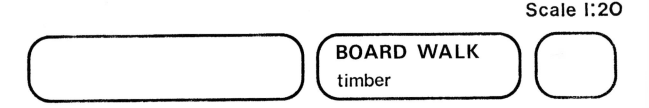

BOARD WALK
timber

PEDESTRIAN BRIDGES

1. GENERAL

'Footbridges in the Countryside' and 'Time Saver Standards for Landscape Architects' provide considerable technical information on this subject. It is not the purpose of this publication to supersede this in any way but to provide a basic summary, which will endorse the need to seek further advice where appropriate. Footbridges occur not only in the countryside but in urban parks and open spaces, gardens and commercial landscapes, business parks, hospital grounds and places of education – universities, colleges and school grounds. It is hoped that the selection of details will provide some assistance to the designer for his/her scheme be it rural or urban, large or small scale. Selection costs will play an important part in the design as will the use of local and/or reclaimed materials, the level of construction skills and the site itself.

2. SITE SELECTION

Having decided that a crossing of a water course is necessary the designer must then decide what means is appropriate, i.e. a footbridge, or a ford or stepping stones. If a footbridge is necessary there may be a choice of location. Factors to be considered, with users in mind, are:

- Which has the shortest span.
- Which has the best foundation conditions.
- Which is closest to the line of the existing footpath.
- Which allows the best approaches to the footbridge. The paths leading up to the footbridge must be on well-drained or drainable ground if messy path erosion problems at either end of the bridge are to be avoided.
- Which gives the best clearance from flooding.
- Which is easiest to reach with plant, men and materials.
- Which has the fewest hazards to make safe, such as precipices, steep paths, exposure to strong winds.
- Which may users prefer. What are the views from each side, is there a pool beneath (for looking at fish), rapids at hand, a waterfall in sight; what are the views from the bridge, from the approaches, from a distance.

A bridge should carry a path across a stream or gap with the minimum interference to the natural waterway when the river is running full. The site for a bridge must be chosen with this in mind. When selecting the site make strict inquiries regarding the level of flood waters. *The surface of a bridge should be at least 0.6 m above flood level.* Streams which flow through tree-covered land are less likely to come down in spate than those which flow through open country. Steep-cut banks often indicate a hard formation and a good site. Sand appears to stand high when cut by the action of the stream, therefore examine the banks carefully. The ideal site is where the river is narrow and where the banks are solid even if it means moving the alignment of an existing path.

Once a site is selected it must be surveyed in detail to enable the designer to produce

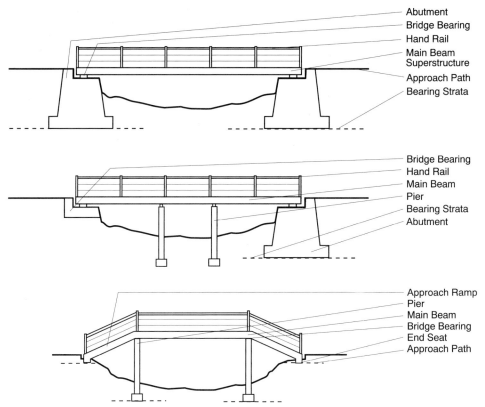

Abutment
Bridge Bearing
Hand Rail
Main Beam
Superstructure
Approach Path
Bearing Strata

Bridge Bearing
Hand Rail
Main Beam
Pier
Bearing Strata
Abutment

Approach Ramp
Pier
Main Beam
Bridge Bearing
End Seat
Approach Path

Bridges – basic components

the appropriate bridge including its foundations and approaches.

3. BRIDGE TYPES

There are five basic types of footbridges:
- the log
- the in-situ construction
- the prefabricated
- the low water
- the suspension

The log footbridge – built for centuries with three basic components – log beams, decking and in some cases one handrail or two. Beams are long, straight timber poles, spanning 3–12 m depending on size and length of log. Decking is sawn planks or half round poles. Handrails can be sawn square timber or round or half-round poles.
The in-situ footbridge is the most common type in the UK and is constructed to fit a

specific site in a variety of configurations as described.

The prefabricated footbridge is made by specialists in the workshop, brought to the site and assembled at a specific crossing. The advantages over in-situ construction are:
- site area disturbance is reduced
- significant cost savings
- can be built regardless of climatic conditions
- can span greater distances
- minimal amount of skill and expertise required at site.

The low water footbridge is constructed to allow water to flow over the top of the bridge under certain conditions. They can be constructed in place or prefabricated from concrete culverts or pipes encased in concrete, precast concrete superstructure and decking, and temporary wooden logs or poles but under high water or flood conditions the surface of the bridge is usually inundated with flowing water.

The advantage of a low water bridge over other bridge types is the reduced length of span required for the same crossing. This situation most often occurs where the width and the required height of the crossing above the stream channel makes the length of an out-of-channel span bridge prohibitively expensive. A low-water bridge can cross the stream at a lower cost and, if properly designed, can be safe and accessible to all users.

One of the disadvantages of low-water bridges is that they collect silt from stream overwash. Another is that a low-water bridge can trap debris and block up during high water causing flooding upstream.

The suspension footbridge is usually built when no other type can span the required distance of the crossing within a budget allocation. It is more applicable in remote sites where it is virtually impossible to construct other kinds of bridges. There are two styles: *rope bridges*, where rope cross bracing is used as the walking surface, and *steel cable* bridges with wood or metal superstructures and decking. It is not unusual for these bridges to clear spans of 50–100 m and simple methods of construction can produce safe and effective clear span crossings of 17–25 m.

4. BRIDGE SELECTION

The basic components of a footbridge are shown in Figure 4.1.

There are many factors to be taken into account when selecting the type of bridge for a specific project (apart from the users), such as:

• Finance available.
• Construction – methods and workers.
• Capability of designer.
• Size – structures up to 9.0 m should only be considered without assistance from an engineer.

Local planning regulations may require not only planning approval but a certificate from a registered Structural Engineer, depending upon the size of the bridge.

Consideration must also be given to what may pass underneath the bridge, especially boat traffic, as well as protection of users on top of the bridge. Depending upon the height of the bridge provision for handrails should be take into account. None would be required for bridges over shallow streams provided that they remain so in periods of heavy rainfall.

The needs for handicapped users including the approaches, landings, surfaces, rest areas, handrails should also be considered, and even bottom rails for wheel guidance should also be considered. If there are any ramps approaching the bridge then there should be a level landing or platform of at least 1500 mm (5 ft). Places to sit or rest could be designed as part of the bridge either at the end or in the middle, if it is a long bridge.

Non-slip surfaces are an essential design factor. Timber decking is the usual material and laminated decks are even stronger and stiffer. The latter can be covered with a bitumen and gravel material.

The width of a bridge should be considered at the design stage. Table 5 provides a guide.

The decision on whether the footbridge should be one way or two will depend on its location.

In urban situations it is likely that footbridges will be two way.

They may be made wider to allow crowd flow in certain situations.

They will usually cater for wheelchairs.

In accessible rural situations footbridges will usually be two way and may cater for wheelchairs depending on the approach paths.

In remote rural situations footbridges will usually be one way only.

In deciding the width of a footbridge other factors to be considered are:

• The width of the approach paths.
• Structural requirements – long span bridges may require to be wider to provide lateral stiffness to the structure.
• Economy – the footbridge should be as narrow as possible to achieve lowest cost.

Selection of main structural members

When a bridge type has been selected, the size and form of the main structural members may be determined in one of the following three ways:

1. **Typical bridge designs**: for spans under (9 m) where no site difficulties exist, a typical footbridge may be built.
2. **Prefabricated bridge designs**: specialist suppliers offer a range of standard bridge types, either in kit form or completed and ready to place in position. Commonly available bridge types include:
   a. Laminated timber beams
   b. Hardwood beams and made-up girders
   c. Steel lattice girders
   d. Aluminium lattice girders
   e. Precast concrete beams
3. **Special designs**: custom-made bridge structures may be designed by experienced engineers, especially for spans exceeding 9 m.

Note:

The material available for bearers (e.g., locally cut unseasoned timber, squared seasoned timber, rolled steel joists or old rails) will decide the type of bridge to be built (i.e. whether it shall be of single span or a bridge with intermediate supports, or some type of framed or trussed bridge). The simplest type will naturally be chosen. Provided that the material available is sufficiently strong and is treated skilfully 'single span bridges' (i.e. bridges without intermediate support), can be constructed to span great widths; however, 6 m can be considered the limit for the rough material available in the field.

Avoiding Flood Damage: Flood damage can be avoided either by (1) specifying longer spans to allow the largest recorded flood to pass safely or (2) setting the bridge high enough to allow passage of the highest flows and to provide clearance for floating branches and other debris. Areas upstream of the bridge should be inspected to determine what can be carried downstream during a flood.

Scour: Scour is one of the most frequent causes of failure in bridges over streams. The dangers of scour around abutments and piers can be minimised by various methods – see Figure 4.2.

Footbridge structures should be fastened down at the abutments so that they do not float off.

The selection chart indicates a few of the structural types appropriate to the span and eliminate or favour certain structures with reference to foundation conditions as published by the Countryside Commission for Scotland.

The clearance required will determine the construction depth available between the deck and the underside of the bridge. The bridge can be raised by using approach ramps or steps, but only at additional cost.

5. BRIDGE SUPERSTRUCTURE

Loading

The loads which a bridge must carry are:
1 The weight of the elements that make up the bridge.

TABLE 5. WIDTHS OF BRIDGES FOR DIFFERING USES

	Pedestrian	Cyclist	Wheelchair	Horse and Rider and Cattle
One way traffic	900 – 1200 mm	min 1170 max 1300	900 – 1200 mm	min 1200 max 1500
Two way traffic	1800 – 2200 mm	min 2100 max 2400	1200 – 1700 mm	Not recommended

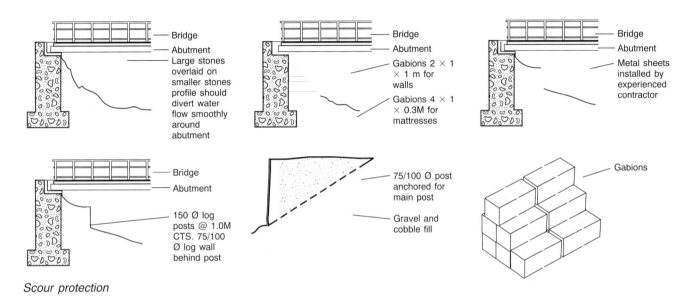

	Bridge
	Abutment
	Large stones overlaid on smaller stones profile should divert water flow smoothly around abutment

	Bridge
	Abutment
	Gabions 2 × 1 × 1 m for walls
	Gabions 4 × 1 × 0.3M for mattresses

	Bridge
	Abutment
	Metal sheets installed by experienced contractor

	Bridge
	Abutment
	150 Ø log posts @ 1.0M CTS. 75/100 Ø log wall behind post

	75/100 Ø post anchored for main post
	Gravel and cobble fill

Gabions

Scour protection

2 The weight of any material which is placed on the structure to allow traffic to cross.
3 The weight of the traffic – people, horses, vehicles which use the bridge plus any climatic factors – snow, wind.
4 Climatic influences – i.e. wind.
5 Flooding.

Points (1) and (2) are termed dead loads as they are inert and point (3) is called a live load. The latter (weight for weight) produces greater stresses in bridge elements than a dead load, especially if suddenly applied.

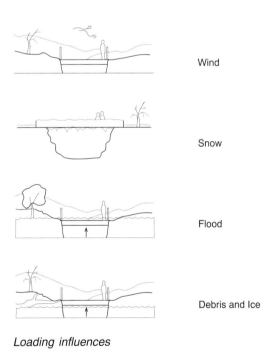

Wind

Snow

Flood

Debris and Ice

Loading influences

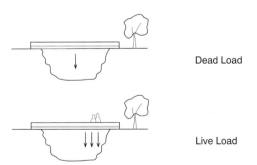

Dead Load

Live Load

In field engineering it is usual to multiply the live load by 2 in order to convert it to an equivalent dead load. This is in order to simplify calculations.

Pedestrian loading

Table 6 provides loads for narrow footbridges in the countryside as a guide but the designer will need to have his/her calculations checked depending upon location and use, especially in urban areas where there may be far more users.

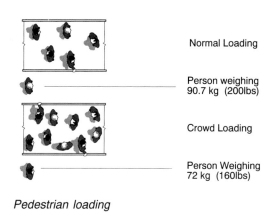

Normal Loading

Person weighing
90.7 kg (200lbs)

Crowd Loading

Person Weighing
72 kg (160lbs)

Pedestrian loading

Deflections

Where possible structures should be built with a precamber which should be at least equal to the dead load of deflection (and limited to 1/240th of the span). The aesthetic appearance of a footbridge can be improved by making this camber substantial, i.e. 10 mm/m of total span to 35 mm/m and also resulting in a grade of 1:15.

Camber

Footbridges found to be susceptible to vibration can be remedied by various ways such as rubber bearings and side guys to suspension spans.

TABLE 6. LOADS FOR FOOTBRIDGES IN THE COUNTRYSIDE 800–1700 mm WIDE

Member	Load type	Loading		Remarks
		Uniformly distributed	**Point load**	
Main beams	Pedestrian – Normal – Crowd Horse and Rider, Cattle or Sheep	2.3 kN/m^2 3.2 kN/m^2 2.3 kN/m^2		For wider foot-bridges and urban sites use BS 5400 Part 2
Short span members	Pedestrian – Normal – Crowd Sheep	The greater of 3.2 kN/m^2 or	1.62 kN on a 75 mm sq up to 1900 span. Thereafter 1.69 kN/m run of member.	All Short Span members may carry crowd loading. Individual timber deck boards may carry point or line load
	Horse and Rider	3.2 kN/m or	8.12 kN on a 175 mm sq	
	Cattle	3.2 kN/m or	6.12 kN on a 120 mm sq	
Handrail (horizontal load)	Pedestrian – Normal	0.74 kN/m, 1000 mm above deck		
	– Crowd	1.4 kN/m, 1100 mm above deck		
	Horse and Rider, Cattle	1.3 kN/m, 1250 mm above deck		
All members	Snow	0.4 kN/m^2		
Unloaded footbridge	Wind: 40 m/sec (horizontal load)	1.4 kN/m^2		Permissible stresses increased by 25%
Loaded footbridge	Wind: 28 m/sec (horizontal load)	0.7 kN/m^2		

TABLE 7. PERMISSIBLE BEARING PRESSURE

Material	Permissible bearing pressure on ground (KN/m^2)
Hard rock	2150
Shale and soft rock	1075
Compact sand or gravel and hard compact clay	430
Firm sand, sandy clay and ordinary fairly dry boulder clay	215
Wet or loose sand and soft clay	105
Made up ground, alluvial, soil peat	Varies up to 55

6. BRIDGE SUBSTRUCTURES

Substructures are parts of the bridge which transmit loads from the bridge span to the ground. They include abutments, wing walls and piers. The forces acting on the substructures include:

from the substructure	— its own self weight
from the bridge superstructure	— the dead load of the bridge the live load from the bridge including traction effects the snow load on the bridge the wind load on the bridge expansion forces from the bridge
from the approaches	— the pressure of any fill material retained by the abutments the pressure from flowing water, floating debris and ice

Foundations

Soil Bearing Capacity
The applied load from the substructure must be resisted by the ground to prevent failure and excessive settlement (see Table 7). In almost all cases, engineering advice is required when estimating soil bearing capacity.

Choice of foundation (footings or piles)
Engineering advice is important for all but the simplest of structures when selecting an appropriate foundation design. Spread footings are usually preferable to piles because they are less expensive and generally pose less risk in terms of encountering unforeseen and expensive technical and contractual problems during construction.

Table 8 lists some of the ground and construction considerations for which footings or piles have been found to be advantageous. For sites with variable bearing qualities of the strata, designers may have to work through a range of types, depths, and sizes of foundation to identify the most acceptable economic solution.

Abutments

An abutment is a structure of stone, brick, concrete or timber which actually carries the shore ends of the load bearers. In order to defend the abutment from the action of the water, walls are built which run back into the bank and form a funnel to allow the water to pour through the bridge. These walls are also termed wing walls as in culverts. The thickness of masonry abutments at their base should be two-fifths of their height.

TABLE 8. GENERAL GUIDE TO CHOICE OF FOUNDATION

Ground	Footings preferred	Piles preferred
Stiff clay, medium-dense dry sand, or gravel	Footings are most often appropriate for footbridges for reasons of cost, reliability, and ease of construction.	Piles may have to be used where very heavy concentrated loads have to be transmitted to ground.
Firm clays, loose dry gravels, or sand and gravel	Some designers prefer to use footings with bearing pressures as low as 100–150 kN/m^2 if significant settlement is expected during or soon after construction.	Piles are often the preferred solution because settlement of a pile group is often as much as one-half or one-third of that of a footing and takes place rapidly.
Stiff stratum at moderate depth with deep water table	Shallow spread footings supported on mass concrete or granular fill which forms a firm stratum are sometimes less expensive than deep footings.	
High water table in permeable ground		Driven or cased bored piles are typically used, but installation can be difficult.
Stiff ground overlying soft ground, e.g. gravel over clay	Shallow footings can be designed to make use of load-spreading quality of the stiff ground.	Use of piles can create driving or boring problems and by concentrating the load above or in the clay can cause larger settlements.
Soft silty clays, peat, and uncompacted fills	Spread footings can be used on fill if the ground can be consolidated in advance by use of a surcharge.	Piles are usually preferred. Measures sometimes have to be taken to prevent damage from lateral loading due to adjacent embankment.
Interbedded sand and silt layers	Excavation can be hindered by water in layers, but installation of bored piles has also given many problems.	
Loose sands increasing in strength with depth	Improving the strength of existing sand often is cheaper than using piles, but it is difficult to predict and monitor these special techniques. Therefore, piles are sometimes preferred.	Driven piles compact the sand and provide high load capacity with minimum settlement. (Note: single size sands can be impossible to compact.)
Chalk	Use footings unless chalk is deeper than the spread footings. Even soft chalk consolidates quickly under a load (usually during construction).	If upper surface is at unpredictable depths due to shallow holes, piles may be better because they can be driven to different depths without delays in the contract. Chalk softens during driving or boring but recovers some strength during following weeks; therefore delay testing test piles at different depths to determine the optimum.
Unpredictable and impenetrable ground, such as boulders or rock with clay matrix	Excavation for footings or installation of piles can be very difficult, with predictions of movement unreliable. Shallow footings can be the more economical.	Steel H piles have been driven either to deep firm stratum or to sufficient depths to mobilize adequate friction.
Compacted fill	Well-compacted, suitable, or selected fill is generally as good as, if not better than, natural deposits of the same material.	
Steeply dipping rock substratum	Mass concrete fill can grip stepped interfaces where piles might glance off.	If stratum is very deep, then precast concrete piles with rock shoes or use steel piles.
Over rivers and estuaries		Piles are usually preferred irrespective of ground conditions.

Source: Adapted from *Building Research Establishment*.

The construction of abutments and the approach paths can be a large part of the overall cost of a scheme and every effort in siting the bridge to limit the work required is worthwhile.

Sophisticated abutments are not necessary for narrow footbridges. Plain mass blocks built in concrete, brick or stone are sufficient and the most economic. Timber could also be used.

Piers

Bridges with long spans require support from piers which must be located on sound foundations depending upon the materials

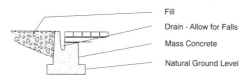

- Fill
- Drain - Allow for Falls
- Mass Concrete
- Natural Ground Level

Typical mass-abutment above natural ground

- Path
- Bridge

Typical mass-abutment with wing walls on slopes

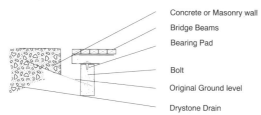

- Concrete or Masonry wall
- Bridge Beams
- Bearing Pad
- Bolt
- Original Ground level
- Drystone Drain

Typical small-abutment detail

Wing walls parallel to abutment. Mass concrete, stone or block.

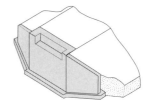

Wing walls at angle to abutment face. Mass concrete, stone or block.

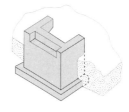

Wing walls parallel to the bridge. Mass concrete, stone or block

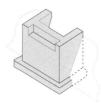

Cantilever wing walls parallel to over-road. Mass concrete, stone or block

Crib wall

Typical abutments

used. The simplest form of structure will be a mass block of concrete, stone brick (or concrete blocks) on a spread footing. Piers in waterways are difficult to construct and are subject to abnormal conditions from flooding. Expert advice should be sought before such a solution is adopted. In a shallow stream, with a slow current, a timber crib pier could be used. This could have its lower half built on the bank and then manoeuvred into position in the stream then completed *in-situ*. Afterwards it should be sunk with stones on the bottom

platform up to the flood level. Above this level it could be left open or filled with soil and planted with appropriate species.

Wing walls

The cost of wing walls can far outweigh the advantages particularly for narrow bridges; this depends upon the materials used and the construction methods. Check first with an engineer to see if they are necessary.

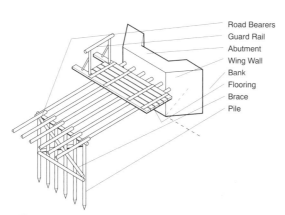

- Road Bearers
- Guard Rail
- Abutment
- Wing Wall
- Bank
- Flooring
- Brace
- Pile

Timber crib pier

TABLE 9. SAFE SPANS FOR TIMBER DECKING

With pedestrian – Normal/Crowd loading on 800–1700 wide footbridges in countryside locations.
DECKBOARDS (Softwood, Hardwood)

Deck Boards		SOFTWOODS Grade GS or MGS Strength Class SC3		Grade SS or MSS Strength Class SC4		HARDWOOD Keruing Grade HS	
t	b	S	C	S	C	S	C
36	100					725	160
	125					925	200
	150					1100	240
50	100	675	150	1000	250	1400	300
	125	850	200	1250	300	1775	375
	150	975	250	1500	350	2000	450
75	125	1900	500	2250	700	2700	775
	150	2000	600	2500	850	3000	900
	200	2300	750	2900	1000	3500	1200
100	150	2500	900	3200	1500		
	200	2900	1300	3750	1750		

BEARERS (Softwood, Grade GS Strength Classification SC3)

Bearer Size		Bearer Spacing	Bearer Span
d	w	s	Y
75	50	900	900
		1000	850
		1200	775
100	50	900	1200
		1000	1100
		1200	1000
150	50	900	1800
		1000	1700
		1200	1500
100	75	900	1300
		1000	1300
		1200	1200
150	75	900	2200
		1000	2100
		1200	1900

With Horse and Rider, Cattle or Sheep on 800–1700 wide foot-bridges in countryside locations.
DECKBOARDS (Softwood, Hardwood)

Deck Boards		SOFTWOODS Grade GS or MGS Strength Class SC3		Grade SS or MSS Strength Class SC4		HARDWOOD Keruing Grade HS	
t	b	S	C	S	C	S	C
50	100					375	80
	125					430	100
	150	260	40	300	60	430	100
75	125	480	105	700	160	990	225
	150	480	105	700	160	990	225
	200	640	140	925	210	1300	300
100	150	850	200	1250	290		
	200	1150	250	1650	390		

BEARERS (Softwood, Grade GS Strength Classification SC3)

Bearer Size		Bearer Spacing	Bearer Span
d	w	s	Y
150	75	Up to 1200	Up to 1200

Decking

The most commonly used material for decking is timber boarding, both transverse and longitudinal. Other materials which can be used are:
- pre-cast concrete slabs
- in-situ concrete slabs
- in-situ concrete topping to form a slab steel or aluminium planks
- epoxy resin sprayed on any of above and granular material spread on top (useful in very wet areas).

Timber
The material is light, strong and easily worked, has a good life and can be easily repaired. The size of board used depends upon:
1. The span between supports
2. The loading
3. The width of the individual boards and the spacing between boards
4. The grade of timber used
5. The additional thickness allowed for wear

Board width should be 100 mm minimum, board thickness should be 50 mm minimum for softwood and 30 mm minimum for hardwood. Spacing between boards should be 6 mm minimum. All softwood should have preservative treatment. Galvanised nails or screws should be used.

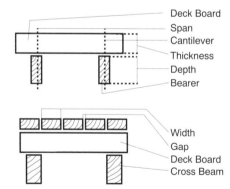

Deck-section details

Handrails

Handrails are usually required on both sides of a footbridge, but for remote or low-

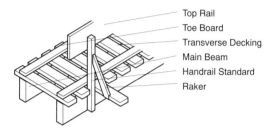

Single handrail

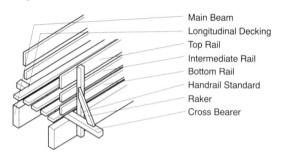

Double handrail

risk bridges one handrail or perhaps no handrail may be appropriate.

Safety of the user must be considered by the designer particularly for high bridges or where inclement weather, such as heavy, and strong winds could cause obvious danger. A handrail must be strong enough for people to lean against.

The simplest handrail is a single horizontal rail mounted at waist height. The addition of midrailings and a bottom railing reduces the risk of accidentally falling or rolling off the bridge. The space between the top railing and the deck can be infilled with vertical members if required.

In certain situations involving young children or animals, the risk of falling off may be so great that a more impenetrable barrier is required. For footbridges over major roads and railways, unclimbable or even solid parapets are advisable.

Dimensions
The height of the handrailing should be adjusted for different types of use and for different locations. For general pedestrian footbridges in the countryside a height of 1000 mm is recommended. Where the drop from the bridge is particularly hazardous

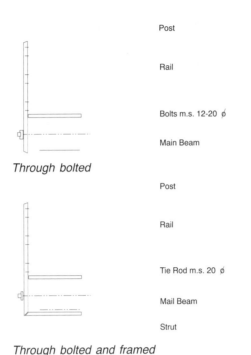

Post

Rail

Bolts m.s. 12-20 ø

Main Beam

Through bolted

Post

Rail

Tie Rod m.s. 20 ø

Mail Beam

Strut

Through bolted and framed

TDR Rail

Post Tapered

Bouts m.s. 12-20 ø

Struts

Through bolted and inclined

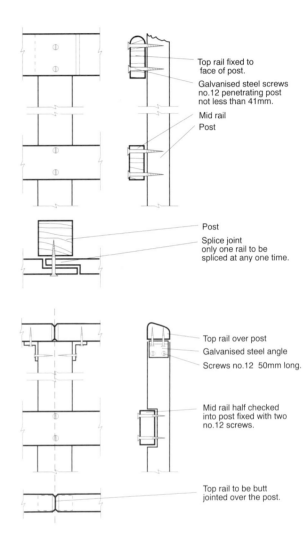

Top rail fixed to face of post.

Galvanised steel screws no.12 penetrating post not less than 41mm.

Mid rail
Post

Post

Splice joint only one rail to be spliced at any one time.

Top rail over post
Galvanised steel angle
Screws no.12 50mm long.

Mid rail half checked into post fixed with two no.12 screws.

Top rail to be butt jointed over the post.

this height should be increased to 1400 mm.
For normal situations three horizontals are adequate. The gap below the bottom rail should not be greater than 100 mm.
The spacing of the handrail posts should be selected so that the full strength of the horizontal rails is used. Aesthetically, panels should be 1½–2 times as long as they are high. This gives spacing of 1500–2000 mm.

Materials
Handrails can be supplied in a variety of materials. For countryside footbridges timber is the most common but steel and aluminium can also be used, in square or round fabrications.

Fixing
Adequate fixing of the handrail to the bridge is essential for safety reasons and examples are shown above.

Timber, when adequately preserved, has a life that is virtually unlimited. Galvanised connectors, metal components and the synthetic resin adhesives used also have a long endurance and bridge life can be indefinite, being limited only by a change or use of loading requirements.

Fastenings

Every hole, split and joint in any part of the bridge structure has the potential of

TABLE 10. HANDRAILS. TABLE OF SPANS BETWEEN POSTS

| Timber size | Loading | Timber strength classification or grade | | | |
		SC3	*SC4*	*SC5*	*Keruing HS*
50 × 75	Normal	1400	1500	1600	1750
	Crowd	1000	1100	1300	1400
50 × 100	Normal	1600	1700	1800	1900
	Crowd	1200	1300	1400	1500
50 × 150	Normal	1800	2000	2000	2250
	Crowd	1500	1600	1600	1800
75 × 50	Normal	1900	2100	2300	2500
	Crowd	1350	1500	1800	1900
75 × 75	Normal	2200	2400	2500	2700
	Crowd	1600	1800	2000	2200

TABLE 11. CANTILEVERED HANDRAIL POSTS. TABLE OF SIZES

| Spacing Ss | Timber Grade SC4 Douglas Fir or Larch | | Timber Grade SC5 Douglas Fir or Larch | | Hardwood Keruing MS | |
	Normal loading	*Crowd loading*	*Normal loading*	*Crowd loading*	*Normal loading*	*Crowd loading*
1000	100 × 75	120 × 100	100 × 75	100 × 100	100 × 75	100 × 100
1250	100 × 100	150 × 100	100 × 75	120 × 100	100 × 75	100 × 100
1500	100 × 100	150 × 100	100 × 100	120 × 100	100 × 75	120 × 100
1750	120 × 100	150 × 100	100 × 100	150 × 100	100 × 100	120 × 100
2000	120 × 100	150 × 150	100 × 100	150 × 100	100 × 100	150 × 100
2250	150 × 100	150 × 150	120 × 100	150 × 100	100 × 100	150 × 100
2500	150 × 100	150 × 150	120 × 100	150 × 100	120 × 100	150 × 100

encouraging fungal decay and/or rust. Good design, detailing and workmanship are essential if these problems are to be avoided or at least minimised. Cutting and fitting at joists requires skilled labour. Metal fasteners for use with timber include nails (including large spikes), screws, lag screws, bolts and washers, timber connectors, metal gussets and cleats, hangers, glands and straps. All metal used in timber fastenings should be protected against corrosion. Hot-dip galvanising or electroplating in zinc and cadmium are common techniques used to protect metals from corrosion. Holes for fastenings should be pre-drilled to prevent splitting of wood. Points to look out for during inspection are:

1. Scouring of river bed and bridge foundations.
2. Natural or man-made damage to banks and adjacent land.
3. Unsafe trees close to bridge.
4. Muddy or worn footpaths, steps, ramps.
5. Decay in timbers, especially at holes, checks and ends.
6. Water lying on horizontal surfaces and in joints.
7. Loose bolts, screws, nails, posts, handrails.
8. Rust.

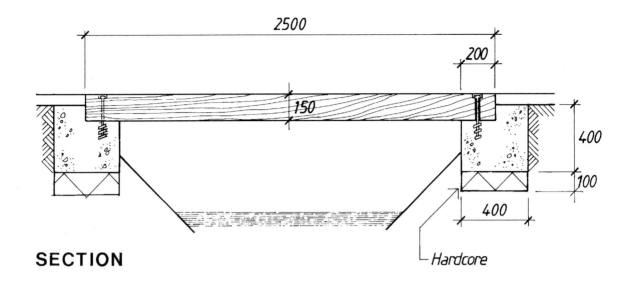

SECTION

2500

200

150

400

100

400

Hardcore

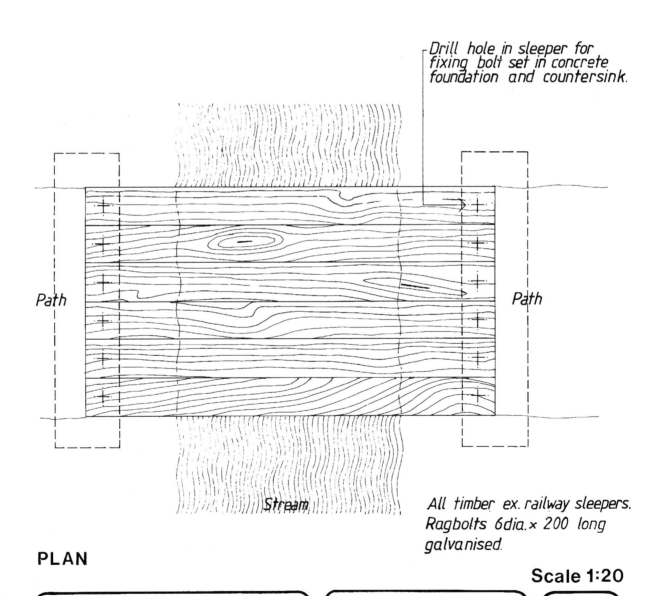

Drill hole in sleeper for
fixing bolt set in concrete
foundation and countersink.

Path

Path

Stream

All timber ex. railway sleepers.
Ragbolts 6dia. × 200 long
galvanised.

PLAN

Scale 1:20

FOOTBRIDGE
Small

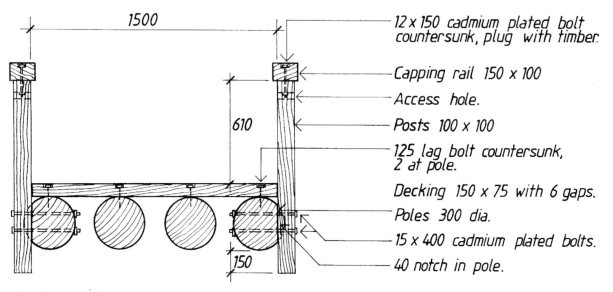

1500

610

150

SECTION

12 x 150 cadmium plated bolt countersunk, plug with timber.

Capping rail 150 x 100

Access hole.

Posts 100 x 100

125 lag bolt countersunk, 2 at pole.

Decking 150 x 75 with 6 gaps.

Poles 300 dia.

15 x 400 cadmium plated bolts.

40 notch in pole.

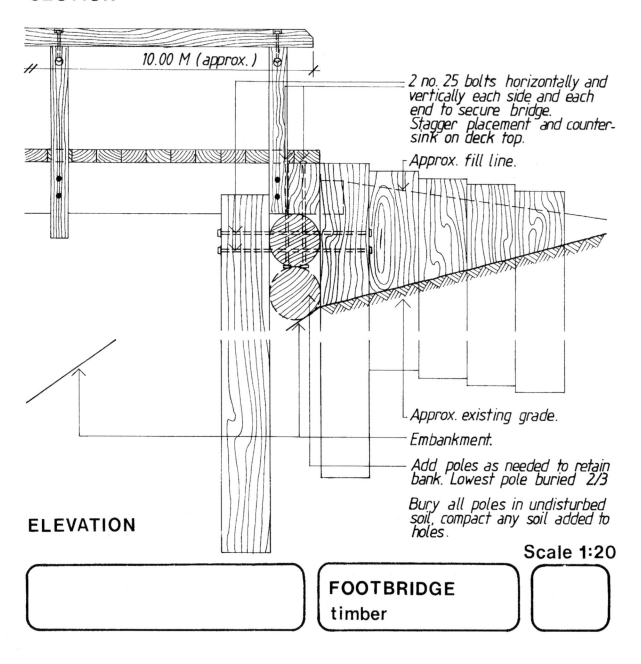

10.00 M (approx.)

2 no. 25 bolts horizontally and vertically each side and each end to secure bridge. Stagger placement and countersink on deck top.

Approx. fill line.

Approx. existing grade.

Embankment.

Add poles as needed to retain bank. Lowest pole buried 2/3.

Bury all poles in undisturbed soil, compact any soil added to holes.

ELEVATION

Scale 1:20

FOOTBRIDGE
timber

91

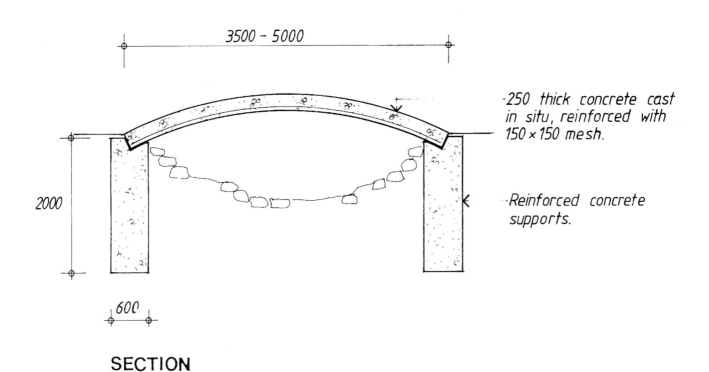

3500 – 5000

-250 thick concrete cast in situ, reinforced with 150 × 150 mesh.

2000

-Reinforced concrete supports.

600

SECTION

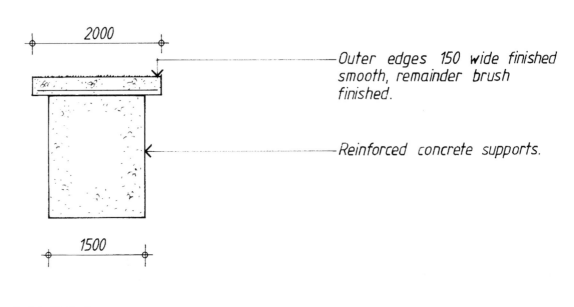

2000

—Outer edges 150 wide finished smooth, remainder brush finished.

—Reinforced concrete supports.

1500

SECTION

Scale 1:50

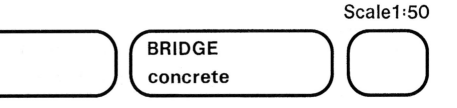

BRIDGE
concrete

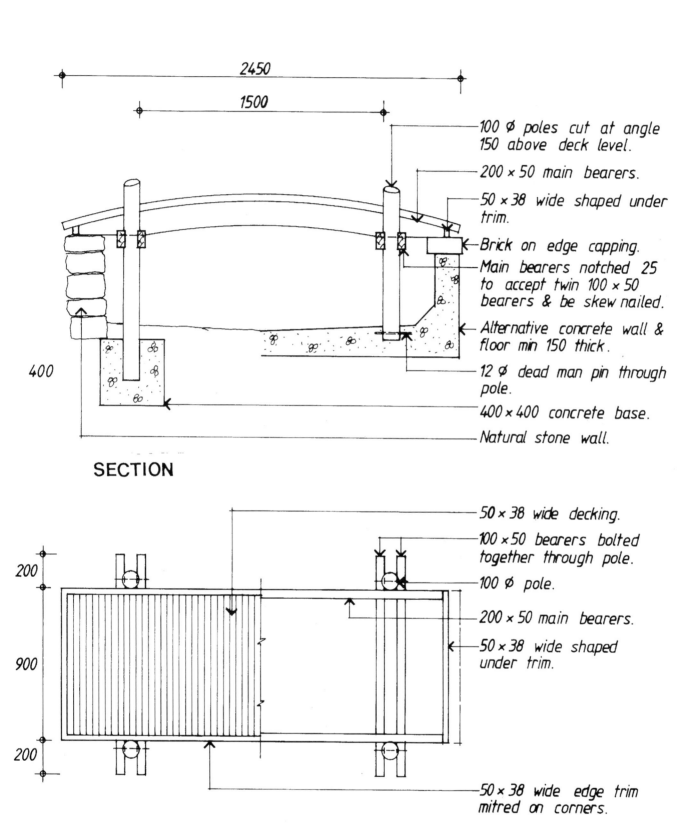

2450

1500

100 ∅ poles cut at angle 150 above deck level.

200 × 50 main bearers.

50 × 38 wide shaped under trim.

Brick on edge capping.

Main bearers notched 25 to accept twin 100 × 50 bearers & be skew nailed.

Alternative concrete wall & floor min 150 thick.

12 ∅ dead man pin through pole.

400 × 400 concrete base.

Natural stone wall.

400

SECTION

50 × 38 wide decking.

100 × 50 bearers bolted together through pole.

100 ∅ pole.

200 × 50 main bearers.

50 × 38 wide shaped under trim.

200

900

200

50 × 38 wide edge trim mitred on corners.

PLAN

Scale 1:20

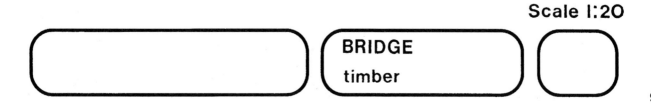

BRIDGE
timber

93

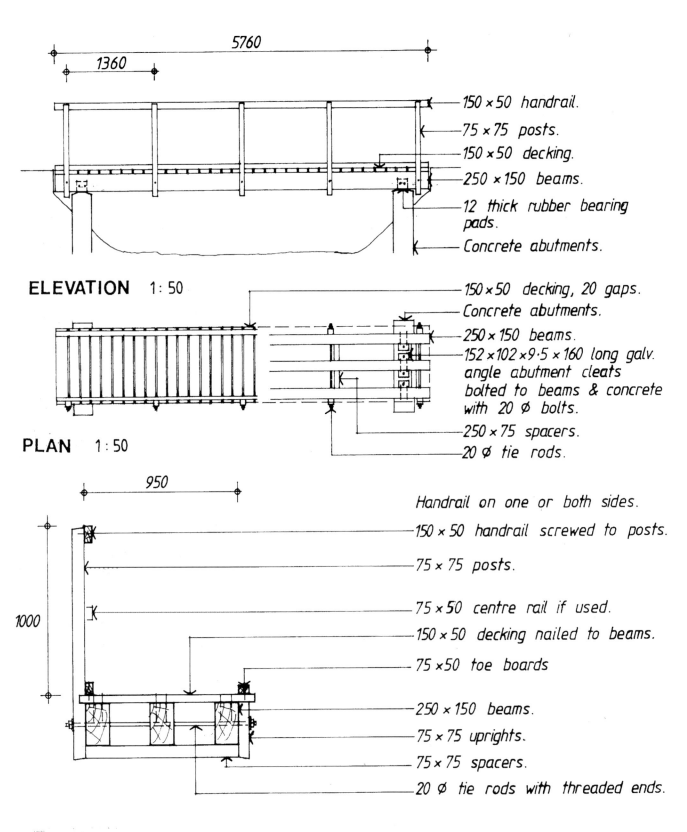

5760

1360

150 × 50 handrail.

75 × 75 posts.

150 × 50 decking.

250 × 150 beams.

12 thick rubber bearing pads.

Concrete abutments.

ELEVATION 1 : 50

150 × 50 decking, 20 gaps.

Concrete abutments.

250 × 150 beams.

152 × 102 × 9·5 × 160 long galv. angle abutment cleats bolted to beams & concrete with 20 ∅ bolts.

250 × 75 spacers.

20 ∅ tie rods.

PLAN 1 : 50

950

Handrail on one or both sides.

150 × 50 handrail screwed to posts.

75 × 75 posts.

75 × 50 centre rail if used.

150 × 50 decking nailed to beams.

75 × 50 toe boards

1000

250 × 150 beams.

75 × 75 uprights.

75 × 75 spacers.

20 ∅ tie rods with threaded ends.

SECTION 1 : 20

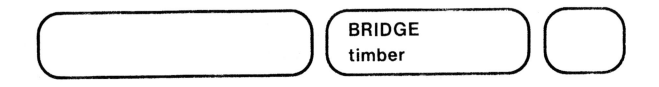

BRIDGE
timber

94

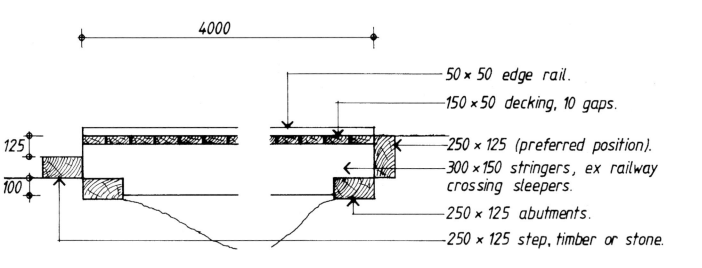

4000

50 × 50 edge rail.

150 × 50 decking, 10 gaps.

125

250 × 125 (preferred position).

300 × 150 stringers, ex railway crossing sleepers.

100

250 × 125 abutments.

250 × 125 step, timber or stone.

ELEVATION

Steps & abutments from half a standard railway sleeper or concrete kerbstone.

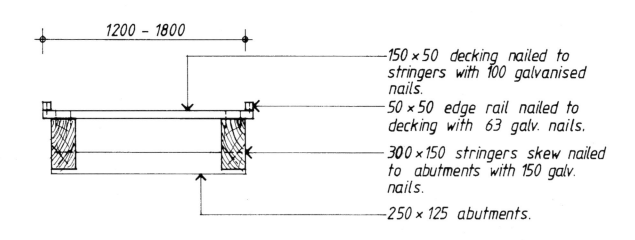

1200 – 1800

150 × 50 decking nailed to stringers with 100 galvanised nails.

50 × 50 edge rail nailed to decking with 63 galv. nails.

300 × 150 stringers skew nailed to abutments with 150 galv. nails.

250 × 125 abutments.

SECTION

Scale 1:20

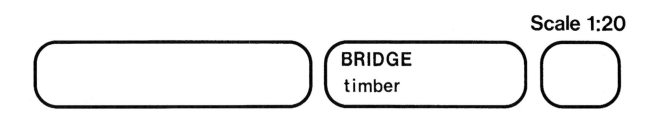

BRIDGE
timber

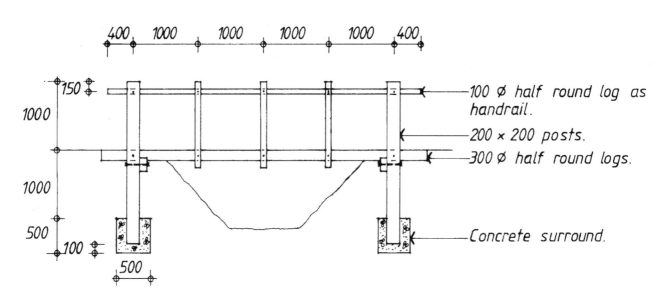

400 | 1000 | 1000 | 1000 | 1000 | 400

150

1000

1000

500

100

500

100 ⌀ half round log as handrail.

200 × 200 posts.

300 ⌀ half round logs.

Concrete surround.

ELEVATION

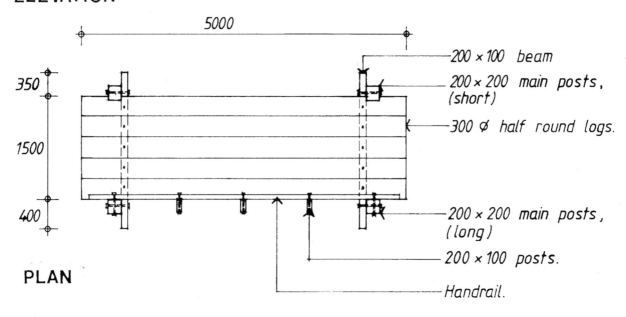

5000

350

1500

400

200 × 100 beam

200 × 200 main posts, (short)

300 ⌀ half round logs.

200 × 200 main posts, (long)

200 × 100 posts.

Handrail.

PLAN

Scale 1:50

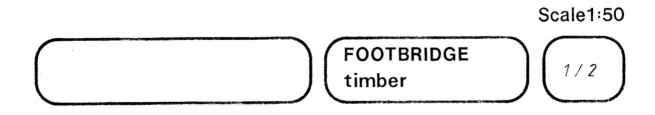

FOOTBRIDGE
timber

1 / 2

96

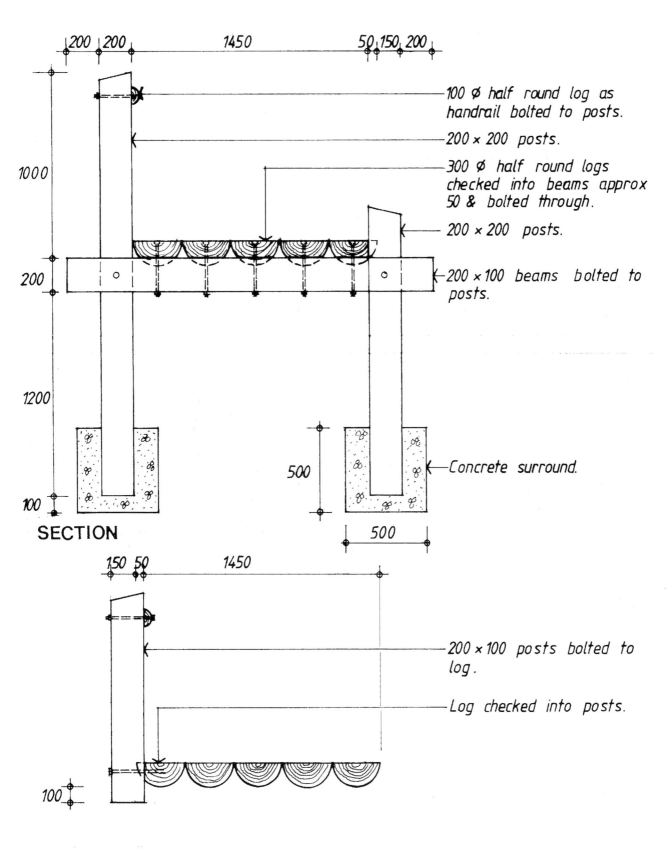

200 | 200 | 1450 | 50 150 200

100 ⌀ half round log as handrail bolted to posts.

200 × 200 posts.

300 ⌀ half round logs checked into beams approx 50 & bolted through.

200 × 200 posts.

1000

200 × 100 beams bolted to posts.

200

1200

500

Concrete surround.

100

SECTION

500

150 50 | 1450

200 × 100 posts bolted to log.

Log checked into posts.

100

SECTION

Scale 1:20

FOOTBRIDGE
timber

2 / 2

97

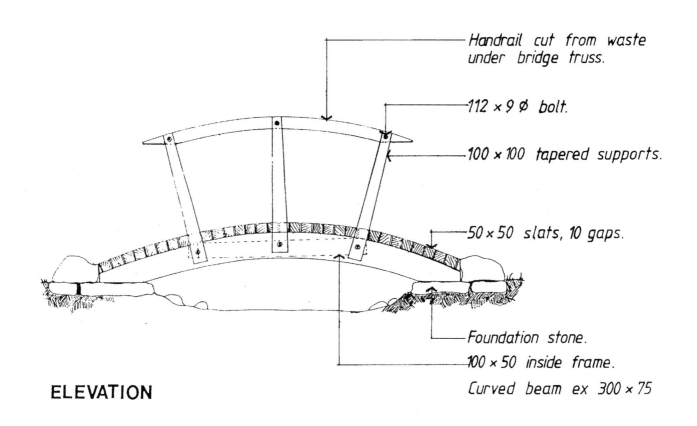

Handrail cut from waste under bridge truss.

112 × 9 Ø bolt.

100 × 100 tapered supports.

50 × 50 slats, 10 gaps.

Foundation stone.

100 × 50 inside frame.

Curved beam ex 300 × 75

ELEVATION

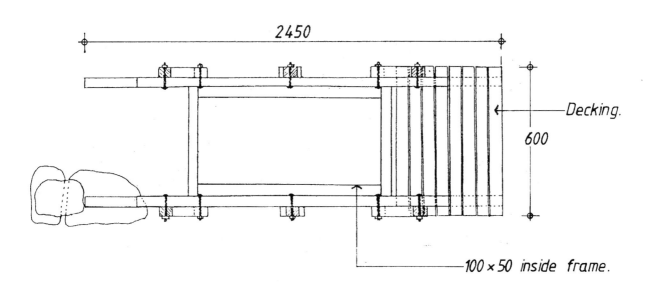

2450

Decking.

600

100 × 50 inside frame.

PLAN

Scale 1:20

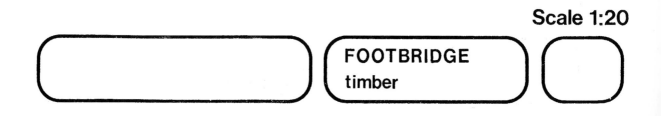

FOOTBRIDGE
timber

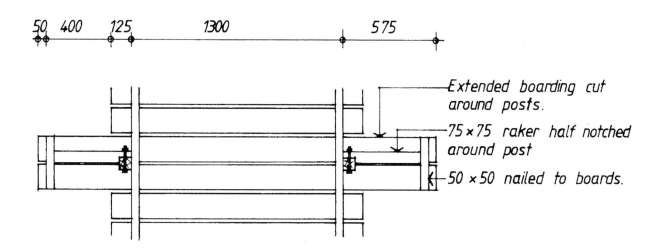

50 400 125   1300   575

PLAN

Extended boarding cut
around posts.

75 × 75 raker half notched
around post

50 × 50 nailed to boards.

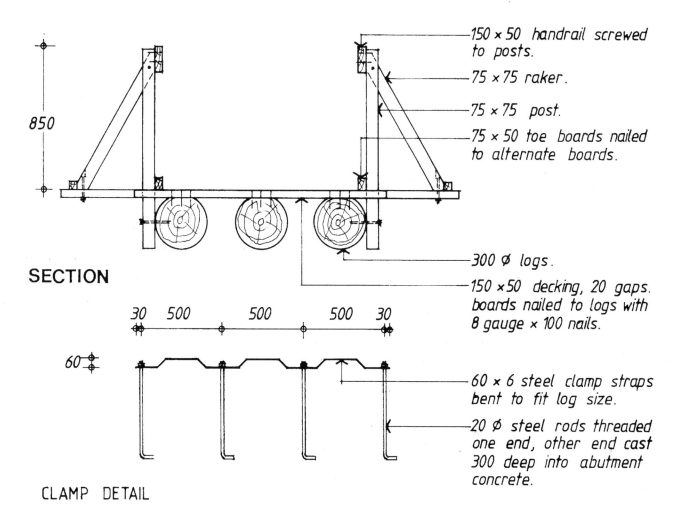

850

SECTION

150 × 50 handrail screwed
to posts.

75 × 75 raker.

75 × 75 post.

75 × 50 toe boards nailed
to alternate boards.

300 Ø logs.

150 × 50 decking, 20 gaps.
boards nailed to logs with
8 gauge × 100 nails.

30 500   500   500 30

60

60 × 6 steel clamp straps
bent to fit log size.

20 Ø steel rods threaded
one end, other end cast
300 deep into abutment
concrete.

CLAMP DETAIL

Scale 1:20

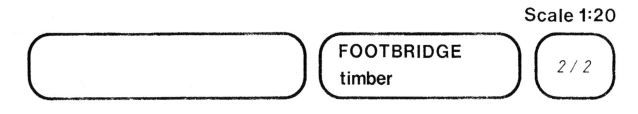

FOOTBRIDGE
timber

2 / 2

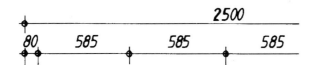

2500

80   585   585   585

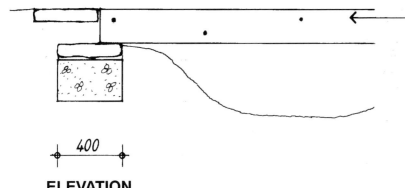

5 in No 200 × 100 timbers held together with 5 in No 15 ⌀ threaded mild steel rods with 10 thick stainless steel washers between timbers to give 10 gaps, nuts to be countersunk into timbers.

400

ELEVATION

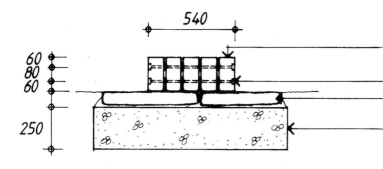

540

60
80
60

250

200 × 100 timbers. (or ex railway sleepers).

15 ⌀ threaded mild steel rods.

Natural stone flags set in mortar.

Concrete base.

SECTION

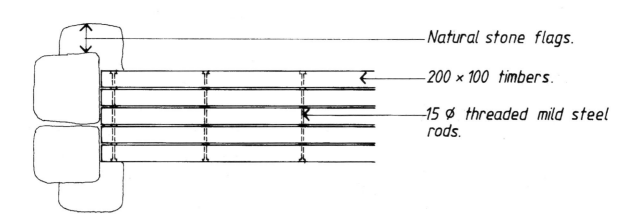

Natural stone flags.

200 × 100 timbers.

15 ⌀ threaded mild steel rods.

PLAN

Scale 1:20

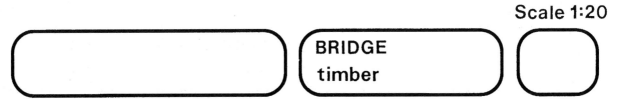

BRIDGE
timber

100

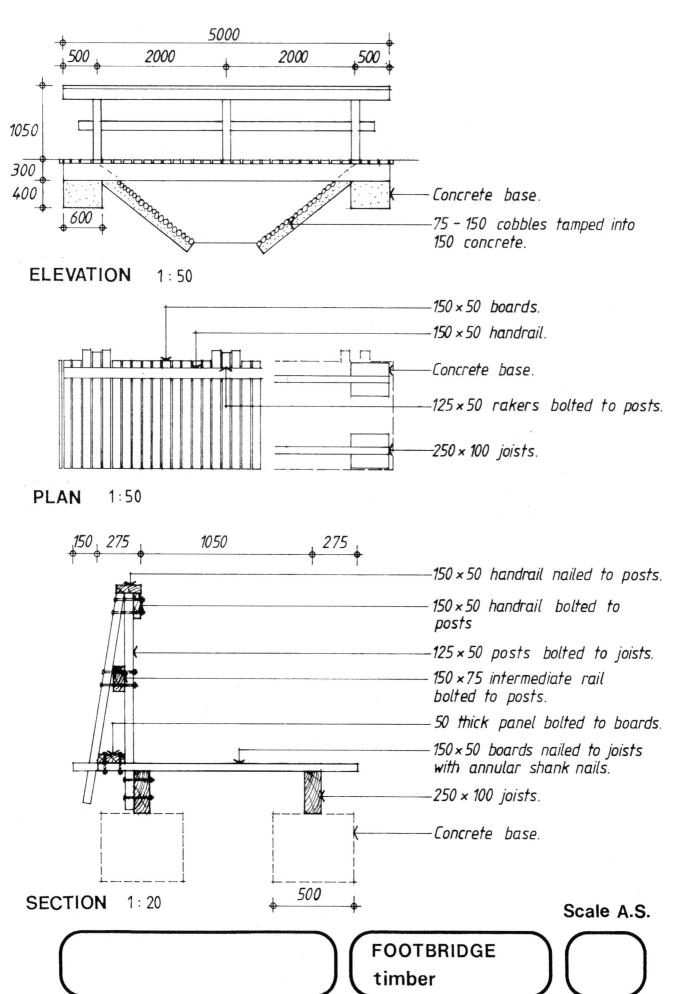

ELEVATION   1 : 50

5000
500 | 2000 | 2000 | 500
1050
300
400
600

Concrete base.

75 – 150 cobbles tamped into 150 concrete.

PLAN   1:50

150 × 50 boards.

150 × 50 handrail.

Concrete base.

125 × 50 rakers bolted to posts.

250 × 100 joists.

SECTION   1 : 20

150 | 275 | 1050 | 275

500

150 × 50 handrail nailed to posts.

150 × 50 handrail bolted to posts

125 × 50 posts bolted to joists.

150 × 75 intermediate rail bolted to posts.

50 thick panel bolted to boards.

150 × 50 boards nailed to joists with annular shank nails.

250 × 100 joists.

Concrete base.

Scale A.S.

FOOTBRIDGE
timber

101

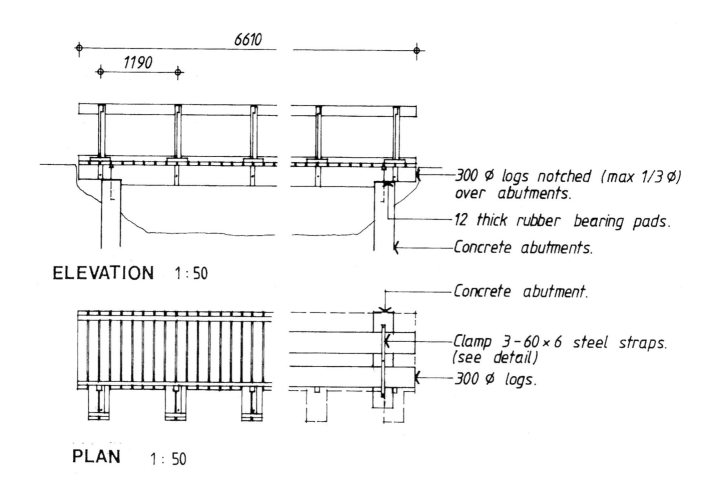

6610

1190

ELEVATION 1:50

300 Ø logs notched (max 1/3 Ø) over abutments.

12 thick rubber bearing pads.

Concrete abutments.

Concrete abutment.

Clamp 3-60 × 6 steel straps. (see detail)

300 Ø logs.

PLAN 1:50

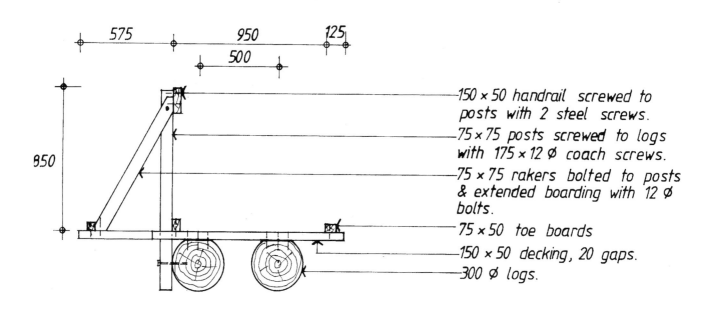

575   950   125

500

850

150 × 50 handrail screwed to posts with 2 steel screws.

75 × 75 posts screwed to logs with 175 × 12 Ø coach screws.

75 × 75 rakers bolted to posts & extended boarding with 12 Ø bolts.

75 × 50 toe boards

150 × 50 decking, 20 gaps.

300 Ø logs.

SECTION 1:20

Scale A.S.

FOOTBRIDGE
timber

102

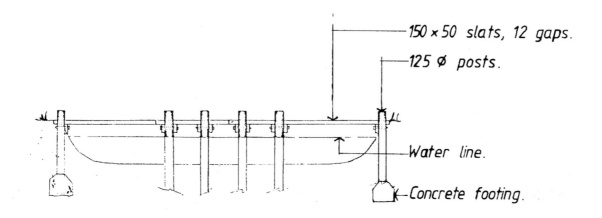

- 150 × 50 slats, 12 gaps.
- 125 ∅ posts.
- Water line.
- Concrete footing.

SECTION

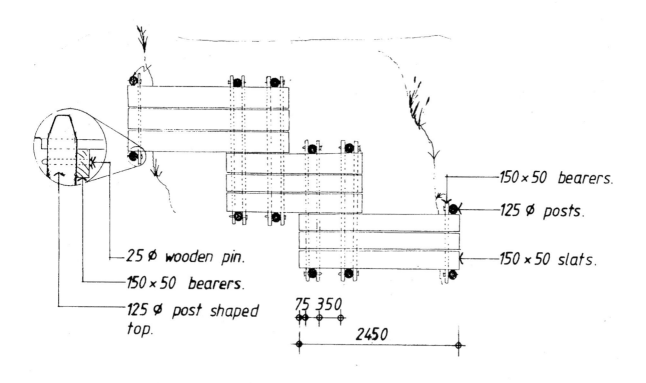

- 150 × 50 bearers.
- 125 ∅ posts.
- 150 × 50 slats.

- 25 ∅ wooden pin.
- 150 × 50 bearers.
- 125 ∅ post shaped top.

75 350

2450

PLAN

Scale 1:50

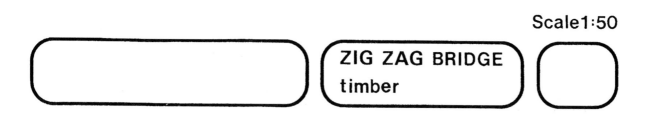

ZIG ZAG BRIDGE
timber

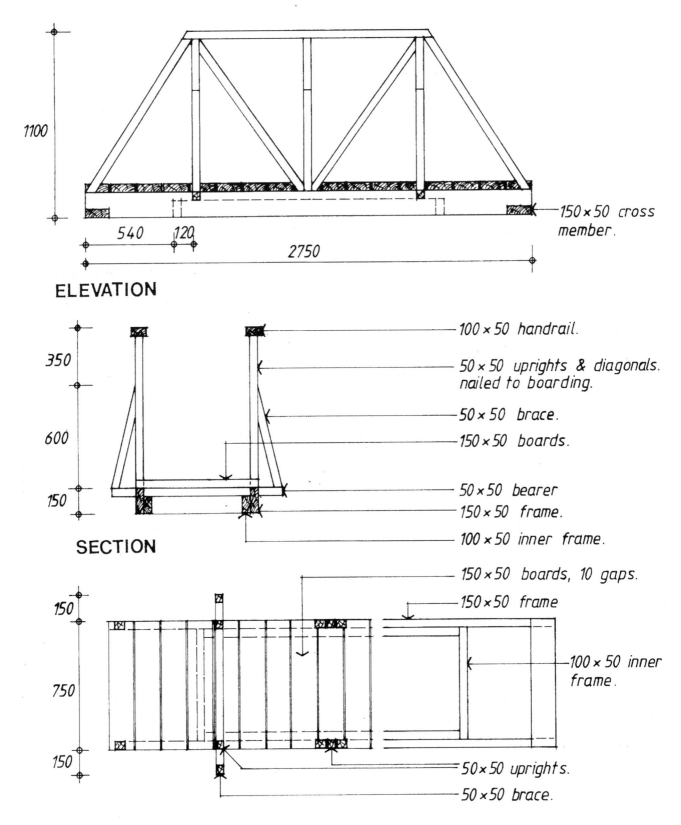

1100

150×50 *cross member.*

540   120   2750

ELEVATION

350

600

150

100×50 *handrail.*

50×50 *uprights & diagonals.*
nailed to boarding.

50×50 *brace.*

150×50 *boards.*

50×50 *bearer*

150×50 *frame.*

100×50 *inner frame.*

SECTION

150   750   150

150×50 *boards, 10 gaps.*

150×50 *frame*

100×50 *inner frame.*

50×50 *uprights.*

50×50 *brace.*

PLAN

Scale 1:20

FOOTBRIDGE
timber

104

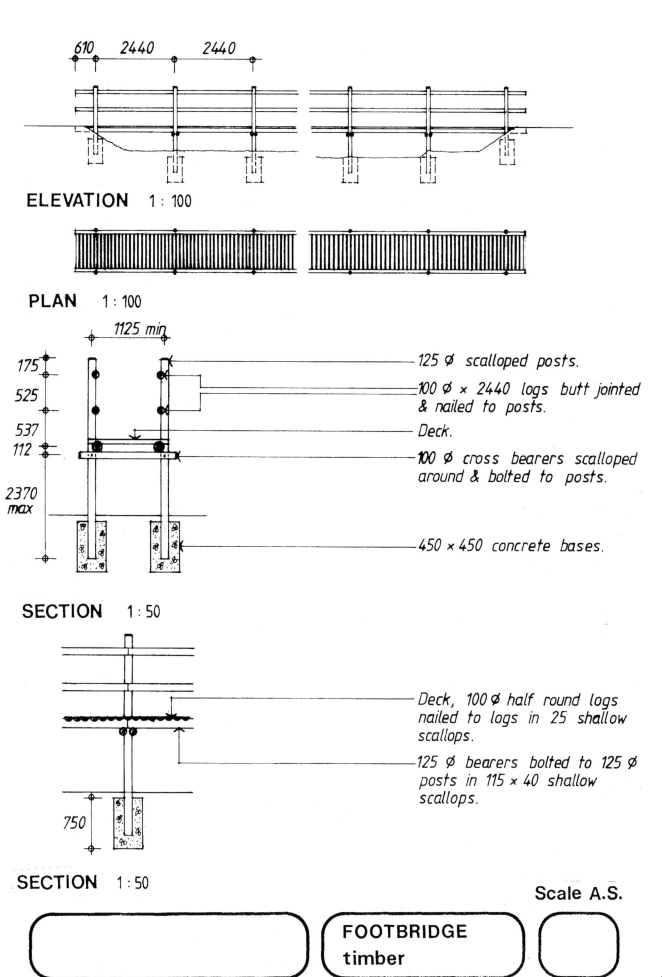

ELEVATION 1 : 100

PLAN 1 : 100

1125 min

175
525
537
112

2370 max

125 Ø scalloped posts.

100 Ø × 2440 logs butt jointed & nailed to posts.

Deck.

100 Ø cross bearers scalloped around & bolted to posts.

450 × 450 concrete bases.

SECTION 1 : 50

Deck, 100 Ø half round logs nailed to logs in 25 shallow scallops.

125 Ø bearers bolted to 125 Ø posts in 115 × 40 shallow scallops.

750

SECTION 1 : 50

Scale A.S.

FOOTBRIDGE
timber

105

OUTDOOR FURNITURE

Seats and Benches

Of the many items of outdoor furniture seats and benches appear to be the most numerous. This is not surprising considering that places for pedestrians to rest after walking, whether associated with daily activities such as going to the shops or to work or to a local recreational facility, is a definite requirement. Unfortunately seats have not always been appropriate for their setting, as can be seen in both urban and rural areas even today.

'The type of seat to be used in any particular area is dependent on its siting. In metropolitan areas the seats should be monumental in character, the design forming part of the urban landscape; in the country they should be rough and workmanlike, the key quality being simplicity, often emphasised by using the local material such as stone, slate or timber, but care must be taken to avoid false rusticity. Scale is important and materials should be in character with the surroundings. In small spaces the simplicity of bench or chair is essential and the attempt to attract attention by an overdressed design, or intricacy of finish, merely looks silly. Visually it is better to have seats designed as benches without backs, a form which is least obtrusive in the landscape, but seating in public places must take into account requirements of old people and other users who will require seats with arms and backs. Seats as an element of design need a background, whether

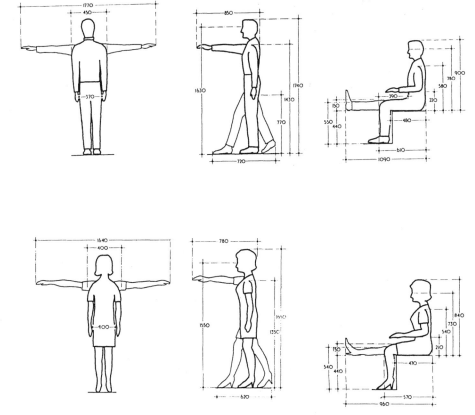

Mean average (50th percentile) dimensions of adult British males

this consists of planting, walls or trees and they should be related to other objects in the landscape and should be co-ordinated wherever possible with other street furniture.[1]

Another criticism which has been levelled at the ubiquitous seat is its lack of comfort. The basic requirements are that the height of the seat should be low enough for the person's feet to be on the ground giving no pressure to the thighs. On average this is possible but as the human body varies in size there will be some occasions when the seat is higher than the length of the person's lower leg and sometimes when it may feel too low, such as to a tall person. The depth of the seat should also be considered, ensuring that it does not cause pressure behind the knees. A typical seat dimension is illustrated.

There are a wide variety of seats made by manufacturers offering far more choice than ever before of excellent quality and design. However, there are occasions when less costly design is required for a garden or landscape project which can be easily made. Some examples can be found in the details contained in this chapter.

Seats on the whole have backs and those that do not have them are generally called benches. Both can be free-standing or be in-situ as part of a wall – retaining walls can often be made wide enough to be a bench.

Seats and benches, while generally rectangular, can also be circular, multi-sided or be combined with other elements, such as tables and walls, to make a sheltered sitting area. Protection from inclement weather is essential.

Consideration must be given these days to the security of seats and benches from theft and vandalism in public places. They must be securely fixed to the ground or walls with no opportunity for any fixings to be easily removed. Seats and benches which have to be fixed should be built with the basic enclosure and other elements of the garden or landscape as part of the permanent design framework. While fixed

seats or benches may take up less room than movable furniture they do not have the flexibility of the latter, and may not be as comfortable.

Fixed items must be able to withstand all climatic conditions and therefore must be made much more durable than movable types which can be easily stored in a shed. Another advantage of fixed seats or benches is their ability to accommodate more people than individual items. On the other hand the cost of movable furniture can be lower than fixed items because of large scale production methods.

Seats and benches, whether fixed or movable, must have the correct heights and angles of seats, tops and backs for active sitting, such as when eating; for more relaxed sitting as when talking or reading or when lounging or sleeping in sun or shade. These three different basic types of seats and benches should be considered at the design stage and selected accordingly for their use and location. The combined bench and table usually seen in park picnic areas around the country gives cause for concern over its measurements. The gap between table and seat does, on many an occasion, appear to be too narrow for many large people to negotiate. The size of this combination should be given far greater attention than has been done so far.

Construction

Benches and seat walls should be approximately 425/450 mm high (17/18 in). Bench heights are limited so they will be comfortable for the average person, but widths and lengths can vary so long as the understructure provides good support. Tops can be boards or plywood, or they can be cut from a panel edge-glued wood. Rails can be used between supports when the top is plywood or a similar material – stretchers contribute rigidity and durability. X-legs are a popular design and can be made with lap joint at the crossing point or by using a spacer and the rail between the legs, as shown. The lap crossing is the stronger of the two.

[1]Landscape Techniques
Outdoor Fittings and Furniture, Ian Purdy.

Materials

The basic materials are wood and metal, although brick, stone and slate are used but to a far lesser extent. Again the design – warm and solid or light and graceful – will determine the material.

Stone seats and benches (and concrete) can be fixed as it is unlikely for them to be moved because of their weight. They can be simple cut slabs or complete curved benches.

Wood is the most versatile of all the materials – teak being the most durable and weather resistant of all woods. The designs of wooden seats made by specialist manufacturers and craftspeople are both numerous and intricate as their catalogues indicate.

Wicker is another variation, although it is not weatherproof and appears to be used inside conservatories and summerhouses, except in prolonged warm, dry weather conditions.

Both wrought and cast iron have been used for seats and benches in designs, particularly where combined with lightness, strength is required. Very often the seat slats are in timber and the frames in metal, either stove enamelled or plastic coated. Painted cast iron and aluminium alloy frames can also be used effectively. Aluminium, in marine environments, should be avoided because of corrosion risks.

All steel bolts and fixings should be galvanised, all softwood timber should be treated, preferably with an environmentally friendly chemical. Likewise the staining of timbers.

Tables

Table structures should be uncomplicated, strong and durable especially when designed for dining. This is one area where function definitely dictates proportions. Table height must permit comfortable seating – table size must allow elbow room for each person. Minimum width for a square table for four is 800 mm. If the table is round, provide a 900 mm diameter for four people, 1200 mm for six. A rectangular table for eight should measure about 900 ×

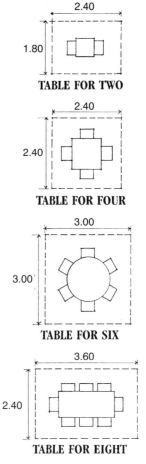

Suggested table sizes

2000 mm. A good general rule is to provide about 600 mm for each person.

The basic frames shown above can be used for any round, square, or rectangular table. Size the frame so overall dimensions are 100 mm less than the dimensions of the top.

Top slabs can be solid wood, plywood, plywood used as a core for another material, or special materials like wide panel, edge-glued wood.

The details show how to assemble various table tops. Solid boards can be butted or spaced. They can be nailed directly to the frame or preassembled with cleats and then secured with corner irons. Corner irons can also be used for plywood tops, whether used alone or as a core for other materials such as tiles.

Litter Bins

These elements in the landscape – be it urban or rural – are more often than not an intrusion, similar to many others such as parking meters, columns containing signs, symbols and lights, etc. There is a need to design the bin as an integral part of other elements, such as seats, benches, shelters, walls and fences. Always ensure that the bin is noticeable by the user and that it can be easily emptied by the collector. The bins should be located at a height which will provide easy deposits of litter and if fitted with a lid it must be easily opened and closed.

Vandalism, whether by people or animals, will demand that the design of a litter bin – depending upon its location – must be given serious consideration.

The design must also ensure that hygiene is included as well as an allowance for drainage of any rain water and liquids.

Types

There are various types such as:
• Bins mounted on columns – lighting, signs, etc.
• Bins mounted on walls or vertical surfaces
• Free-standing bins
• Bins fixed to the ground surface
• Movable bins, generally for temporary use
• Built-in bins – benches, seats, walls, etc.

Materials

There are a wide variety of materials used for bins such as:

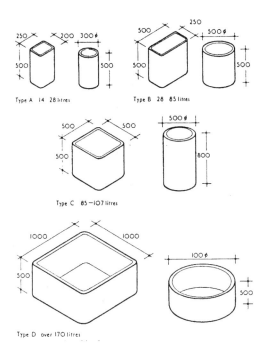

BS4324 Litter bin size ranges

Sheet metal Aluminium Glass fibre	} usually made by a manufacturer.
Timber Concrete	} while this can also be manufactured, designs are available which will allow bins to be individually made *in-situ*.

Very often there is more than one material used, such as metal and timber.

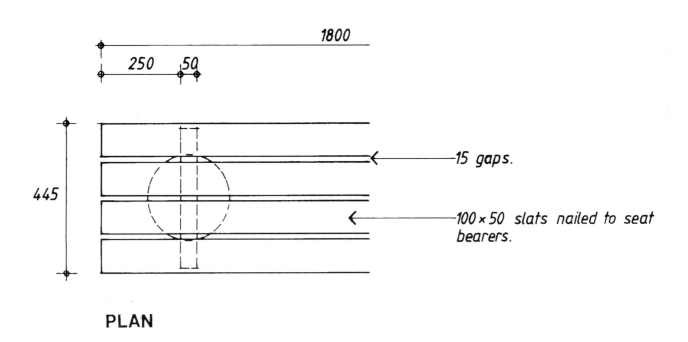

1800

250 50

445

15 gaps.

100 × 50 slats nailed to seat bearers.

PLAN

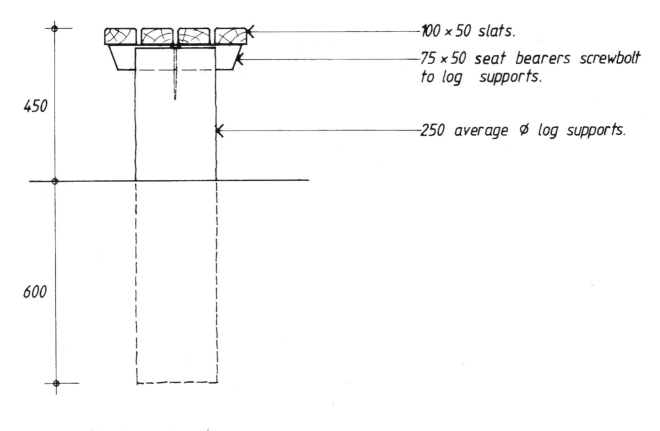

100 × 50 slats.

75 × 50 seat bearers screwbolt to log supports.

450

250 average ∅ log supports.

600

ELEVATION

Scale 1:10

BENCH SEAT
timber

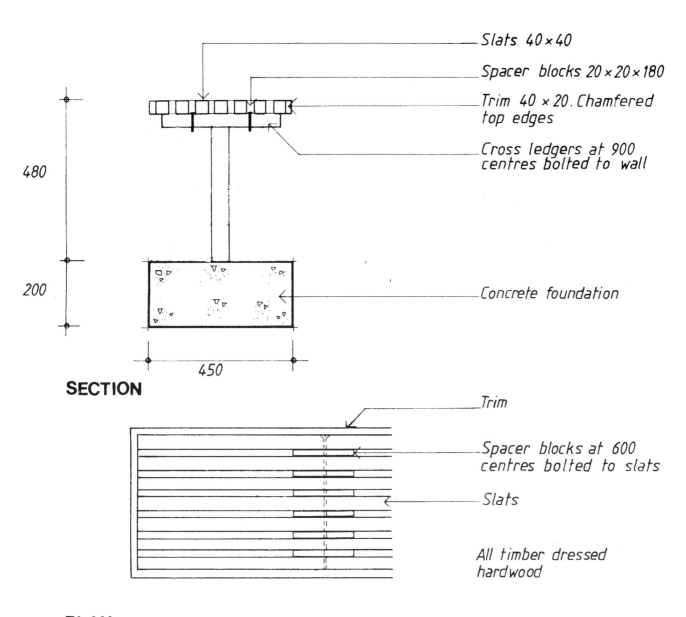

Slats 40 × 40

Spacer blocks 20 × 20 × 180

Trim 40 × 20. Chamfered top edges

Cross ledgers at 900 centres bolted to wall

Concrete foundation

480

200

450

SECTION

Trim

Spacer blocks at 600 centres bolted to slats

Slats

All timber dressed hardwood

PLAN

Scale 1 : 10

BENCH SEAT
timber / block

111

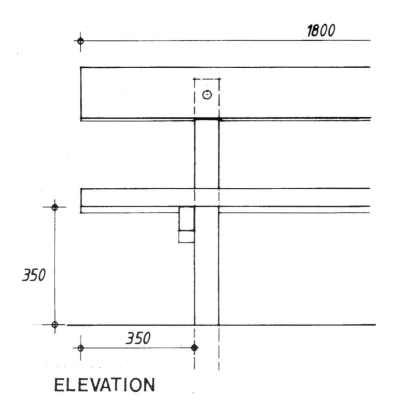

ELEVATION

1800

350

350

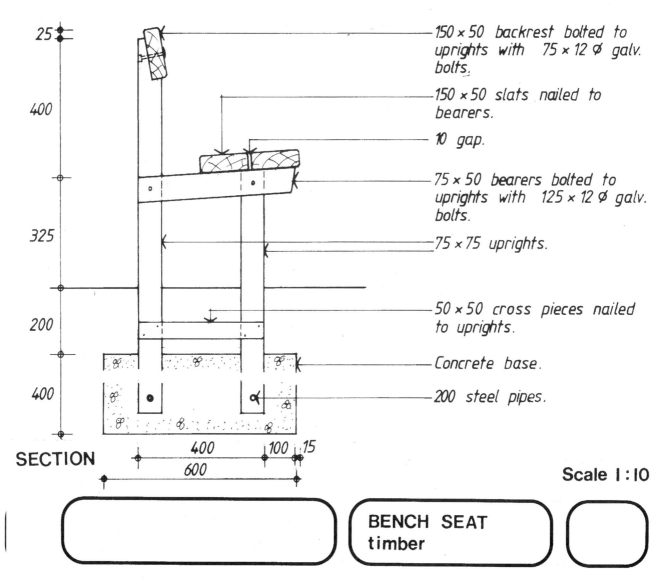

25

400

325

200

400

SECTION

150 × 50 backrest bolted to uprights with 75 × 12 ⌀ galv. bolts.

150 × 50 slats nailed to bearers.

10 gap.

75 × 50 bearers bolted to uprights with 125 × 12 ⌀ galv. bolts.

75 × 75 uprights.

50 × 50 cross pieces nailed to uprights.

Concrete base.

200 steel pipes.

400   100   15

600

Scale 1 : 10

BENCH SEAT
timber

112

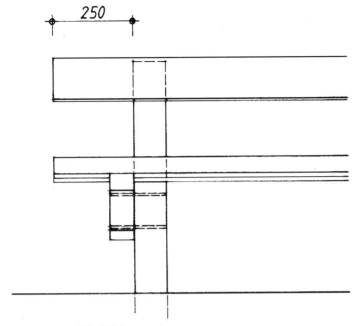

250

ELEVATION

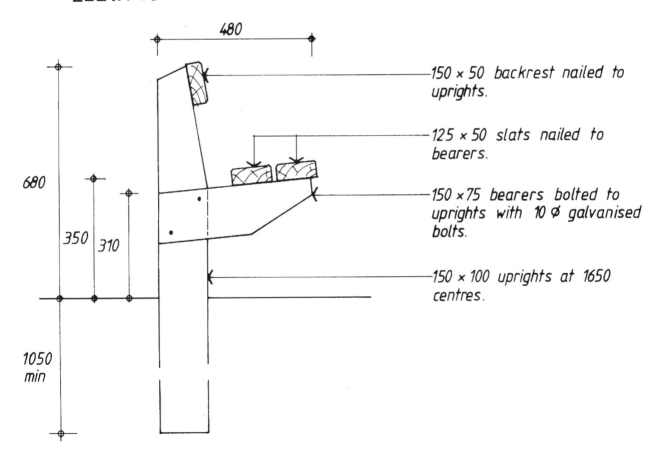

480

680

350 310

1050
min

150 × 50 backrest nailed to
uprights.

125 × 50 slats nailed to
bearers.

150 × 75 bearers bolted to
uprights with 10 Ø galvanised
bolts.

150 × 100 uprights at 1650
centres.

SECTION

Scale I : 10

BENCH SEAT
timber

113

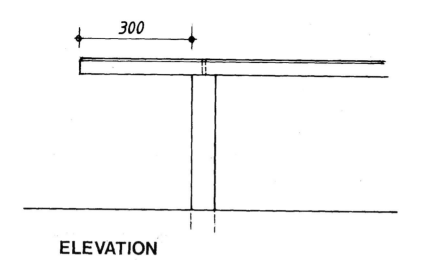

ELEVATION

300

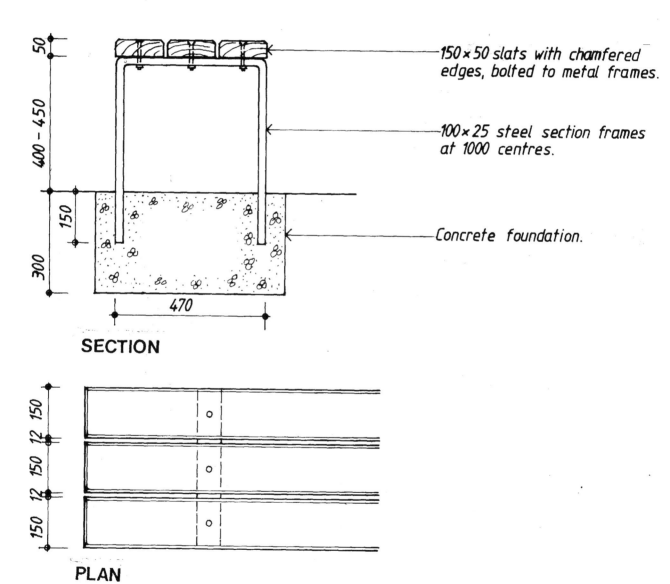

150 × 50 slats with chamfered edges, bolted to metal frames.

100 × 25 steel section frames at 1000 centres.

Concrete foundation.

50

400 – 450

150

300

470

SECTION

150
12
150
12
150
12
150

PLAN

Scale 1:10

BENCH SEAT
timber

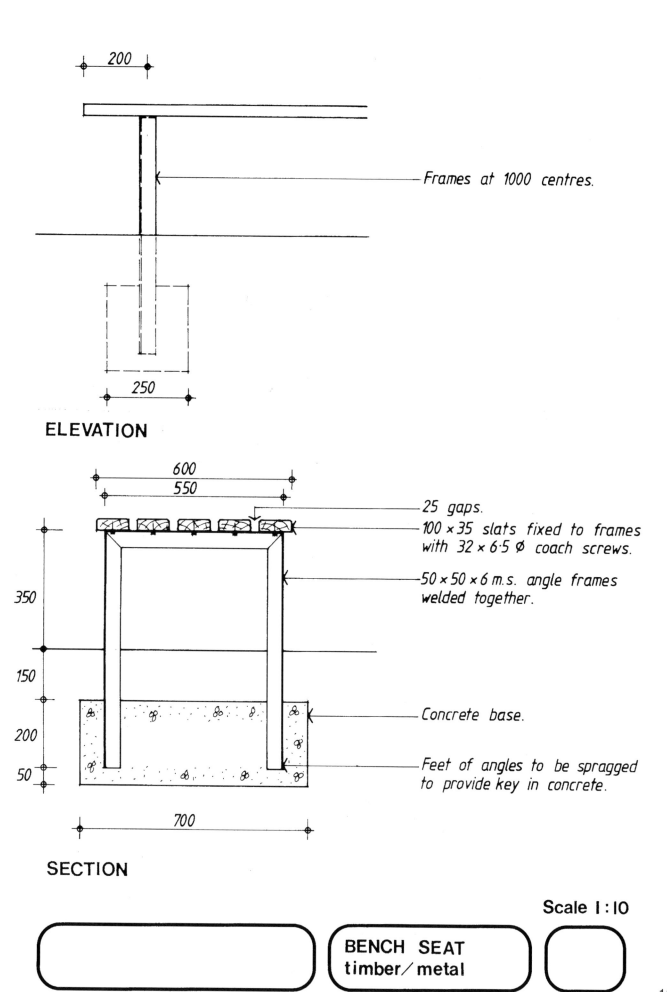

200

Frames at 1000 centres.

250

ELEVATION

600
550

25 gaps.

100 × 35 slats fixed to frames
with 32 × 6·5 ⌀ coach screws.

50 × 50 × 6 m.s. angle frames
welded together.

350

150

200

50

Concrete base.

Feet of angles to be spragged
to provide key in concrete.

700

SECTION

Scale 1 : 10

BENCH SEAT
timber / metal

115

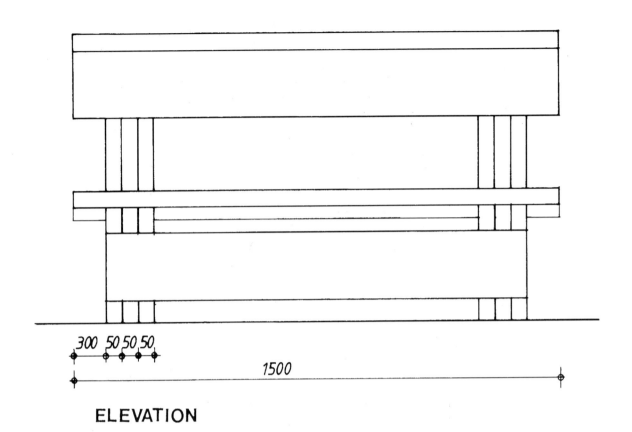

ELEVATION

300 50 50 50

1500

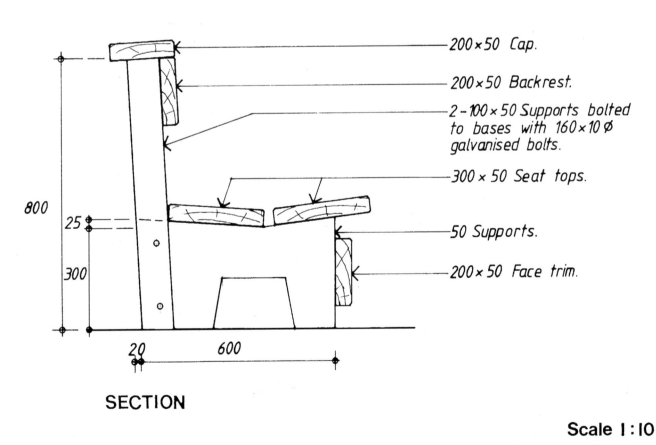

200×50 Cap.

200×50 Backrest.

2-100×50 Supports bolted
to bases with 160×10 Ø
galvanised bolts.

300×50 Seat tops.

50 Supports.

200×50 Face trim.

800

25

300

20 600

SECTION

Scale 1:10

**BENCH SEAT
timber**

116

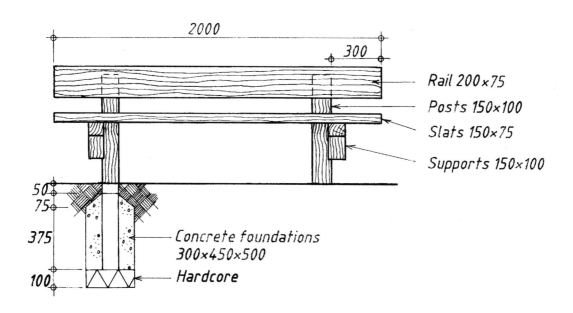

2000

300

Rail 200×75

Posts 150×100

Slats 150×75

Supports 150×100

50
75
375

Concrete foundations
300×450×500

100

Hardcore

FRONT ELEVATION 1:20

Slat

Fix rails to posts
with 165ø bolts c'sk
& plugged.

Post

REAR ELEVATION 1:10

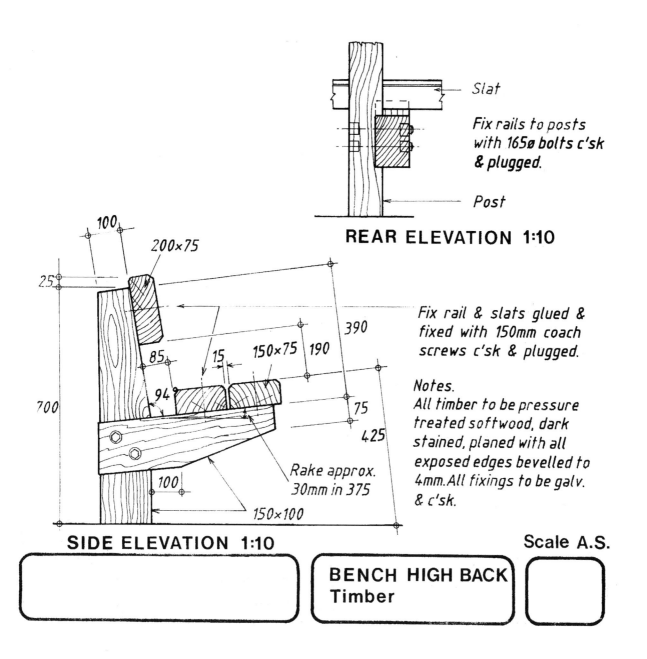

100

200×75

25

390

85

15   150×75   190

94°

75

700

425

Rake approx.
30mm in 375

100

150×100

Fix rail & slats glued &
fixed with 150mm coach
screws c'sk & plugged.

Notes.
All timber to be pressure
treated softwood, dark
stained, planed with all
exposed edges bevelled to
4mm. All fixings to be galv.
& c'sk.

SIDE ELEVATION 1:10

Scale A.S.

BENCH HIGH BACK
Timber

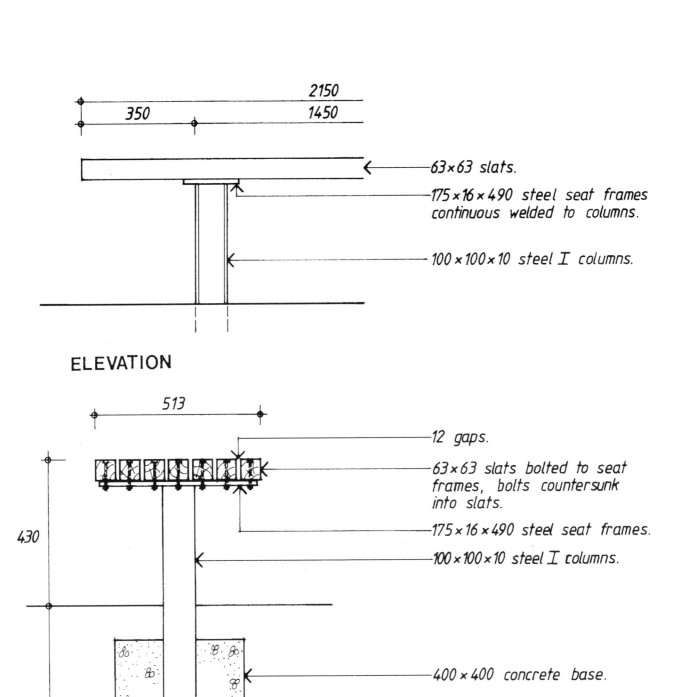

2150

350   1450

63×63 slats.

175×16×490 steel seat frames continuous welded to columns.

100×100×10 steel I columns.

ELEVATION

513

12 gaps.

63×63 slats bolted to seat frames, bolts countersunk into slats.

175×16×490 steel seat frames.

100×100×10 steel I columns.

430

400×400 concrete base.

600

200×10 ∅ steel rod welded to column.

SECTION

Scale 1:10

BENCH SEAT
timber

118

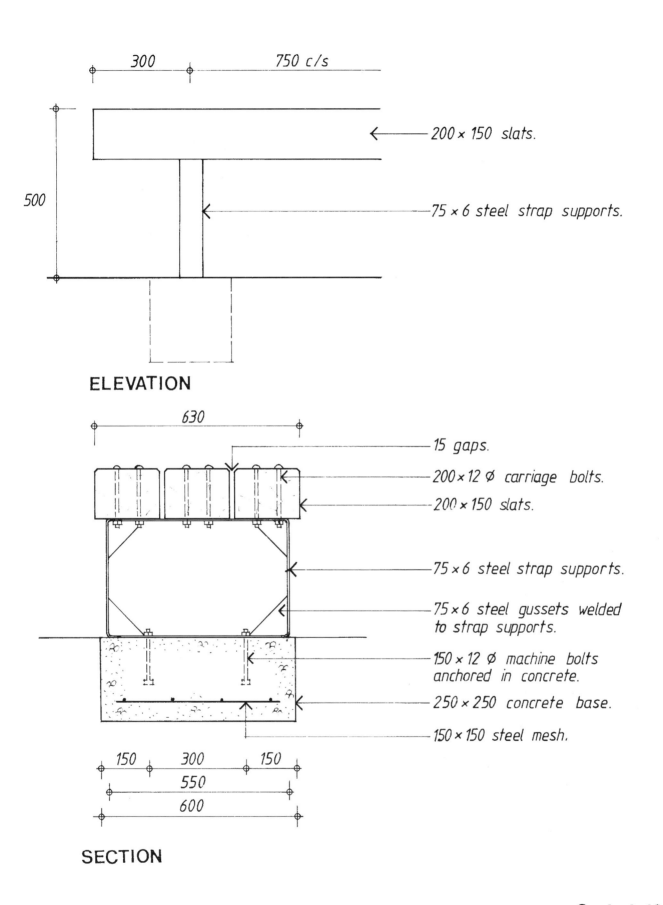

300   750 c/s

500

ELEVATION

← 200 × 150 slats.

75 × 6 steel strap supports.

630

15 gaps.

200 × 12 Ø carriage bolts.

200 × 150 slats.

75 × 6 steel strap supports.

75 × 6 steel gussets welded
to strap supports.

150 × 12 Ø machine bolts
anchored in concrete.

250 × 250 concrete base.

150 × 150 steel mesh.

150   300   150
550
600

SECTION

Scale 1 : 10

BENCH SEAT
timber

119

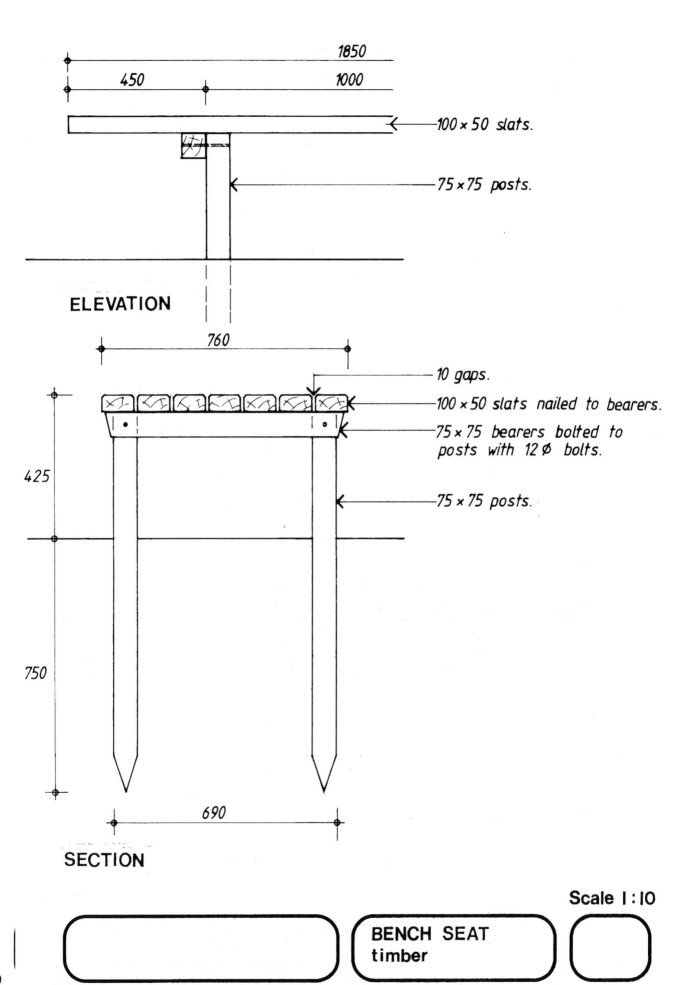

1850

450   1000

—100 × 50 slats.

—75 × 75 posts.

ELEVATION

760

— 10 gaps.

—100 × 50 slats nailed to bearers.

—75 × 75 bearers bolted to
posts with 12 ∅ bolts.

425

—75 × 75 posts.

750

690

SECTION

Scale 1 : 10

BENCH SEAT
timber

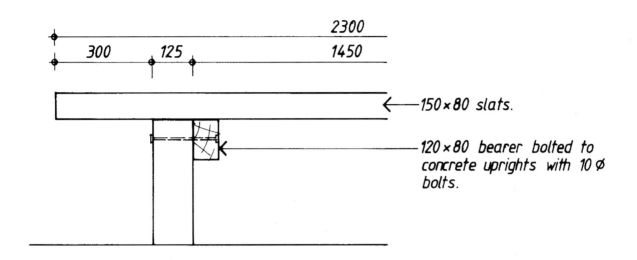

2300

300　　125　　1450

←─150×80 slats.

←─120×80 bearer bolted to concrete uprights with 10 ∅ bolts.

ELEVATION

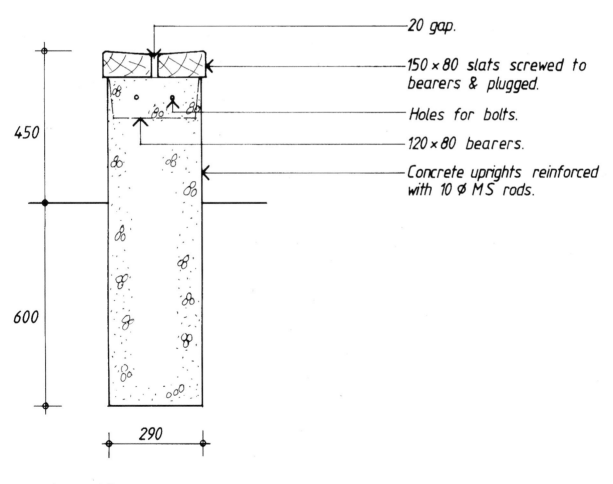

─20 gap.

─150×80 slats screwed to bearers & plugged.

─ Holes for bolts.

─120×80 bearers.

─Concrete uprights reinforced with 10 ∅ MS rods.

450

600

290

SECTION

Scale 1:10

BENCH SEAT
timber/concrete

121

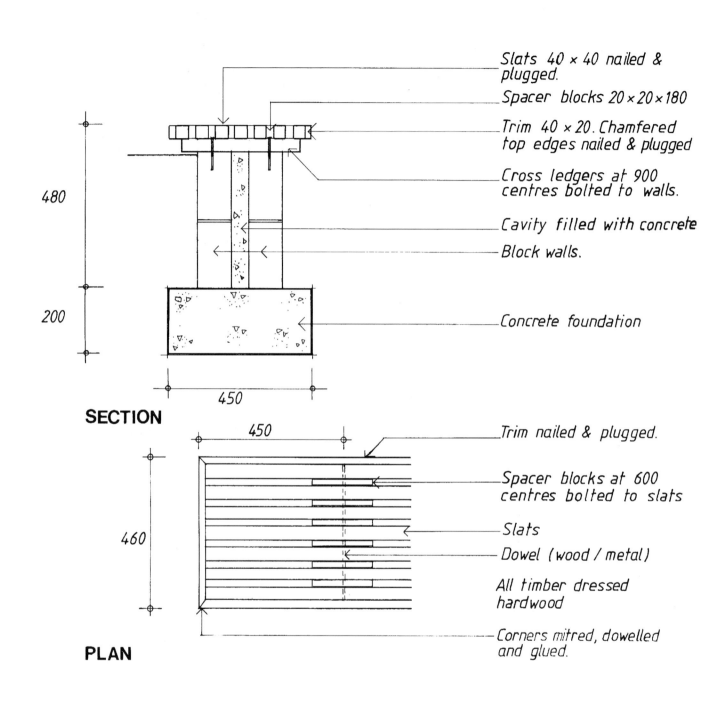

SECTION

480

200

450

Slats 40 × 40 nailed & plugged.

Spacer blocks 20 × 20 × 180

Trim 40 × 20. Chamfered top edges nailed & plugged

Cross ledgers at 900 centres bolted to walls.

Cavity filled with concrete

Block walls.

Concrete foundation

PLAN

450

460

Trim nailed & plugged.

Spacer blocks at 600 centres bolted to slats

Slats

Dowel (wood / metal)

All timber dressed hardwood

Corners mitred, dowelled and glued.

Scale I : I0

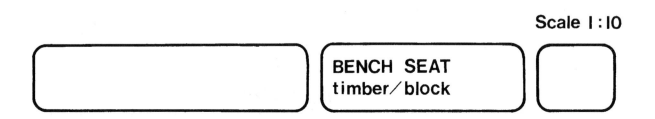

BENCH SEAT
timber/block

122

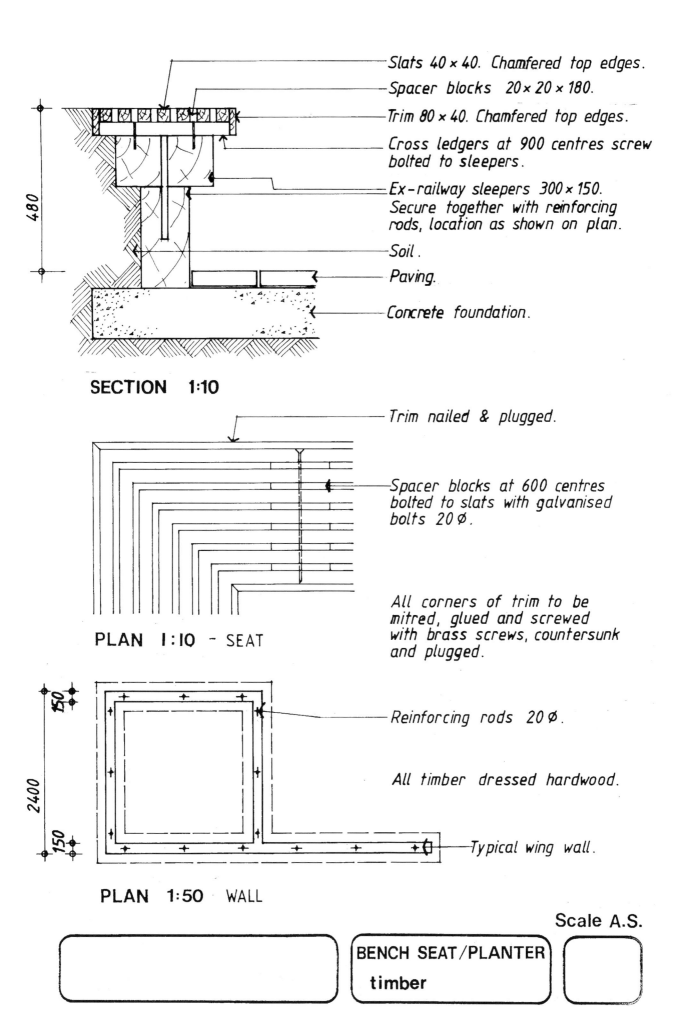

Slats 40 × 40. Chamfered top edges.

Spacer blocks 20 × 20 × 180.

Trim 80 × 40. Chamfered top edges.

Cross ledgers at 900 centres screw bolted to sleepers.

Ex-railway sleepers 300 × 150. Secure together with reinforcing rods, location as shown on plan.

Soil.

Paving.

Concrete foundation.

SECTION 1:10

Trim nailed & plugged.

Spacer blocks at 600 centres bolted to slats with galvanised bolts 20 Ø.

All corners of trim to be mitred, glued and screwed with brass screws, countersunk and plugged.

PLAN 1:10 – SEAT

Reinforcing rods 20 Ø.

All timber dressed hardwood.

Typical wing wall.

PLAN 1:50 WALL

Scale A.S.

BENCH SEAT/PLANTER

timber

123

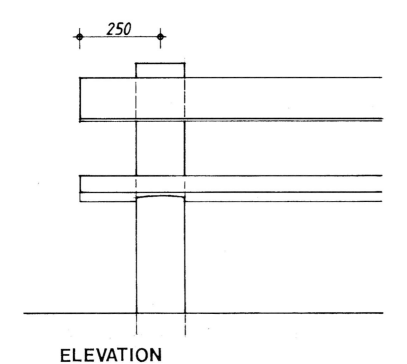

250

ELEVATION

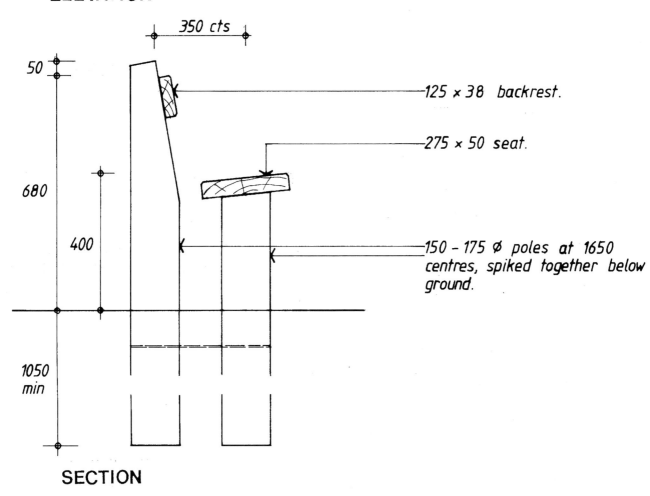

350 cts

50

680

400

1050 min

125 × 38 backrest.

275 × 50 seat.

150 – 175 ⌀ poles at 1650 centres, spiked together below ground.

SECTION

Scale 1:10

BENCH SEAT
timber

124

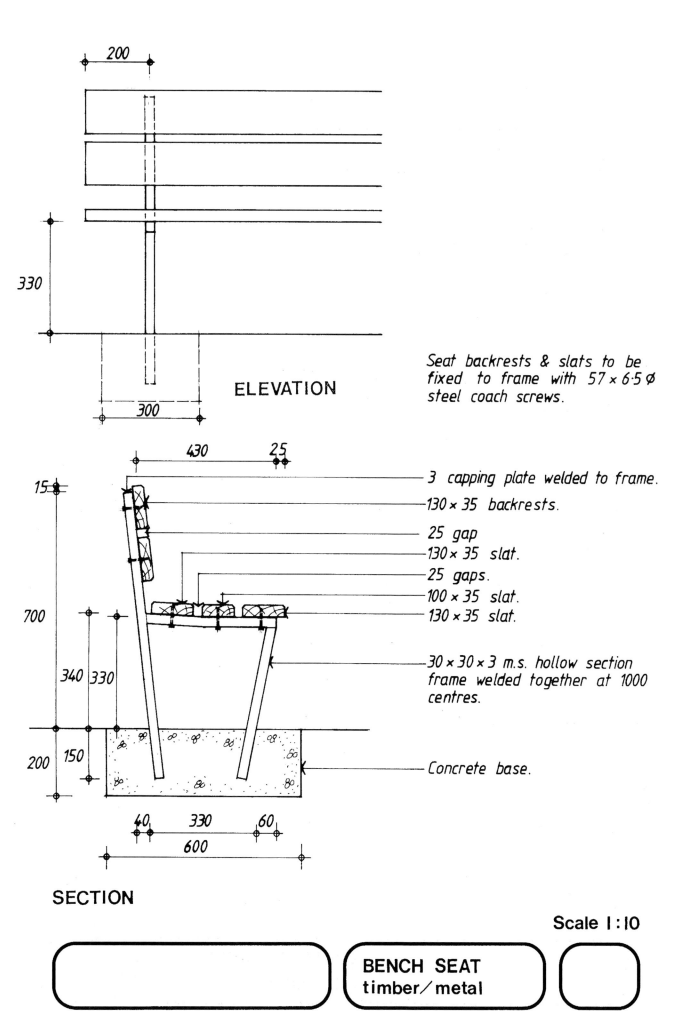

200

330

300

ELEVATION

Seat backrests & slats to be fixed to frame with 57 × 6·5 ⌀ steel coach screws.

430   **25**

15

700

340 **330**

200 **150**

— 3 capping plate welded to frame.

—130 × 35 backrests.

— 25 gap
—130 × 35 slat.
— 25 gaps.
—100 × 35 slat.
—130 × 35 slat.

—30 × 30 × 3 m.s. hollow section frame welded together at 1000 centres.

— Concrete base.

40   **330**   **60**
600

SECTION

Scale 1:10

BENCH SEAT
timber/metal

125

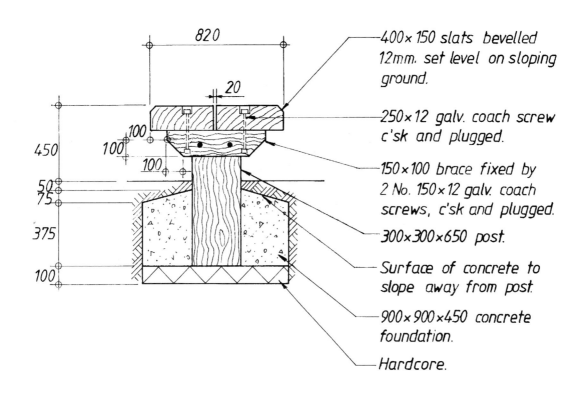

820

20

450

100 100 100

100

50
75

375

100

400×150 slats bevelled
12mm. set level on sloping
ground.

250×12 galv. coach screw
c'sk and plugged.

150×100 brace fixed by
2 No. 150×12 galv. coach
screws, c'sk and plugged.

300×300×650 post.

Surface of concrete to
slope away from post.

900×900×450 concrete
foundation.

Hardcore.

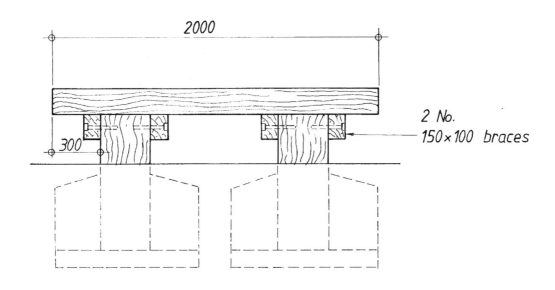

2000

300

2 No.
150×100 braces

Scale 1:20

BENCH BACKLESS
Timber

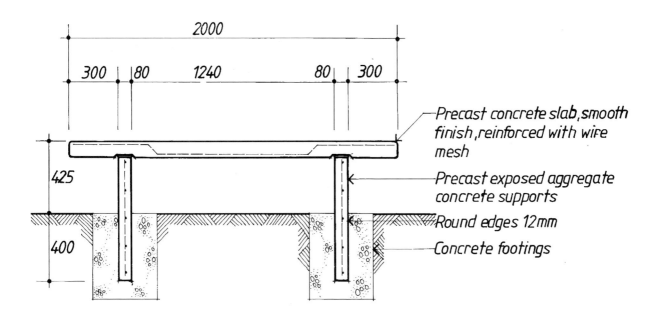

FRONT ELEVATION

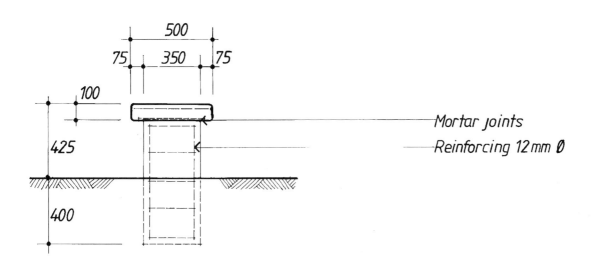

END ELEVATION

Precast concrete slab, smooth finish, reinforced with wire mesh

Precast exposed aggregate concrete supports

Round edges 12mm

Concrete footings

Mortar joints

Reinforcing 12mm ⌀

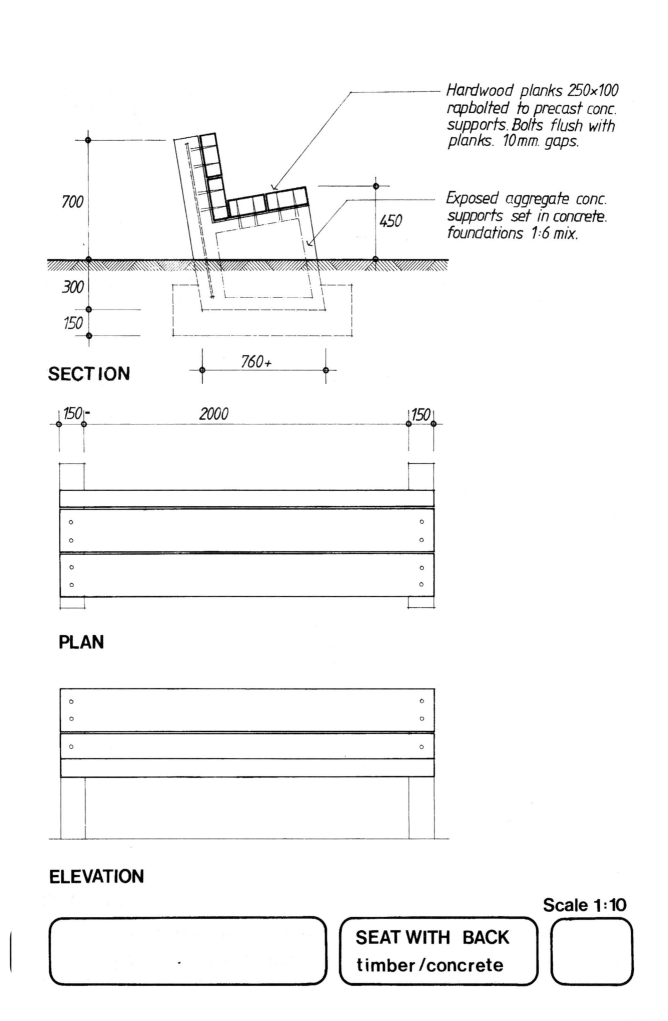

Hardwood planks 250×100
rapbolted to precast conc.
supports. Bolts flush with
planks. 10mm. gaps.

Exposed aggregate conc.
supports set in concrete.
foundations 1:6 mix.

700

450

SECTION

300

150

760+

150−   2000   150

PLAN

ELEVATION

Scale 1:10

SEAT WITH BACK
timber /concrete

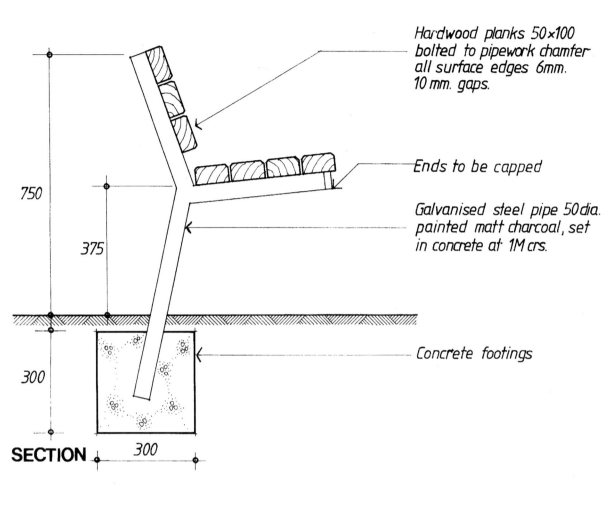

Hardwood planks 50×100
bolted to pipework chamfer
all surface edges 6mm.
10 mm. gaps.

Ends to be capped

Galvanised steel pipe 50 dia.
painted matt charcoal, set
in concrete at 1M crs.

Concrete footings

750

375

300

SECTION   300

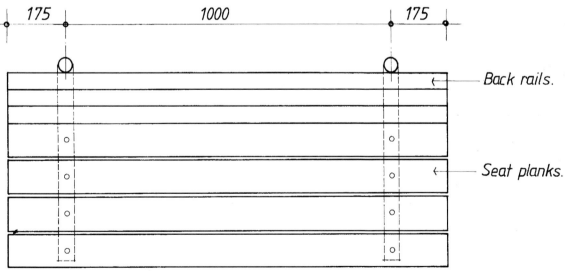

175   1000   175

Back rails.

Seat planks.

PLAN

Scale 1:10

SEAT WITH BACK
timber & steel

129

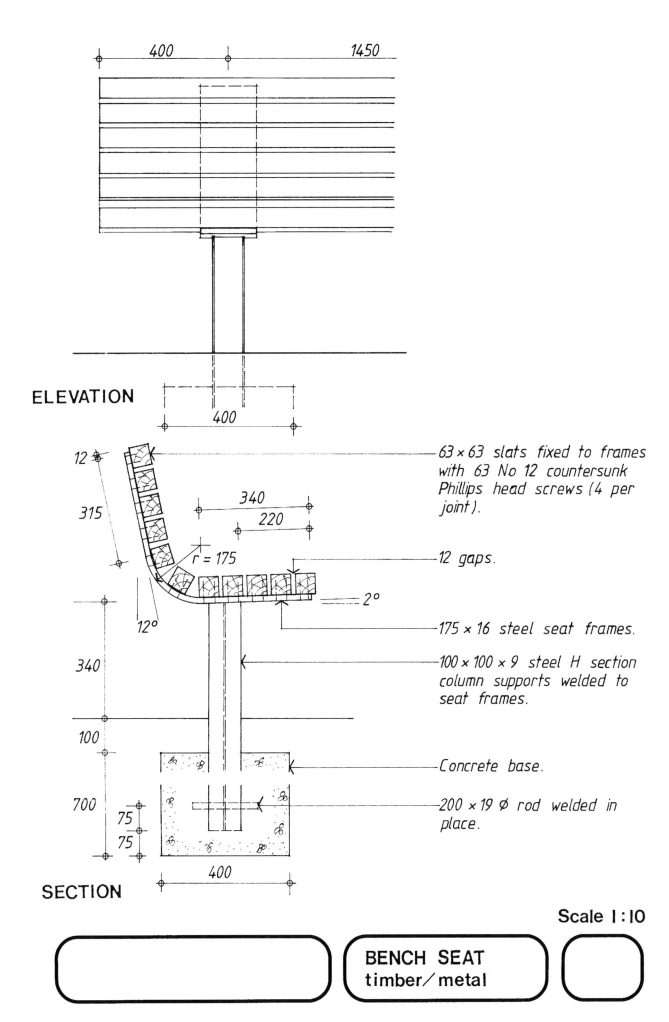

ELEVATION

400   1450

400

SECTION

12
315
340
220
r = 175
12°
340
100
700
75
75
400
2°

63 × 63 slats fixed to frames
with 63 No 12 countersunk
Phillips head screws (4 per
joint).

12 gaps.

175 × 16 steel seat frames.

100 × 100 × 9 steel H section
column supports welded to
seat frames.

Concrete base.

200 × 19 ∅ rod welded in
place.

Scale 1 : 10

BENCH SEAT
timber / metal

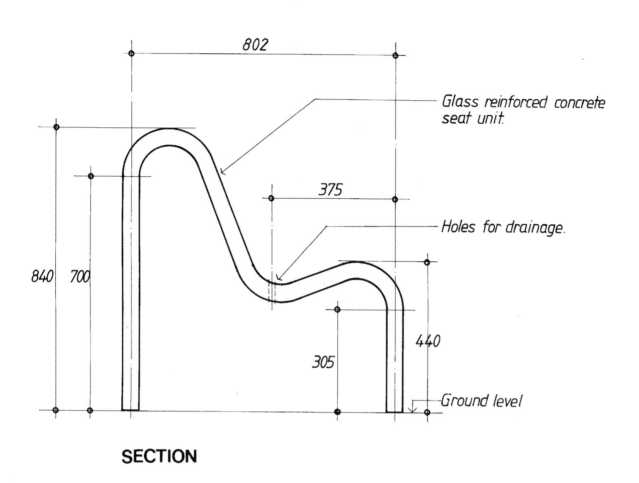

802

Glass reinforced concrete
seat unit.

375

Holes for drainage.

840 700

305

440

Ground level

SECTION

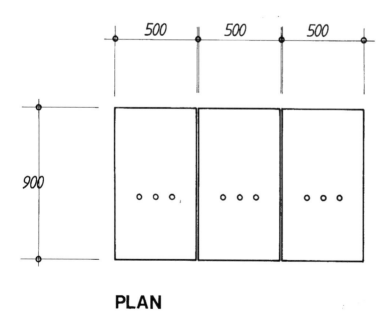

500   500   500

900

PLAN

Scale 1:10

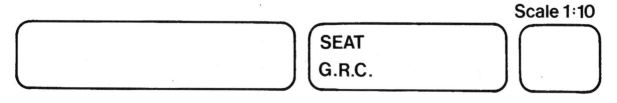

SEAT
G.R.C.

131

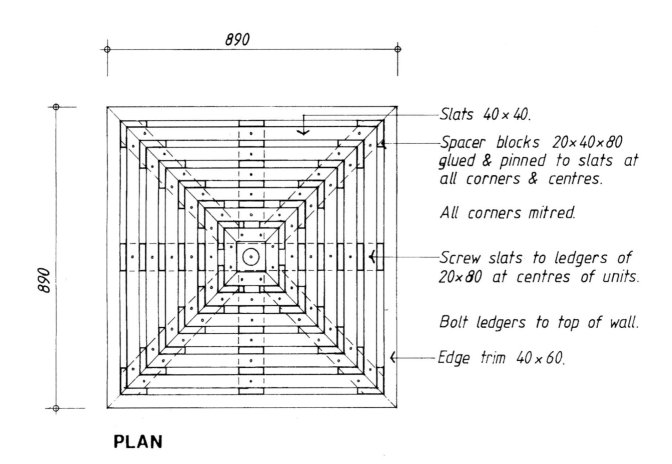

PLAN

Slats 40 × 40.

Spacer blocks 20×40×80 glued & pinned to slats at all corners & centres.

All corners mitred.

Screw slats to ledgers of 20×80 at centres of units.

Bolt ledgers to top of wall.

Edge trim 40 × 60.

890

890

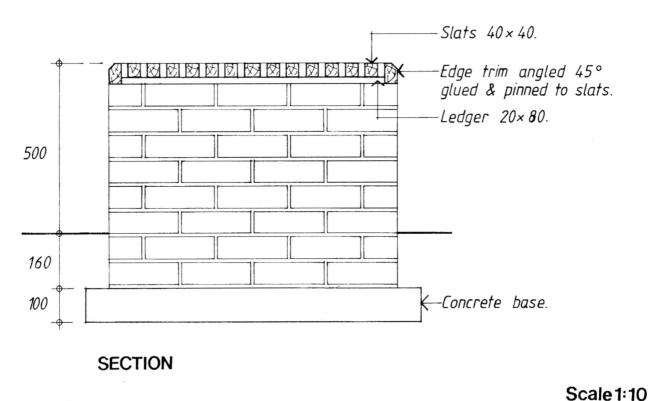

SECTION

Slats 40 × 40.

Edge trim angled 45° glued & pinned to slats.

Ledger 20 × 80.

Concrete base.

500

160

100

Scale 1:10

**SEAT
brick & timber**

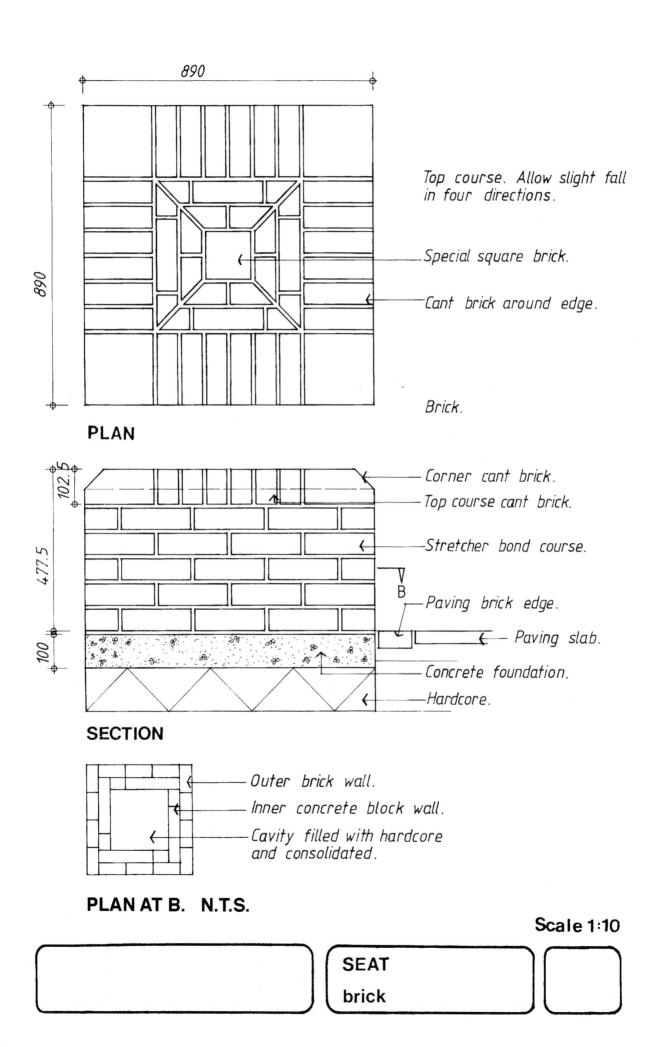

890

890

PLAN

Top course. Allow slight fall in four directions.

Special square brick.

Cant brick around edge.

Brick.

102.5

477.5

100

SECTION

Corner cant brick.

Top course cant brick.

Stretcher bond course.

B

Paving brick edge.

Paving slab.

Concrete foundation.

Hardcore.

PLAN AT B. N.T.S.

Outer brick wall.

Inner concrete block wall.

Cavity filled with hardcore and consolidated.

Scale 1:10

SEAT

brick

133

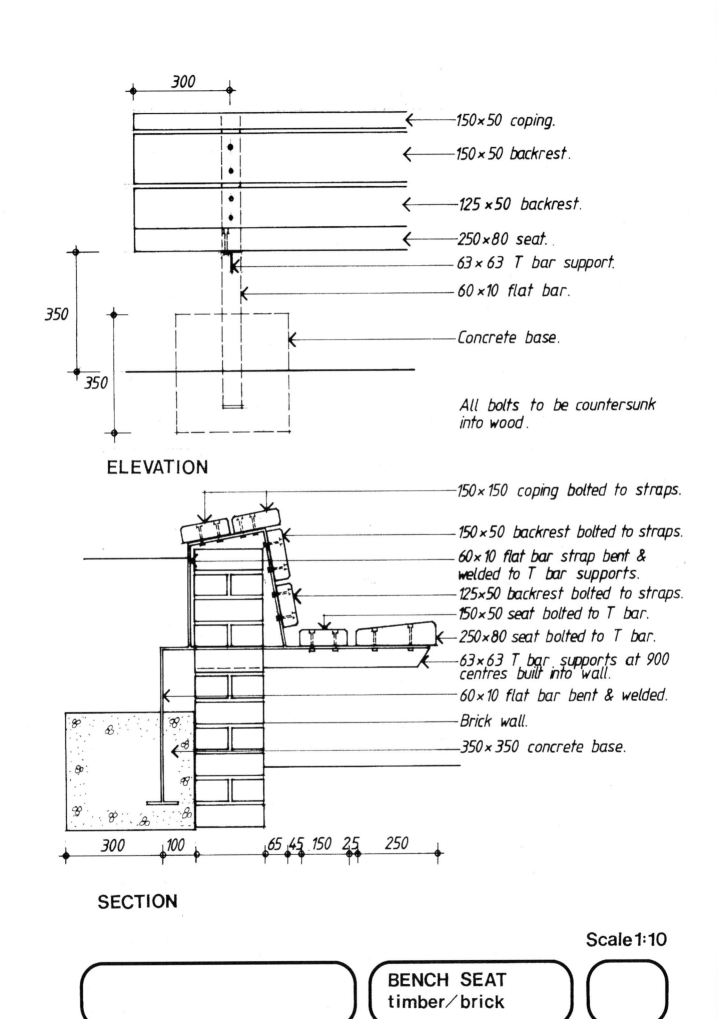

300

150×50 coping.

150×50 backrest.

125×50 backrest.

250×80 seat.

63×63 T bar support.

60×10 flat bar.

Concrete base.

350

350

All bolts to be countersunk into wood.

ELEVATION

150×150 coping bolted to straps.

150×50 backrest bolted to straps.

60×10 flat bar strap bent & welded to T bar supports.

125×50 backrest bolted to straps.

150×50 seat bolted to T bar.

250×80 seat bolted to T bar.

63×63 T bar supports at 900 centres built into wall.

60×10 flat bar bent & welded.

Brick wall.

350×350 concrete base.

300   100   65 45 150 25   250

SECTION

Scale 1:10

BENCH SEAT
timber/brick

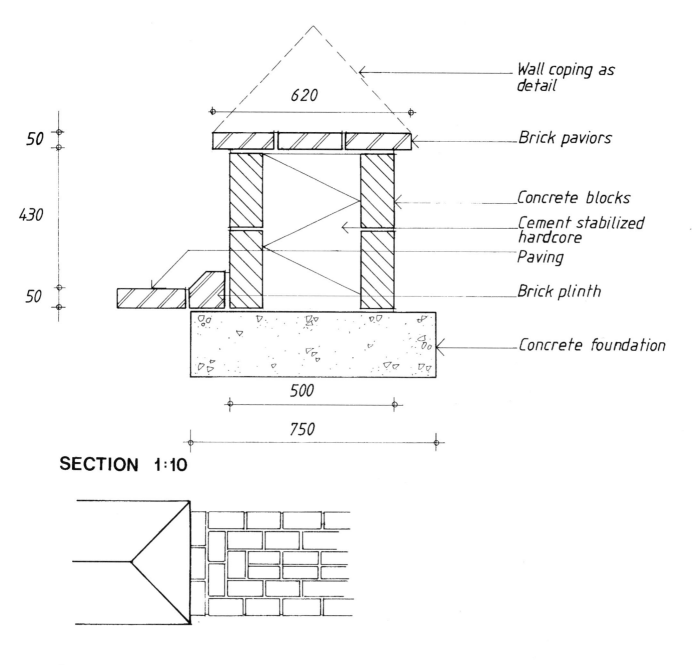

620

50

430

50

Wall coping as detail

Brick paviors

Concrete blocks

Cement stabilized hardcore

Paving

Brick plinth

Concrete foundation

500

750

SECTION 1:10

PLAN 1:20

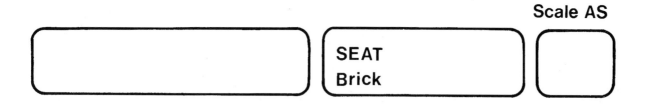

Scale AS

SEAT
Brick

135

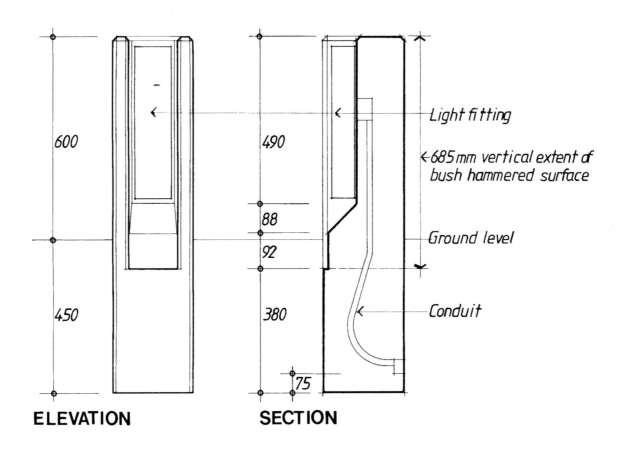

ELEVATION

600

450

SECTION

490

88

92

380

75

— Light fitting

←685 mm vertical extent of bush hammered surface

— Ground level

— Conduit

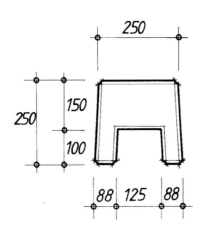

PLAN

250

250

150

100

88 125 88

BOLLARD
lighting

Scale 1:10

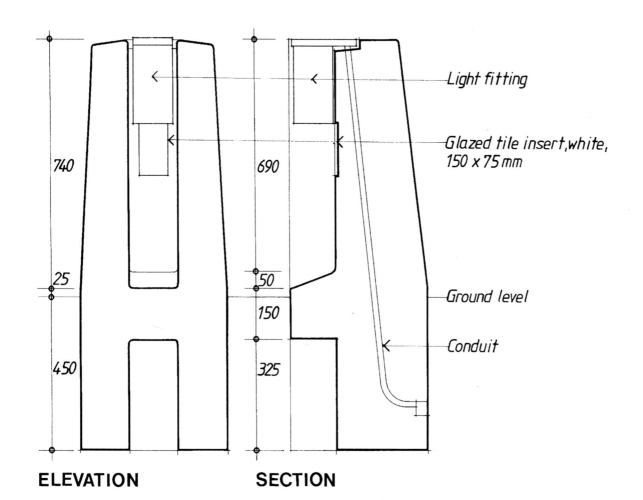

ELEVATION **SECTION**

Light fitting

Glazed tile insert, white,
150 x 75 mm

Ground level

Conduit

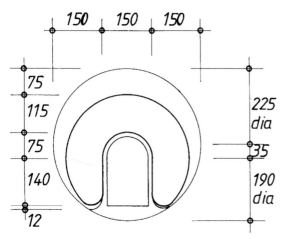

PLAN

Scale 1:10

BOLLARD
lighting

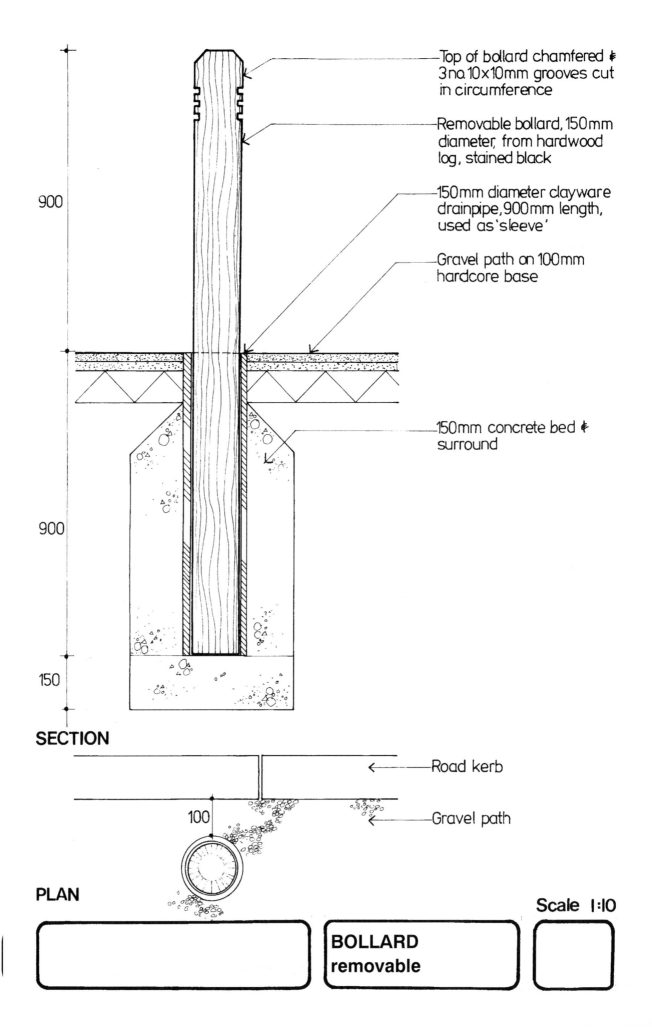

Top of bollard chamfered &
3 no. 10 x 10mm grooves cut
in circumference

Removable bollard, 150mm
diameter, from hardwood
log, stained black

150mm diameter clayware
drainpipe, 900mm length,
used as 'sleeve'

Gravel path on 100mm
hardcore base

150mm concrete bed &
surround

900

900

150

SECTION

Road kerb

Gravel path

100

PLAN

Scale 1:10

**BOLLARD
removable**

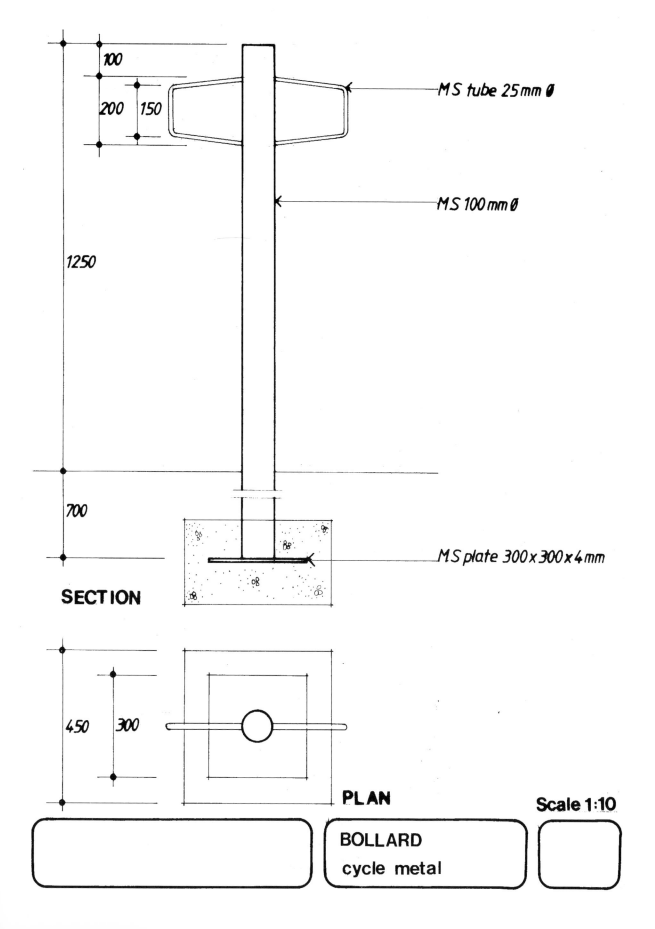

100

200 150

1250

700

SECTION

MS tube 25mm ∅

MS 100 mm ∅

MS plate 300x300x4mm

450 300

PLAN

Scale 1:10

BOLLARD

cycle metal

139

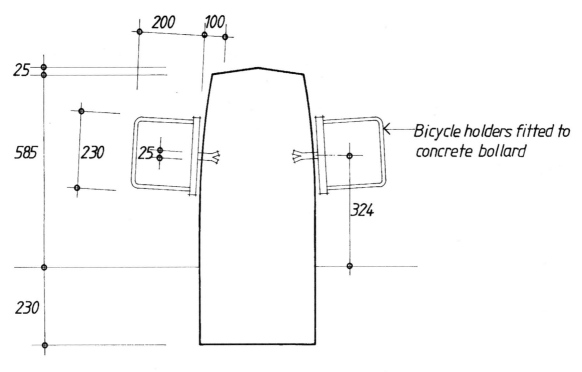

200 **100**

25

585 **230** **25**

324

Bicycle holders fitted to concrete bollard

230

SECTION

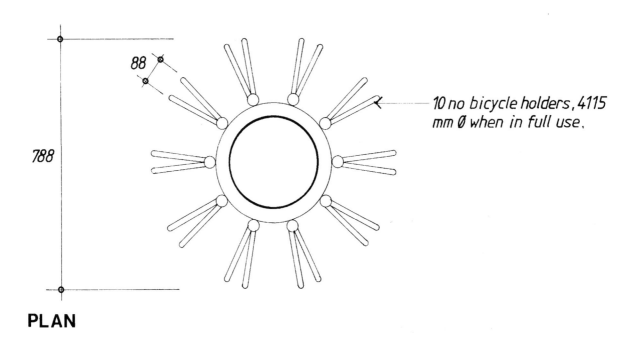

88

788

10 no bicycle holders, 4115 mm Ø when in full use.

PLAN

Scale 1:10

BOLLARD
cycle

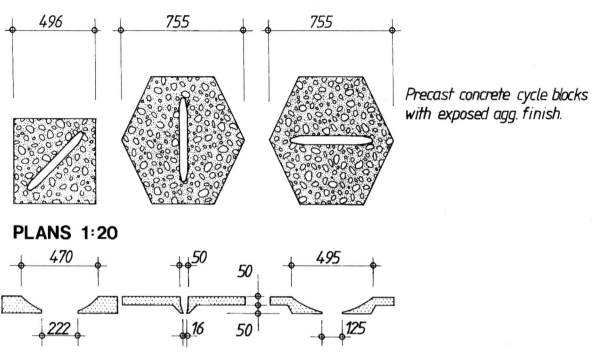

Precast concrete cycle blocks with exposed agg. finish.

PLANS 1:20

SECTIONS 1:20

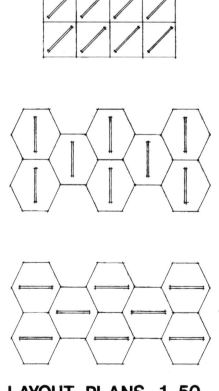

LAYOUT PLANS 1:50

CYCLE BLOCKS

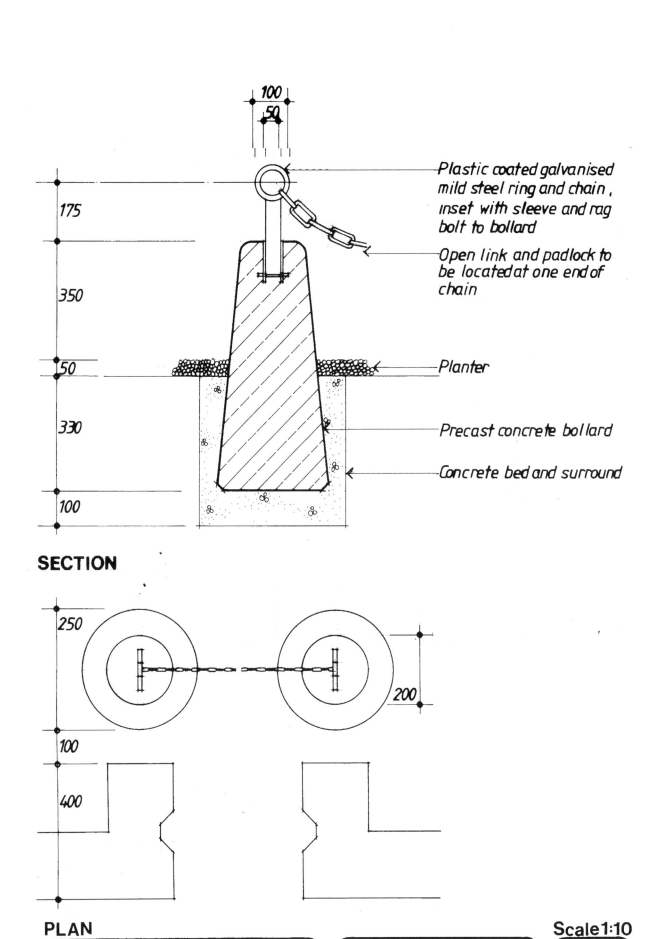

100

50

Plastic coated galvanised mild steel ring and chain, inset with sleeve and rag bolt to bollard

Open link and padlock to be located at one end of chain

175

350

50

Planter

330

Precast concrete bollard

Concrete bed and surround

100

SECTION

250

200

100

400

PLAN

BOLLARD
car park entrance

Scale 1:10

142

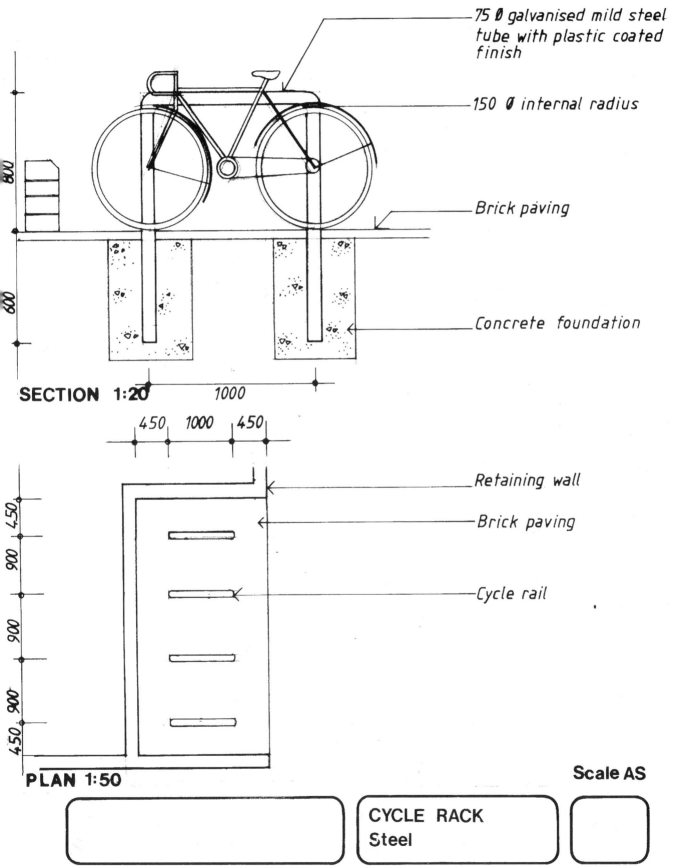

75 Ø galvanised mild steel tube with plastic coated finish

150 Ø internal radius

Brick paving

Concrete foundation

800

600

SECTION 1:20

1000

450 1000 450

Retaining wall

Brick paving

Cycle rail

450

900

900

900

450

PLAN 1:50

Scale AS

| | CYCLE RACK Steel | |

143

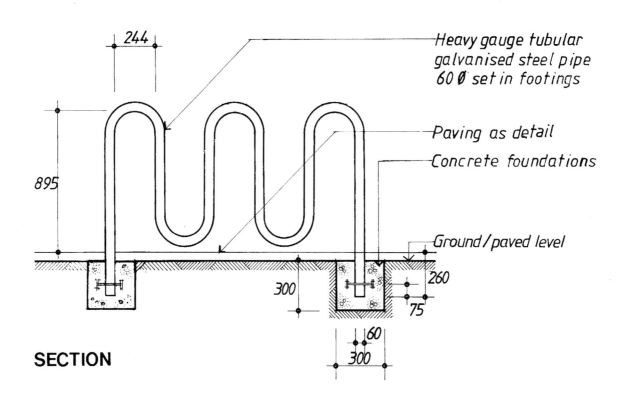

244

895

Heavy gauge tubular
galvanised steel pipe
60 Ø set in footings

Paving as detail

Concrete foundations

Ground / paved level

300

260

75

60

300

SECTION

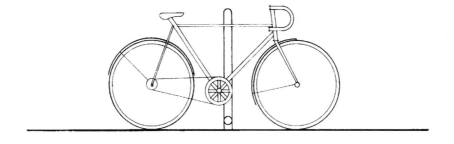

Scale 1:20

CYCLE RACK

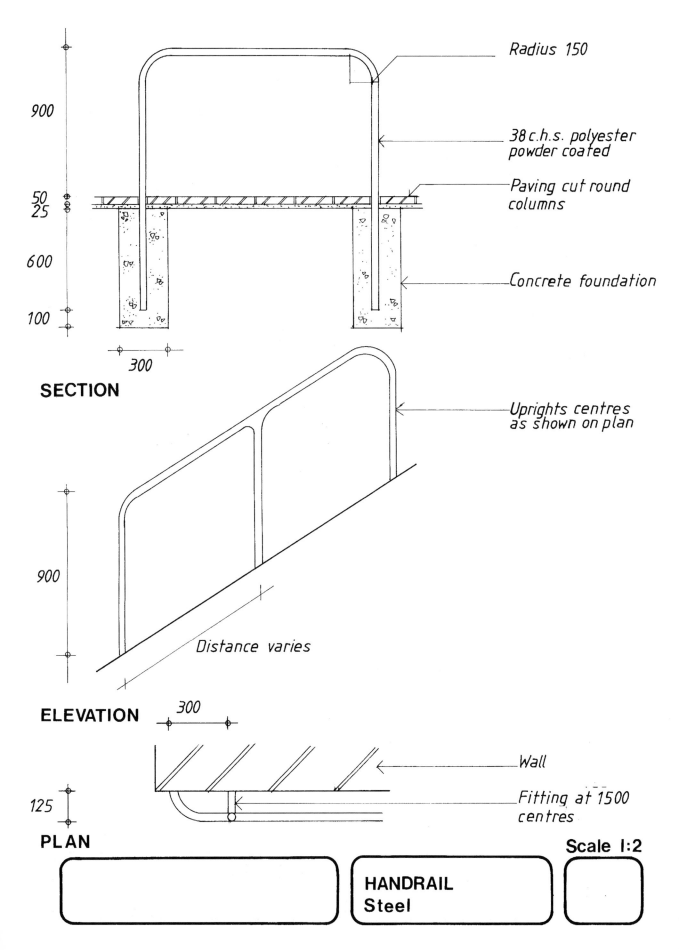

Radius 150

38 c.h.s. polyester
powder coated

Paving cut round
columns

Concrete foundation

900

50
25

600

100

300

SECTION

Uprights centres
as shown on plan

900

Distance varies

ELEVATION

300

Wall

125

Fitting at 1500
centres

PLAN

Scale 1:2

HANDRAIL
Steel

145

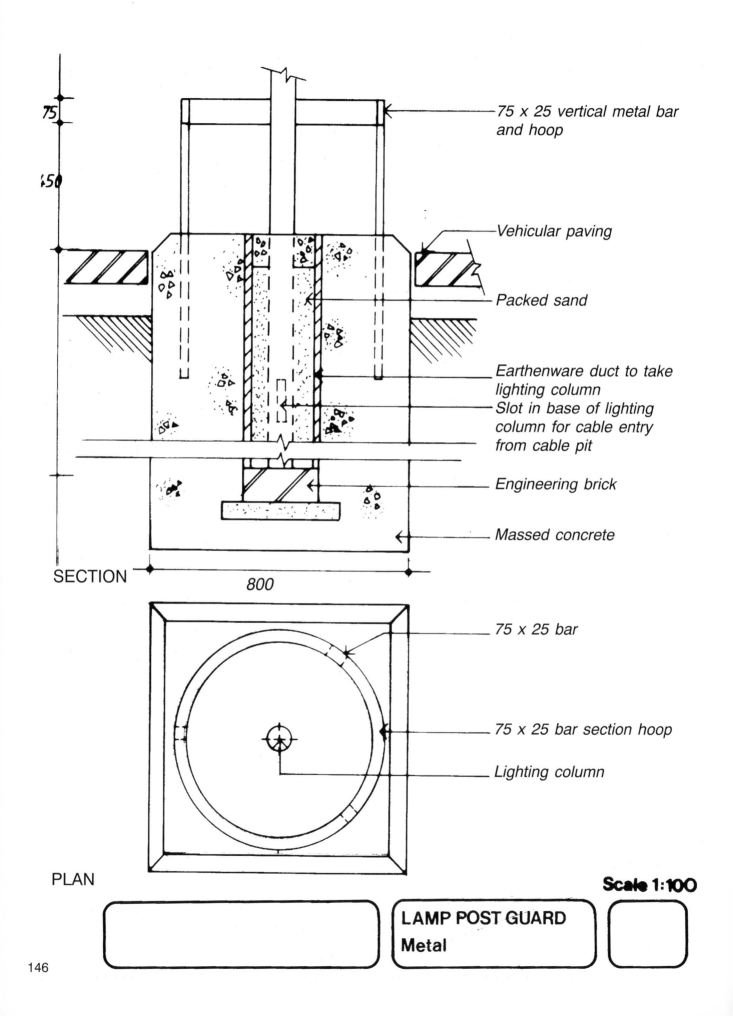

75

650

75 x 25 vertical metal bar
and hoop

Vehicular paving

Packed sand

Earthenware duct to take
lighting column

Slot in base of lighting
column for cable entry
from cable pit

Engineering brick

Massed concrete

SECTION

800

75 x 25 bar

75 x 25 bar section hoop

Lighting column

PLAN

Scale 1:100

LAMP POST GUARD
Metal

146

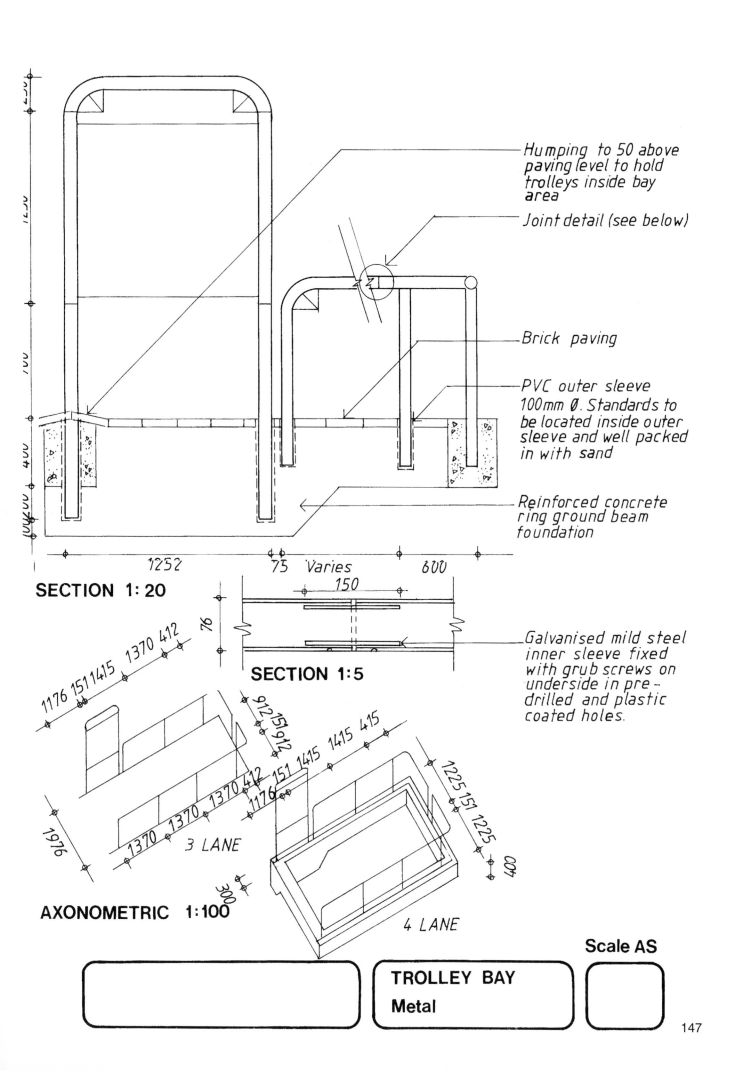

Humping to 50 above
paving level to hold
trolleys inside bay
area

Joint detail (see below)

Brick paving

PVC outer sleeve
100mm Ø. Standards to
be located inside outer
sleeve and well packed
in with sand

Reinforced concrete
ring ground beam
foundation

SECTION 1:20

1252   75 Varies   600

150

SECTION 1:5

Galvanised mild steel
inner sleeve fixed
with grub screws on
underside in pre-
drilled and plastic
coated holes.

76

1176 151 1415 1370 412

912 151 912

1176 151 1415 1415 415

1370 1370 1370 412

3 LANE

1976

300

1225 151 1225   400

4 LANE

AXONOMETRIC 1:100

TROLLEY BAY

Metal

Scale AS

147

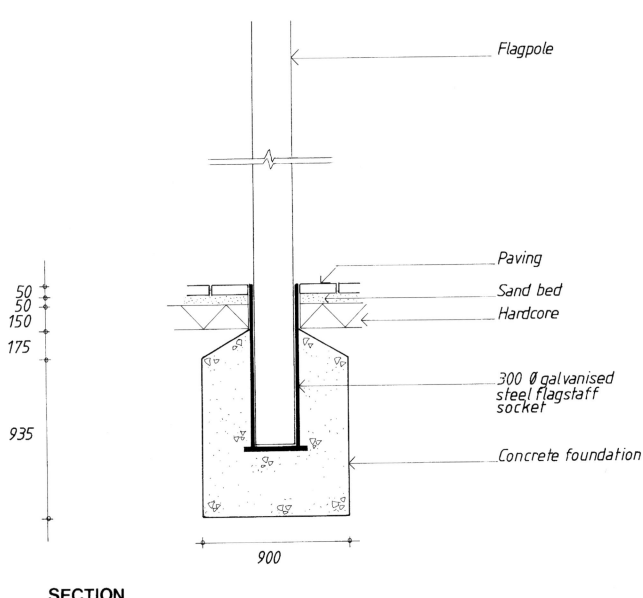

Flagpole

Paving

Sand bed

Hardcore

300 Ø galvanised
steel flagstaff
socket

Concrete foundation

50
50
150

175

935

900

SECTION

Scale 1:20

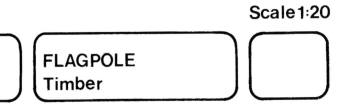

FLAGPOLE
Timber

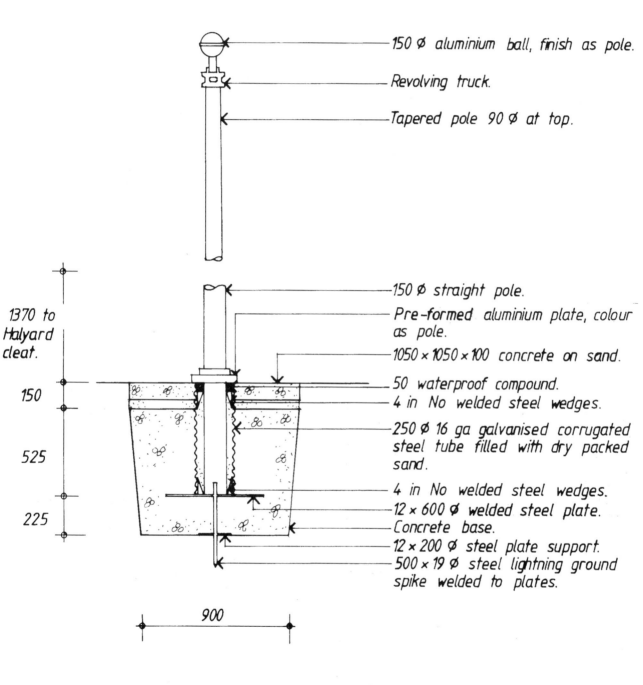

150 ⌀ aluminium ball, finish as pole.

Revolving truck.

Tapered pole 90 ⌀ at top.

1370 to Halyard cleat.

150 ⌀ straight pole.

Pre-formed aluminium plate, colour as pole.

1050 × 1050 × 100 concrete on sand.

50 waterproof compound.

4 in No welded steel wedges.

250 ⌀ 16 ga galvanised corrugated steel tube filled with dry packed sand.

4 in No welded steel wedges.

12 × 600 ⌀ welded steel plate.

Concrete base.

12 × 200 ⌀ steel plate support.

500 × 19 ⌀ steel lightning ground spike welded to plates.

150

525

225

900

SECTION

Scale 1:20

FLAGPOLE
metal

149

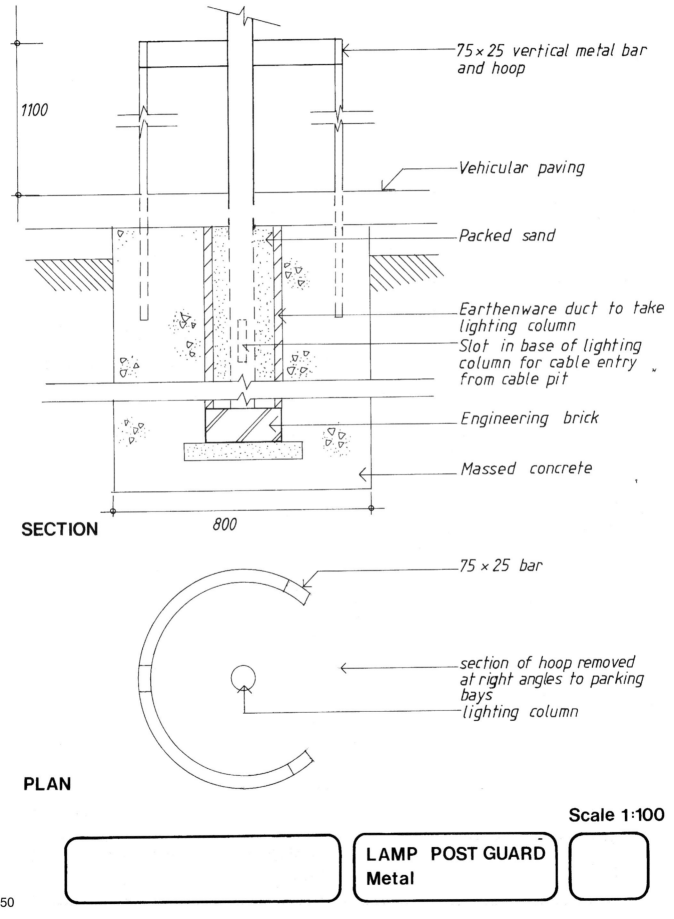

75 × 25 vertical metal bar and hoop

1100

Vehicular paving

Packed sand

Earthenware duct to take lighting column

Slot in base of lighting column for cable entry from cable pit

Engineering brick

Massed concrete

SECTION

800

75 × 25 bar

section of hoop removed at right angles to parking bays

lighting column

PLAN

Scale 1:100

LAMP POST GUARD
Metal

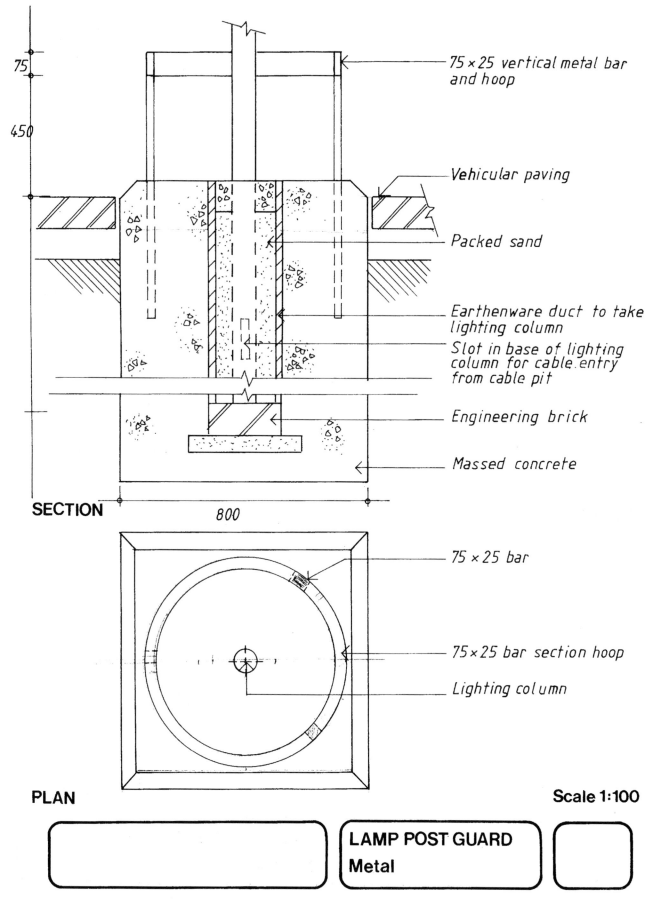

75 ——————— 75 × 25 vertical metal bar and hoop

450

Vehicular paving

Packed sand

Earthenware duct to take lighting column

Slot in base of lighting column for cable entry from cable pit

Engineering brick

Massed concrete

SECTION   800

75 × 25 bar

75 × 25 bar section hoop

Lighting column

PLAN   **Scale 1:100**

LAMP POST GUARD
Metal

151

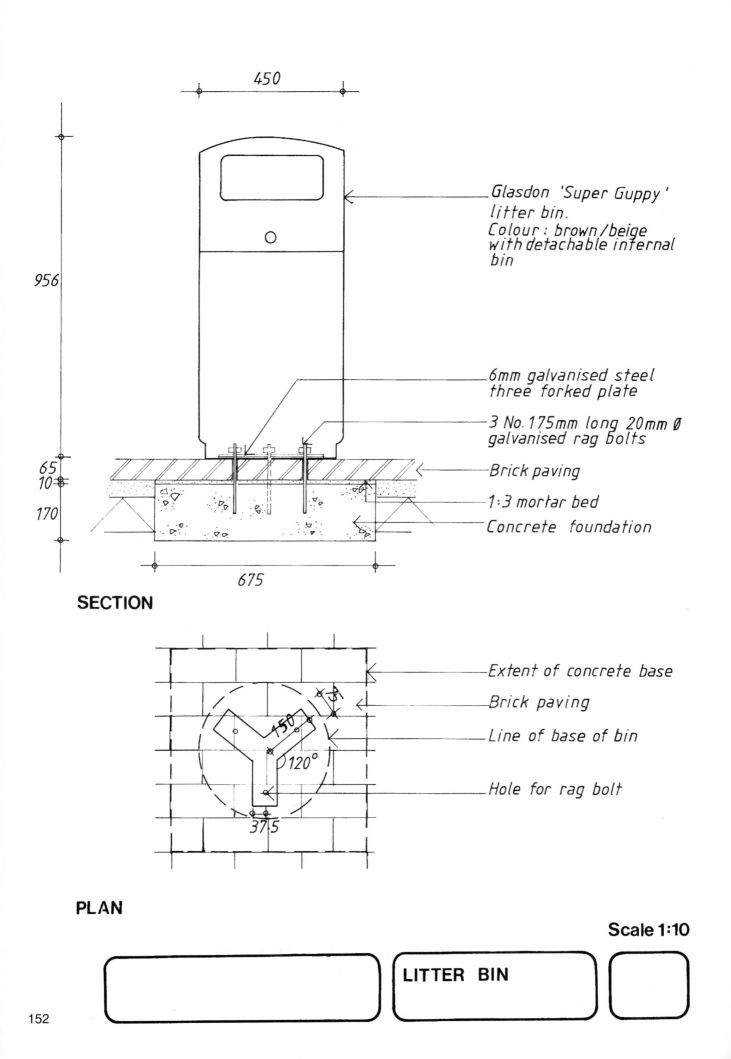

450

956

65
10

170

Glasdon 'Super Guppy'
litter bin.
Colour : brown/beige
with detachable internal
bin

6mm galvanised steel
three forked plate

3 No.175mm long 20mm Ø
galvanised rag bolts

Brick paving

1:3 mortar bed

Concrete foundation

675

SECTION

Extent of concrete base

Brick paving

Line of base of bin

Hole for rag bolt

150

120°

375

PLAN

Scale 1:10

LITTER BIN

400

SECTION

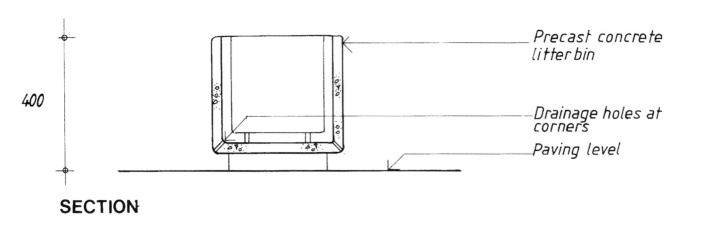

Precast concrete
litter bin

Drainage holes at
corners

Paving level

400

PLAN

400

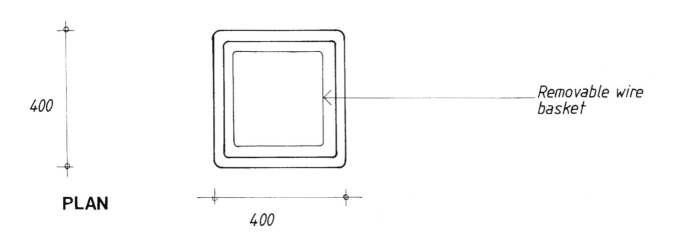

Removable wire
basket

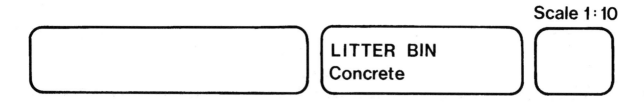

Scale 1:10

LITTER BIN
Concrete

153

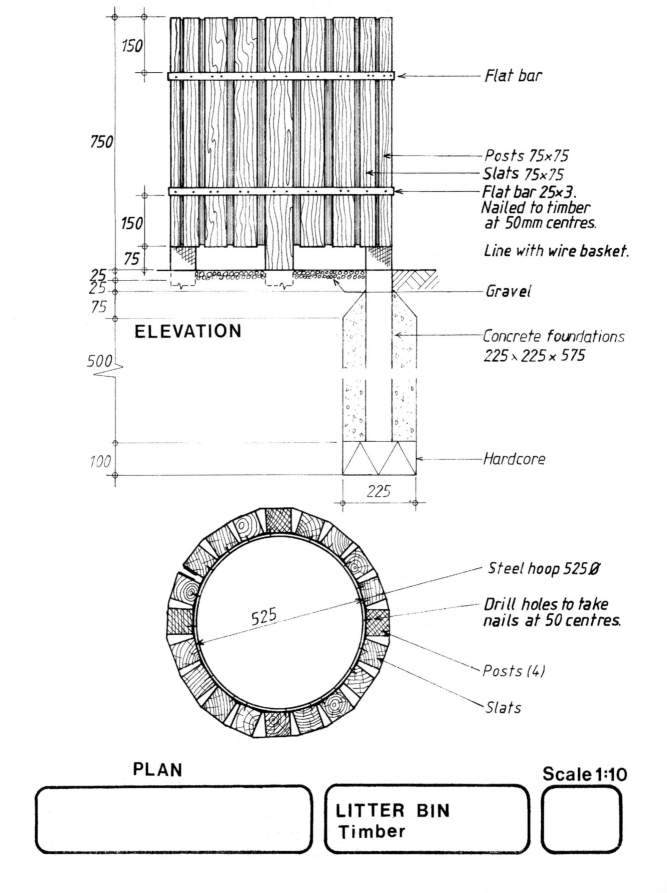

150

750

150

75

25
25
75

ELEVATION

500

100

225

Flat bar

Posts 75×75
Slats 75×75
Flat bar 25×3.
Nailed to timber
at 50mm centres.

Line with wire basket.

Gravel

Concrete foundations
225 × 225 × 575

Hardcore

Steel hoop 525Ø

Drill holes to take
nails at 50 centres.

Posts (4)

Slats

525

PLAN

LITTER BIN
Timber

Scale 1:10

154

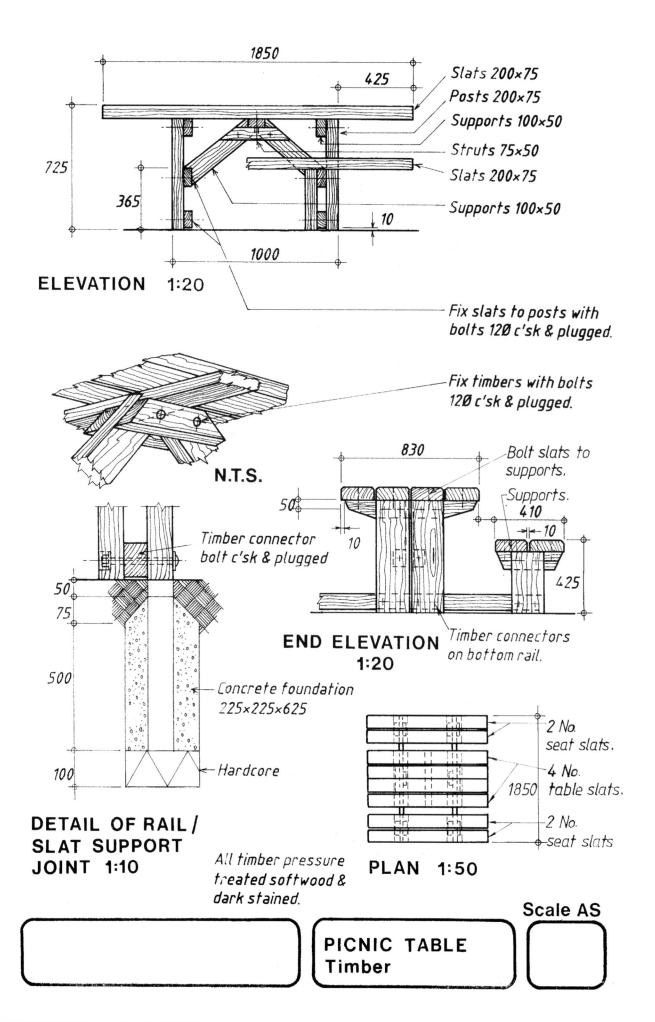

1850

425

Slats 200×75
Posts 200×75
Supports 100×50
Struts 75×50
Slats 200×75
Supports 100×50

725

365

10

1000

ELEVATION   1:20

Fix slats to posts with
bolts 120 c'sk & plugged.

Fix timbers with bolts
120 c'sk & plugged.

N.T.S.

Timber connector
bolt c'sk & plugged

50

75

500

100

Concrete foundation
225×225×625

Hardcore

**DETAIL OF RAIL /
SLAT SUPPORT
JOINT 1:10**

All timber pressure
treated softwood &
dark stained.

830

Bolt slats to
supports.

Supports.
410

50

10

10

425

**END ELEVATION
1:20**

Timber connectors
on bottom rail.

2 No.
seat slats.

4 No.
1850 table slats.

2 No.
seat slats

PLAN 1:50

Scale AS

**PICNIC TABLE
Timber**

155

SIGNS AND INFORMATION

Standardisation can be visually depressing, depending upon the elements; a typical example is the modern indoor shopping centre with the same shop fronts, layouts, etc.

However, there are occasions when standardisation is necessary, not only for economic reasons, but for creating a sense of corporate identity, providing that the elements are incidental to the overall design. For the purposes of giving information, standardisation can actually be of benefit to people, since repetition creates familiarity. Similar styles among signs and other outdoor furniture provide immediate signals for a person in time of need (providing the object has been seen and identified before by the person, it is easily recognised when searching for it on other occasions).

Requirements

Signs should ensure:
- instant recognition
- a clear message
- uniformity of appearance
- consistent application of symbols, colour and typography
- standard support structures
- uniform positioning
- legibility and 'retention value'
- suitability for their location, both in size and materials so that they can be seen, day and night.

The height of signs will vary depending whether they are for motorists or pedestrians. For the former they should be 900–1200 mm from the ground to the bottom of the sign.

For pedestrians the reduction in obstructions on pavements is essential and signs should be fixed to walls and other structures where possible.

Methods

There are various methods for the manufacture of information signs, such as:

- silk screen reproduction
- transfer lettering
- printed adhesive coatings
- laminated photographic reproduction
- three-dimensional materials:
  hand-painted
  carved or sculptured

Materials

Materials will be determined by cost, appearance, durability, location and maintenance.

Aluminium is economic, resists corrosion, light in weight and sheets can be embossed.

Vitreous enamel on a steel base has a long life and is colourfast, but can be damaged by flying objects such as stones.

Plastic in the form of acrylic sheeting, solid or transparent, can withstand corrosive atmospheres and offers low maintenance.

Timber – plywood and blockboard are the most suitable.

Perspex, and laminated glass, stainless steel can also be used.

Advice should be sought from the sign maker at the conceptual design stage.

Lettering

The selection of the appropriate type face for a sign is extremely important, particularly as it will be seen in two or three dimensions which are usually seen flat in publications.

Lettering has to be seen at a distance and it should be bold, simple and confined to a few type faces to avoid 'visual disturbance' to the viewer. Professional advice should be sought from experienced typographers as not every sign maker has the necessary knowledge of typography and typographical layout.

Lettering can be made out of a whole range of materials if an embossed effect is required. Alternatively, letters can be recessed by using a routing machine, but considerable patience and care is required if the type face selected has serifs on the letters.

Fixings

Signs can be hanging (as in a pub sign); flat mounted onto a wall or other vertical structure; or free standing on posts set in concrete. Whichever method is selected all signs must be fixed to avoid damage to people and property, as well as be as vandal-proof as possible.

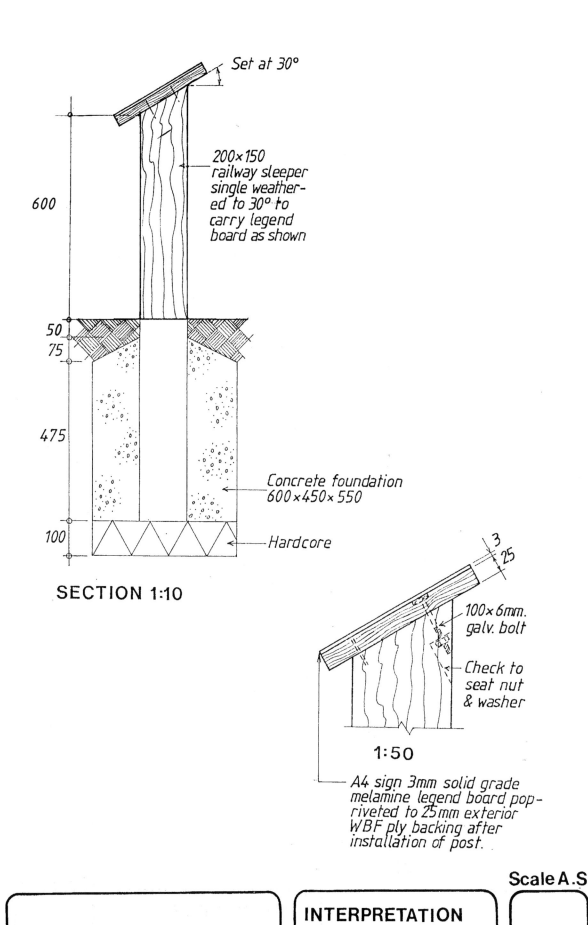

Set at 30°

200×150
railway sleeper
single weather-
ed to 30° to
carry legend
board as shown

600

50
75

475

Concrete foundation
600×450×550

100

Hardcore

SECTION 1:10

3
25

100×6mm.
galv. bolt

Check to
seat nut
& washer

1:50

A4 sign 3mm solid grade
melamine legend board pop-
riveted to 25mm exterior
WBF ply backing after
installation of post.

Scale A.S

INTERPRETATION
BOARD

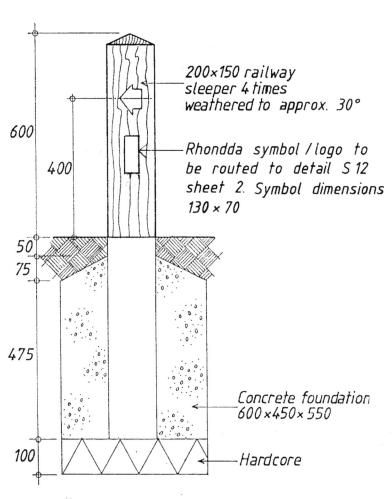

200×150 railway
sleeper 4 times
weathered to approx. 30°

Rhondda symbol / logo to
be routed to detail S 12
sheet 2. Symbol dimensions
130 × 70

600

400

50

75

475

100

Concrete foundation
600×450×550

Hardcore

SECTION 1:10

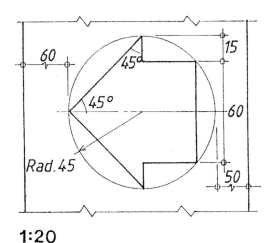

60

45°

45°

15

60

Rad. 45

50

Arrow to be routed

1:20

	WAYMARKER	Scale A.S

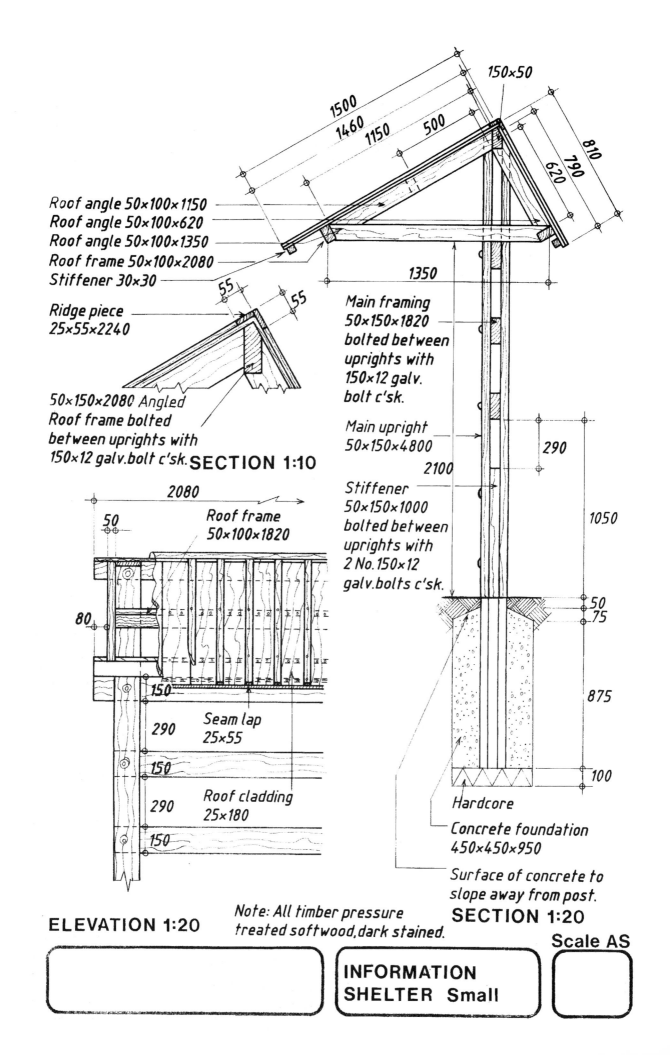

Roof angle 50×100×1150
Roof angle 50×100×620
Roof angle 50×100×1350
Roof frame 50×100×2080
Stiffener 30×30

Ridge piece
25×55×2240

50×150×2080 Angled
Roof frame bolted
between uprights with
150×12 galv.bolt c'sk. **SECTION 1:10**

1500
1460
1150
500

150×50

810
790
620

55
55

1350

Main framing
50×150×1820
bolted between
uprights with
150×12 galv.
bolt c'sk.

Main upright
50×150×4800

290

2100

1050

Stiffener
50×150×1000
bolted between
uprights with
2 No.150×12
galv.bolts c'sk.

2080

50

Roof frame
50×100×1820

80

150

290

Seam lap
25×55

150

290

Roof cladding
25×180

150

50
75

875

100

Hardcore

Concrete foundation
450×450×950

Surface of concrete to
slope away from post.

ELEVATION 1:20

Note: All timber pressure
treated softwood, dark stained.

SECTION 1:20

Scale AS

**INFORMATION
SHELTER Small**

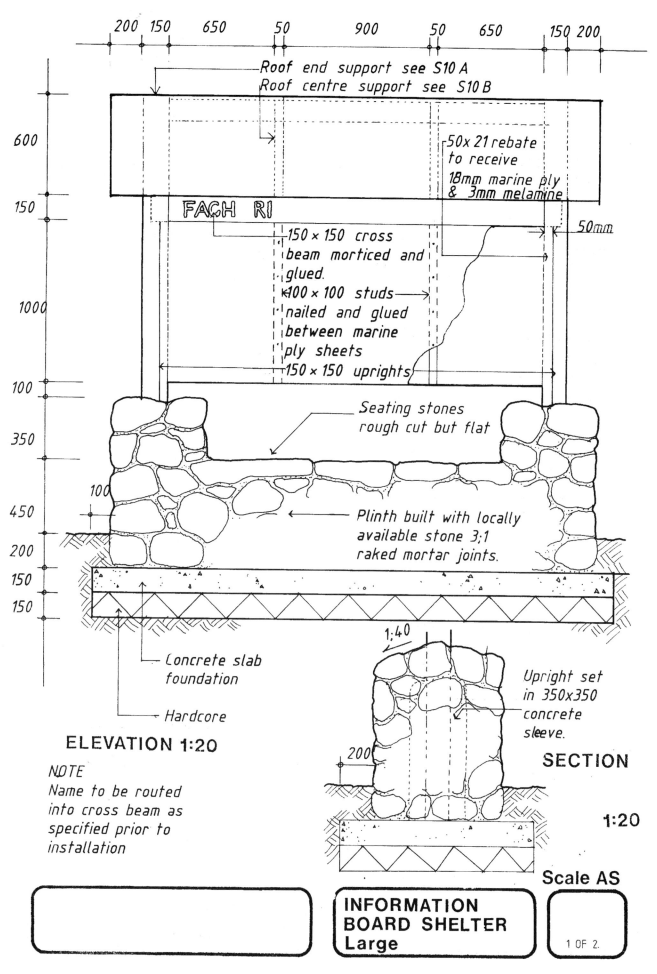

200 150 650 50 900 50 650 150 200

Roof end support see S10 A
Roof centre support see S10 B

600

50x 21 rebate
to receive
18mm marine ply
& 3mm melamine

150

FACH RI

50mm

150 × 150 cross
beam morticed and
glued.
100 × 100 studs
nailed and glued
between marine
ply sheets
150 × 150 uprights

1000

100

350

Seating stones
rough cut but flat

Plinth built with locally
available stone 3;1
raked mortar joints.

100

450

200

150

150

Concrete slab
foundation

Hardcore

ELEVATION 1:20

NOTE
Name to be routed
into cross beam as
specified prior to
installation

1:40

200

Upright set
in 350x350
concrete
sleeve.

SECTION

1:20

Scale AS

**INFORMATION
BOARD SHELTER
Large**

1 OF 2.

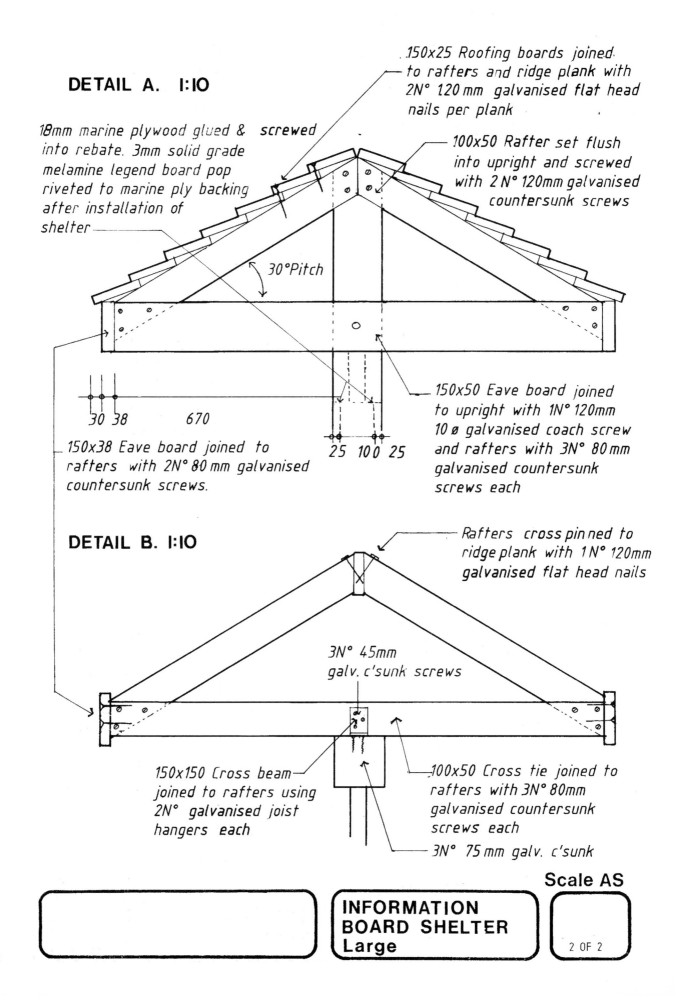

DETAIL A. 1:10

150x25 Roofing boards joined to rafters and ridge plank with 2N° 120 mm galvanised flat head nails per plank

18mm marine plywood glued & screwed into rebate. 3mm solid grade melamine legend board pop riveted to marine ply backing after installation of shelter

100x50 Rafter set flush into upright and screwed with 2 N° 120mm galvanised countersunk screws

30°Pitch

30 38   670

25 100 25

150x38 Eave board joined to rafters with 2N° 80 mm galvanised countersunk screws.

150x50 Eave board joined to upright with 1N° 120mm 10 ø galvanised coach screw and rafters with 3N° 80 mm galvanised countersunk screws each

DETAIL B. 1:10

Rafters cross pinned to ridge plank with 1N° 120mm galvanised flat head nails

3N° 45mm galv. c'sunk screws

150x150 Cross beam joined to rafters using 2N° galvanised joist hangers each

100x50 Cross tie joined to rafters with 3N° 80mm galvanised countersunk screws each

3N° 75 mm galv. c'sunk

Scale AS

INFORMATION BOARD SHELTER Large

2 OF 2

162

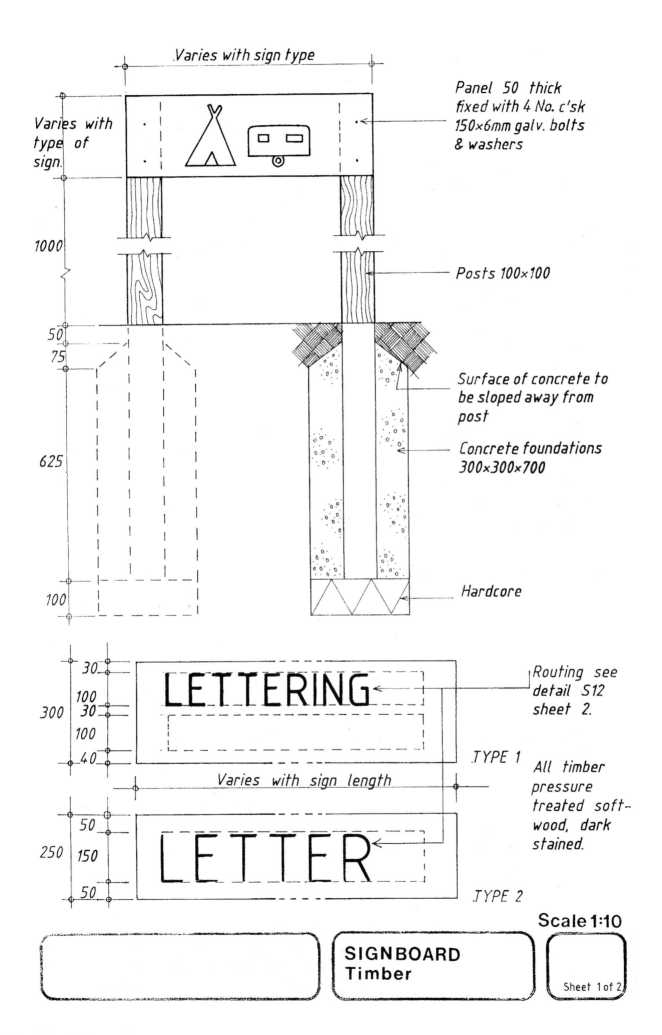

Varies with sign type

Panel 50 thick
fixed with 4 No. c'sk
150×6mm galv. bolts
& washers

Varies with
type of
sign.

1000

Posts 100×100

50

75

Surface of concrete to
be sloped away from
post

Concrete foundations
300×300×700

625

100

Hardcore

30
100
300
30
100
40

LETTERING

Routing see
detail S12
sheet 2.

TYPE 1

Varies with sign length

All timber
pressure
treated soft-
wood, dark
stained.

50
250
150
50

LETTER

TYPE 2

Scale 1:10

SIGNBOARD
Timber

Sheet 1 of 2

163

Prepare an actual size tracing of the words in the typeface required and using transfer paper or office carbon paper trace the outline onto a prepared board.

A standard set of packing case stencils can also be used to pencil the outline on to the board.

When a satisfactory layout has been achieved, rout about 3mm deep.

Finally the lettering may be infilled with a contrasting colour.

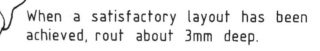

ROUTING

Sheet 2 of 2

ROOFS

Design Factors

1. Structural loadings
2. Drainage
3. Membrane
4. Planting medium
5. Irrigation
6. Materials
7. Features
8. Services
9. Safety

In designing a residential garden or a commercial landscape on a building above the ground there are special factors to be considered compared to ground level developments. These are:

Access – to the roof from the ground, especially during the construction phase and afterwards for maintenance.

Location – if the building and roof are very exposed on all sides considerable protection from wind and sun, as well as climatic extremes of hot and cold.

Roof – whether the existing roof is capable of having a garden or whether it can be amended to take the additional weight of a garden.

Drainage – there must be quick and positive surface and subsurface drainage to prevent flooding due to heavy rains. The weight of accumulated ice and snow must not exceed the weight limits of the roof's structural system.

Planting Medium – this must be lightweight, long lasting, good water permeability, air retention capacity and root penetration, with a high water intake and storage followed by a slow and continuous supply of water to the plants.

Irrigation – this is essential to ensure the survival of plants in a hostile environment and must be allowed for in the design.

Materials – it is essential that these are lightweight but robust to resist harsh climate conditions.

Features – the design of features must ensure the protection of the integrity of the roof and structure, particularly water.

Services – these are integral to the success of the roof garden/landscape and need to be considered at the outset.

Safety – the need for fire escape is a priority and the design of the roof landscape must ensure that there is not restriction of fire exits/ladders.

Protection of users going close to the edge is equally important.

1. STRUCTURAL LOADINGS

Provision has to be made for the weight of soil, materials, plants and for people on a roof garden. A structural engineer should always be consulted before commencing any type of roof design.

Structural movement joints are one of the points likely to fail and should not be covered by any planters/plants. If it is unavoidable there are ways to design a solution to the problem.

2. DRAINAGE

Adequate falls on the existing roof are necessary to ensure the removal of surplus water along with the appropriate number of drains. Roof drains, like all others used in the garden, should be designed to collect both surface and lateral subsurface drainage water.

This type of planting medium used on roofs ensures downward percolation of water direct to the sealed surface. Positive lateral drainage is then necessary through the subsurface of the soil to the drains.

There are a number of typical drainage details that can be used on roof landscapes and these are shown in illustrative form. Provision should be made for cleaning of the drains at periodic intervals.

3. MEMBRANE

It is essential that the material chosen for the waterproof membrane is appropriate as there are for the project two types – continuous membranes and jointed membranes. For projects with a large area the only continuous membrane is asphalt. Smaller projects would use jointed membranes.

A typical section through a roof consists of the structural framing or reinforced concrete slab, sometimes a sloping layer of thin concrete to provide drainage to roof drains, a layer of waterproofing material, a layer of insulation, and a layer of lightweight concrete to protect the insulation and the waterproof membrane. This final layer of lightweight concrete is sloped to carry off surface drainage.

The most important consideration is to protect the roof and its waterproofing at all times and it is the designer's responsibility to ensure that this is achieved. This starts with the bottom of the subdrainage layer to the finished roof.

4. PLANTING MEDIUM

The critical factors in the formulation of a suitable planting medium for roof garden planting are lightweight, the ability to hold nutrients for plant growth, and the capability of developing a firm but easily drained soil structure.

There have been various mediums used in roof gardens. A base layer of lightweight clay granules topped with lightweight compost containing vermiculite, perlite or polystyrene with a 50/50 mix of loam and peat substitute is common. Grodan – a lightweight soil substitute produced from volcanic rock could be used; in addition to being a uniform growing substrate it has sound and temperature insulation qualities. It is available in slab form and placed over a reservoir of lightweight aggregates and, providing water is replenished regularly, capillary action ensures that the root zone is kept moist and the water/air balance constant.

Ready-mixed soils are available commercially, but a suitable soil mixture can be prepared for each project following the given formula per cubic metre:

½ m^2 fine sand
½ m^2 pine bark
500 gms calcium nitrate
1½ kg single superphosphate
500 gms sulphate of potash
3½ kg dolomite lime

When this mix is too heavy it may be lightened by substituting 3 parts expanded shale in No. 8 screen and 3 parts expanded shale No. 10 (texture of fine sand) for the sand elements. Expanded shale is commonly used in place of gravel in lightweight concrete and is generally available from suppliers of concrete materials.

Fine sand

The fine sand used in soil mixes is of critical importance in terms both of the soil's drainage characteristics and of its ability to function without blocking the permeability of the filter blanket.

Soil amendments

Organic materials such as fertilisers – particularly nitrogen, but also other minerals which go into solution – will gradually dissolve and be leached away by watering. Local public water supplies may also lack calcium, magnesium and sulphur. Thus, periodic replacement of these and other materials by surface application may be needed. At least once a year, soil tests should be made by a competent soils laboratory to determine deficiencies and to recommend additives.

Roof weight reduction

If optimum soil depths result in excessive weight on the structure, then lightweight soil mixes can be used. If the subsurface drainage system fails and the soil becomes saturated, the planting mix can reach a weight of about 120 pounds per cubic foot (pcf). If the roof cannot withstand a loading of this magnitude then various ways must be used to create voids beneath the soil medium. See sketch details. The most common methods used include casting a false bottom or using large blocks of high-density styro foam, which is commonly sold in blocks 1200 × 2400 × 250 mm thick.

A roof structure can be designed to provide a recessed planting area over a column for a large tree.

Depths and weights of planting medium and plants

Table 12 shows the minimum soil depths needed for different types of roof-top plantings. Table 13 shows typical dry and damp weights of various planting media, and Table 14 shows the weight of container and field-grown plants.

A method to change grades between an on-grade footpath and roof deck without using excessive depths of planting media and one way to reduce weights for plants in containers are illustrated.

5. IRRIGATION

Roof gardens cannot survive without water as the planting medium dries out quite quickly which causes damage to plants or even their loss. Unlike ground level planted areas, roof plants do not have access to

TABLE 12. MINIMUM SOIL DEPTHS

Planting	Minimum soil depths*	
	in/ft	*mm/m*
Lawns	8–12 in	200–300 mm
Flowers and ground covers	10–12 in	260–300 mm
Shrubs	24–30 in	600–750 mm[†]
Small trees	30–42 in	750–1200 mm
Large trees	5–6 ft	1.5–1.8 m

*On filter blanket and drainage medium.
[†]Depending on ultimate shrub size.

TABLE 13. WEIGHT OF PLANTING MEDIUM

Material	Dry		Damp	
	lb/ft³	*kg/m³*	*lb/ft³*	*kg/m³*
Fine sand	90.00	1446.42	120.00	1928.56
Cedar shavings with fertiliser	9.25	148.66	13.00	208.93
Peat moss	9.60	154.28	10.00	165.53
Red lava (8 mm) maximum	50.00	803.57	53.70	863.03
Redwood compost and shavings	14.80	237.86	22.20	356.78
Fir and pine bark humus	22.20	356.78	33.30	535.17
Perlite	6.50	104.46	32.40*	520.71*
Vermiculite				
Coarse	6.25	100.45		
Medium	5.75	92.41		
Fine	7.50	120.53		
Topsoil	76.00	1221.42	78.00	1253.56

*Applies to wet – not damp – perlite.

TABLE 14. WEIGHT OF CONTAINER AND FIELD-GROWN PLANTS

Container size		Container grown in mushroom compost		Field-grown	
Imperial	Metric	lb	kg	lb	kg
15 gal	56L can	80	36	–	–
20 in	510 mm box	200	90	400	180
24 in	610 mm box	400	180	725	325
30 in	760 mm box	800	360	1500	675
36 in	900 mm box	1300	585	2500	1125
48 in	1220 mm box	3500	1575	6000	2700
54 in	1370 mm box	4000	1800	7000	3150
60 in	1520 mm box	5000	2250	8000	3600
72 in	1830 mm box	7000	3150	12000	5400
84 in	2130 mm box	9000	4050	16000	7200
96 in	2440 mm box	12000	5400	20000	9000
120 in	3050 mm box	14000	6300	24000	10800

Note: All the above are shipping weights, including the box.
Source: *Time-Saver Standards for Landscape Architecture.*

subsurface water to sustain them so irrigation in some form is essential.
This can be achieved by:

1. Hand watering – using a hose from an outside tap depending upon the area; this is very labour intensive.
2. Hose from an outside tap linked to snap-on sprinkler heads.
3. An irrigation system installed with the building of the garden. This can have an automatic timer which can be programmed to water plants at convenient times.

For a sophisticated irrigation system it is well worthwhile to contact a specialist company and discuss the different methods of watering systems which are available.

As a check list:
- Piping should be installed directly on top of the filter blanket.
- The riser heads should be tested, under pressure, before the planting medium is installed.
- Sprinkler controls should be in a locked cabinet in a convenient location.
- Complete drainage of the system should be provided in areas subject to freezing temperatures.
- Access to electrical power is necessary.
- Close co-operation will be necessary between the various trades, such as plumbing, electrical, buildings, etc., particularly if the lighting is being undertaken by a separate electrical contractor.
- Clear and concise specifications for the work will be necessary.
- Consideration should also be given for using the irrigation system for feeding plants with liquid fertiliser.
- Alternative supplies of water for irrigation purposes must be considered in view of restrictions in dry climatic periods from mains supplies. Facilities for storage of roof water should be provided particularly as the volume required, even for a modest scheme, could amount to hundreds of cubic metres.

6. MATERIALS

All constructional elements, such as walls, fences, screens, pergolas, light columns,

TABLE 15. WEIGHT OF COMMON BUILDING MATERIALS

Material	lb/ft³	kg/m³
Granite	170	2757
Marble	170	2757
Slate	160–180	2595–2919
Limestone	155	2514
Sandstone	145	2352
Shale	162	2627
Expanded shale	40–45	649–730
Field stone	95	1541
Gravel	120	1946
Pebbles	120	1946
Pumice	40	649
Concrete		
Lightweight	80–100	1298–1622
Precast	130	2108
Reinforced	150	2433
Concrete block: 8 in	50–60	811–973
Brickwork (average)	115	1865
Cast iron	450	7297
Steel	490	7945
Bronze	513	8318
Timber		
Hardwood (average)	45	730
Softwood (average)	35	568
Sand		
Dry	90–110	1460–1784
Wet	110–130	1784–2108
Sand and gravel: mixed	115	1865
Clay soil		
Compacted, dry	75–100	1216–1622
Compacted, wet	125	2027
Loam		
Dry	80	1298
Wet	120	1946
Special commercial soil: wet	110	1784
Topsoil		
Dry	80	1298
Wet	120	1946
Peat		
Dry	50	811
Wet	60	973
Humus		
Dry	35	568
Wet	82	1330
Water	62.428	1013
Flagstone and setting bed	25 lb/ft²	122 kg/m²
Tile and setting bed	15–73 lb/ft²	73–353 kg/m²

Source: A. E. Weddle, *Landscape Techniques*, Van Nostrand Reinhold, New York, 1983; C. G. Ramsey and H. R. Sleeper, *Architectural Graphic Standards*, 7th ed.,Wiley, New York, 1981; Olwen C. Marlowe, *Outdoor Design*, Watson-Guptill, New York, 1977; American Institute of Steel Construction, Inc.

TABLE 16. WEIGHT OF WOOD

	Green				Dried to 12% moisture content			
	lb/ft³	*kg/ft³*	*lb/fbm*	*kg/fbm*	*lb/ft³*	*kg/ft³*	*lb/fbm*	*kg/fbm*
Douglas fir	38	17	3.17	1.43	34	15	2.83	1.27
Redwood	52	23	4.33	1.95	28	13	2.33	1.05
Cedar, western red	27	12	2.25	1.01	23	10	1.92	0.86

Note: 1 ft³ = board ft (fbm) of lumber.
Source: Courtesy of the California Redwood Association.

and paving, have to be considered in relationship to the structural limitations of the roof and its support below. The factor of weight has a strong influence on the type of materials to be used.

All elements need to be made of lightweight materials and to be anchored securely to the roof or other parts of the building.

When viewed from above paving materials can strongly contrast with the planting and any water surfaces create stronger visual impressions than in the ground level garden.

Materials should also be selected for their light weight and durability. Brick pavers, tiles, textured wood decking (where permitted by local codes), and coloured or exposed aggregate concrete are all excellent choices for roof-top developments. All structural elements need to be carefully anchored on a roof without penetrating the waterproof roofing or structural slab. Sketch drawings show details of how this can be achieved but nothing should be done without reference to the architect or engineer.

Furniture – chairs, benches, tables – do not need to be fixed in place but can be left free to be moved as required depending upon the climatic elements.

7. FEATURES

Water – The use of water and water effects can greatly increase the interest and enjoyment of a roof garden. The following factors should be considered in the design:

- the weight of the water and its container
- construction of the existing roof including location of columns
- the depth of water in the pool
- the surface treatment of the pool
- the material to be used in the construction of the pool
- water movement techniques, i.e. fountains, falls, etc.
- allowance for electricity and plumbing, plus location of cables and pipes
- where possible the heaviest water elements should be located directly over columns.

The illusion of greater water depth can be achieved by colouring the bottom and sides of the pool or basin dark grey or black. Satisfactory water effects can be achieved in depths as shallow as 4–16 in (100–400 mm), especially if the surface is kept agitated so that visibility to the bottom is obscured.

Where weight constraints are stringent and the roof cannot be strengthened, a shallow pool made of 6 mm preformed, shaped fibreglass can be used.

A satisfactory water surface can be obtained with a very shallow depth. This detail is often used in ponds to give them a natural appearance.

If fountains are to be included, allowance must be made for more frequent and stronger winds.

Pool walls should be properly anchored and sealed otherwise serious leaks could occur. The sketch drawings show different methods of achieving a positive leakproof seal. In areas where freezing occurs in the winter, pools should be drained for the duration of the season to prevent damage to the waterproof structure.

Structures

Fences – These are required for wind protection and screening and their design must ensure that they resist any damage by strong winds. Almost any fence will be obvious if it is silhouetted against the sky but the impact can be reduced by ensuring that they are not located on the parapet edge. This will allow any planting to grow under and/or through them, depending upon the design.
Fences should not be on more than two sides of a four-sided roof garden. Trellis or similar open fence with climbing plants are preferable to any solid style, except for around sitting areas when closely spaced pales or split bamboo could be used for greater protection and privacy.

Arbours, Pergolas and Gazebos – If these structures are included in the design they will require to be firmly anchored to the roof and/or the building, particularly if they are covered with climbing plants.

8. SERVICES

Electrical – an electrical supply will be for lighting, irrigation, fountain, etc. Low-voltage lighting is probably cheaper and easier to install for a residential roof garden, whereas the standard 230v will be necessary for commercial projects.
All electrical supply conduits should be enclosed in metal for protection from digging, given the shallow soil conditions, although low-voltage lighting may be supplied by flexible cable. The subsurface distribution system should be placed prior to installing the planting medium and/or paving. Electrically operated or optically controlled timing devices are additional conveniences for gardens which are regularly lighted at night.

Water – A clean water supply is needed for irrigation, ornamental pools and fountains, which must contain suitable back flow

prevention devices to guard against contamination of portable water sources. Recycled water could be used for cleaning of paved surfaces and fire protection.

Controls – Provision should be made for indoor locations of lighting and irrigation control and other mechanical equipment needed for the garden, as well as for gardening tools and supplies.

9. SAFETY

Physical barriers are necessary for protection to users, especially children being near the edge and these could be in the form of plants in a raised bed. There may be special places where people could have access to a railing on the roof's parapet in order to see downward towards the ground.
The spaces between railings and posts should be closed in with wire fabric, safety plate glass, fibreglass or other skiable material to prevent easy or accidental penetration by small children, pets or others.

HARD PAVING FOR TERRACES, ROOF GARDENS AND DECKS

Reprinted from Architect's Journal, 24 June 1987

The selection of hard paving for roof gardens, terraces, pedestrian decks, atria and so on is more difficult than for external works paving because of the need to incorporate a waterproof membrane underneath the paving in most cases. The designer must consider the paving, bedding, waterproofing and insulation together as a total system to ensure success.

Criteria for selecting hard paving

Appearance will usually be a very important criterion for the selection of a hard paving material. Many types give very pleasant mixtures of texture and colour, particularly if selected to complement or contrast with soft landscaping. Different paving materials can often be mixed, such as concrete flags and paving bricks, to interesting effect. However, appearance is a subjective judgment not covered in detail here. In any case, the selection of paving materials for appearance is best done from samples and built examples.

The basic functional criteria for the selection of hard paving are summarised in Table 17. It must be emphasised that external paving is subject to severe weather exposure including long periods of damp and frost. Durability will be an extremely important factor in most hard paving unless it is protected from the elements, such as in a covered atrium. Remedial work in cases of failure is usually costly and disruptive.

Strength may not be critical for moderate pedestrian use but will be critical in other situations such as shopping precincts and car parks. Resistance to wear and slip/skid resistance can also be important in heavily used public areas and where the paving is used by vehicles. Different uses and situations therefore call for a change of emphasis between all the criteria listed in Table 17, together with appearance.

Types of hard paving available

The more common types of external paving available are set out in Table 18, with notes on standards, composition, manufacture, finishes, typical sizes and indicative relative costs. In terms of quantity, precast concrete flags in the many types available still dominate the market. However, the increased emphasis on the quality of the external environment has meant an increased use of more decorative finishes to concrete slabs and a reawakening of the possibilities of brick paving. Precast concrete paving blocks and, more recently, paving bricks are increasingly being used for flexing paving for external works, but their use for hard paving for roof gardens, pedestrian decks, and so on, is more unusual.

In addition to those materials covered in Table 18, natural stone pavings such as York stone and slate are still available, although expensive. Used stone paving is sometimes available and can be mixed with other materials to good effect. Granite setts are often laid as deterrent paving or in small areas for textural interest.

Many patterns, sizes and finishes are available in most of the materials. Designers need to consult manufacturers' literature for the latest information.

Comparison of performance

Table 19 gives a brief comparison of the performance of the various hard paving materials discussed in Table 18. The strengths and weaknesses of each type should be related to the requirements of the specific situation. Most failures of hard paving relate to inadequate specification for durability or inadequate detailing, especially of edges and bedding. The importance of good workmanship must also be emphasised at the start of operations on site.

The total roofing and paving system

As stated in the introduction, hard paving for roof gardens, pedestrian decks and so on must be related to the total construction system. Table 20 sets out basic functional requirements of the total system, the two most important aspects being the waterproofing reliability and the durability of the whole system. Failures of these two aspects are, unfortunately, all too common and the designer must be prepared to look closely at all aspects of the design problem. The client must also be prepared to pay for the proper solution.

The structure of buildings with roof gardens, decks and so on, will normally be in reinforced concrete although other types including steel framed structures and composite structures are becoming more common. Consider the specification and detailing of the paving and waterproofing in relation to the basic characteristics of the structural type, such as the long term shrinkage and creep of concrete frames, the greater reversible movements and deflections of some steel framed structures.

Movement
Whatever the type of structure used, the architect and structural engineer must minimise and accommodate movement of the structure below the paving. Building movement is caused by irreversible initial movements caused by drying out, cyclical thermal and moisture movements, application of load and long term creep. For heavy reinforced concrete construction, the proper allowance for irreversible shrinkage is the most important consideration, particularly if there are large paved areas. Clay paving will suffer irreversible expansion over time, which can maximise differential movement between it and a concrete frame. Large buildings, particularly of complex shape, will require movement joints in the structure and any hard paving on top of the movement joint will have to be detailed to accommodate this movement. Movement joints have a long history of failure—do *not* cut corners and expense here.

Movement joints
Good general principles for the design of movement joints in paving are:
• do not drain to or over movement joints; keep that at high points in the layout of drainage falls
• detail to allow for easy examination and repairs if necessary. It is dangerous to have them buried and inaccessible
• flush movement joints are much more difficult to waterproof than ones with upstands. Movement joints in paving areas normally have to be flush, although it may be possible to create an upstand in the waterproofing membrane
• if possible movement joints should be constructed by a specialist. Some companies even offer a guarantee.

Waterproofing
The type of waterproofing selected will depend upon the many factors outlined in Table 20.

Mastic asphalt is normally favoured for reinforced concrete structures which give the relatively 'brittle' waterproofing a firm base. For non-rigid, lighter weight structural decks in timber or steel, modern 'high performance' membranes should be selected after detailed discussions with the manufacturer.

Hard paving and roof insulation

Care must be taken in selecting any insulation in relation to the type of paving. In particular, the insulation must have sufficient bearing strength to support both the dead load of the paving and the imposed loads of pedestrians, vehicles, planters and so on. Some forms of insulation used in normal roof construction, such as standard density expanded polystyrene, may not be suitable for paved areas. The selection of a particular insulation under hard paving should be discussed with the manufacturers of both the insulation and the waterproof membrane. Ideally, the insulation and waterproofing membrane should be supplied and laid by the same specialist subcontractor.

The more rigorous thermal requirements of the past decade have led to the specification of thicker and less dense materials. In some cases two types of insulation are specified—one thermally efficient type and another screed or board type to give the falls or to provide a stronger base under the paving.

These requirements often lead to a very complex sequence of construction, which is exposed to rain during the various construction stages. Water can therefore be entrapped in the construction leading to problems later unless great care is taken.

Inverted roof construction

These problems led to the development of the inverted roof where a water and vapour resistant, dimensionally stable insulation is placed above the waterproof membrane. The insulation specified is normally extruded closed cell polystyrene which is tough enough to stand up to the requirements of this situation and does not waterlog. It is laid unbonded on to the waterproof membrane and weighed down with paving or gravel. The inverted roof system can claim the following advantages:

• water entrapment is virtually eliminated
• condensation problems are unlikely and installation of a separate vapour barrier is not necessary
• fewer and more easily organised site operations
• roof membrane is more easily accessible for inspection and repair
• roof drainage is easier.

The specification of the inverted roof with hard paving seems particularly appropriate for many roof gardens and pedestrian decks. It has been used for shopping precincts, although its use in these situations is still in the minority. Precast concrete flags are normally used with the inverted roof so the pallette of materials is more limited than with a traditional roof construction.

Recently, insulation for inverted roofs has been available with a factory-applied topping so that no further treatment is required. This topping is suitable for maintenance traffic only, although one importer now supplies insulation with an exposed aggregate finish suitable for light pedestrian traffic.

Hard paving and roof falls

Accommodating falls in paving has caused many problems, such as badly cut paving slabs and inadequate upstands to the waterproofing. Architects have therefore tended to specify the minimum recommended falls. Ponding has often been the result. Ponding of rainwater is not only unsightly but, in freezing weather, can be lethal.

To prevent ponding, it is necessary to specify falls of approximately 1 in 40 so that at least 1 in 60 will actually be achieved. Falls of this order generally necessitate large amounts of screed to achieve them, leading to problems at entrances because of high upstands and so on. Reducing the area to be drained to each gulley reduces the average depth of screed but at the cost of extra drainage. If the structural slab can be laid to falls, this will eliminate the need for excessively thick screeds and assist the general drainage. The advantages and disadvantages of draining to channels or central gullies are summarised in 8. The designer should also refer to BS 6367:1983 *Code of practice for drainage of roofs and paved areas*.

Bedding of paving on the roof membrane

Traditionally, all paving on flat roofs was laid on a full mortar bed. While this bed gave a stable even surface, it made access for maintenance beneath very difficult. To achieve satisfactory results with solid bedding and mortar pointing, good workmanship is essential. No paving surface is completely impervious to water and outlets that drain at both paving and waterproof membrane levels are required. Small paving units such as bricks will require solid bedding, although the use of brick and concrete block flexible paving bedded on compacted sand has been tried in a few cases in recent years. In this case a filter membrane is required around the drainage outlets so that the sand bedding does not wash away. Edge restraint is required for flexible paving which may cause detailing problems for suspended slabs.

To overcome some of these problems, various methods of laying paving with open joints and partial bedding have evolved. Mortar dabs were first used although careful workmanship is essential. Many roofing manufacturers recommend pads made of layers of roofing felt although it is difficult to vary the height of the paving to suit falls in the roofing membrane underneath. Proprietary supports have been introduced from the continent to support paving slabs and ensure a consistent joint, some of which have a height adjustment device.

Specification and details

There are considerable differences of opinion on the specification of paving for roof gardens, pedestrian decks and so on. Although there are British Standards for the manufacture of most of the paving units themselves, there is little advice in codes of practice for laying them on roof membranes that is up-to-date and relevant. Tables 21 to 24 give suggestions for total paving and roofing systems for a range of situations varying from areas subject to maintenance traffic only to areas subject to very heavy pedestrian use such as shopping precincts. The importance of careful specification and detailing of shopping precincts, including car parks, cannot be overemphasised. The designer should consult fully with manufacturers on all elements in the system including their interaction. Trade associations such as the C&CA and the BDA have published some useful guidance, see references. Claims by manufacturers of an easy, fool-proof solution should be treated with scepticism.
It will be advantageous in many cases to make one specialist subcontractor responsible for the total paving and roofing system. Trouble-free hard paving for roof gardens is possible, but only if all members of the design and construction team give it the most careful consideration.

TABLE 17. KEY FUNCTIONAL REQUIREMENTS OF HARD PAVING

Durability (linked with strength and frost resistance)
The required durability will depend upon the type of use, situation and budget. Premature failure of paving in roof gardens and particularly public areas such as pedestrian precincts can have serious repercussions. Durability of paving materials is hard to assess by testing (the BRE and others are still trying to devise reliable tests). The best evidence is satisfactory durability of paving over a period in use for at least three years in a similar situation.

Strength
All hard pavings have adequate strength for light pedestrian use, but careful consideration is necessary for heavy pedestrian use or where vehicles may be present, even if only occasionally. New British Standards for concrete and clay flexible paving units contain some strength requirements. The strength of the paving will also depend upon the bedding and the roof membrane/insulation specification. Displaced pavings can form trips and lead to early failure of the bedding or roof membrane underneath.

Frost resistance
All external paving is subject to severe exposure from rain, snow and freeze/thaw cycles. Again, there is no satisfactory test for frost resistance; satisfactory performance in use in a similar situation is the only reliable criterion. Most concrete and clay paving materials are resistant to deterioration caused by de-icing treatments.

Freedom from efflorescence
As all external paving is subject to severe wetting/drying cycles, freedom from efflorescence is desirable for all paving, and for clay bricks and coloured concrete paving in particular. Clay paviors, engineering pavers and concrete pavings are normally free from significant efflorescence. If facing bricks are used for paving, the manufacturer should be asked to give evidence that efflorescence is not worse than moderate, and preferably slight, when tested to BS 3921:1985 *Clay bricks and blocks*.

Resistance to organic growth
Some growth is almost inevitable where paving is shaded, frequently damp and with little or no cleaning carried out. Moss and algae can be very dangerous as they are slippery when damp. Generally, the harder and denser the surface, the better the resistance to organic growth.

Resistance to wear
This varies with the type of traffic, for example, access for maintenance as compared with a pedestrian precinct. Soft materials such as stock bricks should only be used for very light pedestrian traffic. Wear will reduce the slip resistance of the paving.

Slip/skid resistance
Good slip resistance is important in public pedestrian areas, particularly on ramps and steps. The new BSs on concrete and clay flexible paving units mention the need for skid resistance and tests are being developed to measure skid resistance for wheeled traffic. Placing the main running joints across the direction of traffic will help slip resistance, as will slightly recessed joints. Many paving materials are made with a roughened or otherwise textured surface to improve slip resistance. With softer materials this can be worn away fairly quickly. Watch exposed aggregate finishes: wet smooth pebbles can be very slippery.

Resistance to oil, petrol and salts
Not normally important for pedestrian areas but can be a crucial consideration for car parks and other vehicular areas. Clay and concrete paving have good resistance to petrol and oil, but the designer must also sometimes consider the roofing/insulation underneath.

Colour permanence and consistency
Colour permanence is desirable, but complete permanence is not possible with some paving materials. Colours are also affected by dirt collection within the surface texture of the paving material. Colour consistency between delivered batches can be important, say for uninterrupted paving in shopping centres.

TABLE 18. COMMON TYPES OF EXTERNAL PAVING (FOR USE IN ROOF GARDENS, ACCESS BALCONIES, CAR PARKS)

Promenade tiles in fibre cement	Precast concrete flags (paving slabs)	Clay paving (including paviors, engineering pavers, facing bricks and interlocking types)	Precast concrete paving blocks	Mastic asphalt
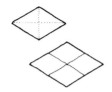	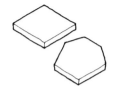	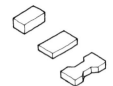	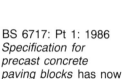	

Relevant standards

Not covered by British Standards but similar to other forms of fibre cement slates and cladding	BS 368: 1971 *Precast concrete flags* give details of specification and sizes for most basic types of paving slabs. Decorative types generally to this specification	BS 3921: 1985 *Clay bricks and blocks* defines types and qualities of bricks in general but does not specifically cover their use in paving; BS 6677: Pt 1: 1986 *Clay and calcium silicate pavers: specification for flexible pavements* may be relevant	BS 6717: Pt 1: 1986 *Specification for precast concrete paving blocks* has now superseded the C&CA/Interpave specification	BS 988: 1973 & BS 6577: 1985 specify limestone and natural rock mastic asphalt respectively for buildings, that is, suitable for roofing grade. BS 1446: 1973 & BS 1447: 1973 specify natural rock (roads) and limestone aggregate mastic asphalt (footways) paving grade

Specification details

Mixture of Portland cement, reinforcing fibres, fillers and water. Produced to tight dimensional tolerances with clean and sharp edges	Cement: To BS 12: 1978 or BS 146: 1973. Aggregate, crushed or uncrushed natural materials to relevant BS, 14 mm nominal maximum size. Pigments, if required to BS 1014: 1975. All arrises clean and and sharp. Surface finish to be agreed. Samples are tested for water absorption, mechanical strength of aggregate and transverse strength. Some decorative types may not be up to BS 368: 1971 strength tests, etc	Bricks used for paving should be 'FL' quality as defined in BS 392: 1985. Strength—min 5.2 N/mm^2 but for paving normally higher. Efflorescence—not worse than moderate, preferably slight or nil. Frost resistance—proven in use or three year exposure test or min 43.5 N/mm^2 or water absorption not greater than 7 per cent. Pavers for flexible paving come in two strength classes: PA and PB. Water absorption is low	Binder—ordinary Portland to BS 12, other types to BS may be mixed with OPC. Aggregates—to BS 882 other types to BS permitted. Excludes fine aggregates containing significant acid soluble material. Portland cement content 380 kg/m^3, with other binders increasing this. Clean arrises, tight dimensional tolerances. Slight surface variations permitted. Minimum strength-average 49 N/mm^2 40 N/mm^2 min for individual blocks	The BSs above define proportions of: asphalt; cement; either bitumen, lake asphalt, asphalite or blends of these with flux oils; fine aggregates, either natural rock asphalt which is limestone naturally impregnated with bitumen, or limestone which is crushed to a fine powder; coarse aggregate, either crushed stone such as granite or limestone; or naturally occurring siliceous material such as grit

Manufacture

Fibre cement tiles are produced using sophisticated automatic production plant. Many are produced by an injection moulding technique after carefully controlled mixing of the materials. This technique ensures tiles of uniform shape and size	Various methods are used, the most common being hydraulic pressing. This process gives a dense and durable structure and surface free of blow holes. Other processes combine pressure and vibration using earth-dry concrete. All processes are carried out on machinery of large throughput	Manufacture varies considerably depending upon types. Prepared clay is either moulded, pressed or extruded and cut to size. It is then dried and fired under controlled conditions	Paving blocks are generally produced in sophisticated vibration presses from earth-dry concrete. During and after manufacture the units are protected from frost and stored to prevent undue loss of moisture during curing	Suitably graded mineral matter and asphaltic cement are combined in carefully defined proportions in the presence of heat, thoroughly mixed and cast into blocks. Blocks are delivered to site (with relevant BS markings), melted in a melter/mixer and laid hot without compaction

TABLE 18. COMMON TYPES OF EXTERNAL PAVING (FOR USE IN ROOF GARDENS, ACCESS BALCONIES, CAR PARKS) (continued)

Promenade tiles in fibre cement	Precast concrete flags (paving slabs)	Clay paving (including paviors, engineering pavers, facing bricks and interlocking types)	Precast concrete paving blocks	Mastic asphalt
Finishes Light grey or white, no colouring is added, colour depends upon whether white or grey cement is used. Surface texture is very slightly grained. A raised chequered pattern is sometimes cast into surface for better slip resistance	Colours are subdued, a range of greys, browns, reds, yellows and greens. Stronger colours achievable with exposed aggregates. Textures can be smooth, dimpled, dibbed, machine rubbed, simulated stone, exposed aggregate, imitation setts/pavers. 'Deterrent' (keep off) patterns are made with a heavily moulded surface	A wide range of colours is available from light brown, reds, browns, dark browns, blue, black in multi-ranges and brindled. Textures are sanded, slight grainy texture from wire cutting. Engineering pavers have various surfaces—panelled, chequered, dimpled, plain. Interlocking paviors may have chamfered edges	Natural grey is cheapest, but limited range of other subdued colours; red, light brown, dark brown, buff, charcoal; a few multi-colour ranges. Texture—slight roughness to face, most types have a chamfered edge	Mastic asphalt is normally black although a brick red is available to special order. Surface is normally sanded to minimize surface crazing. It can also be dimpled with a roller while hot to improve slip resistance
Weight as laid Lightweight, 16–22 kg/m^2 including bitumen bedding	Heavyweight (varies with thickness but including proprietary slab supports): 50 mm thick approx 155 kg/m^2	Heavyweight (varies with density and thickness but including 25 mm mortar bed): 35 mm thick approx 105 kg/m^2	Heavyweight (varies with thickness specified but including 25 mm sand bed) 65 mm thick approx 190 kg/m^2	Mediumweight— 2.4 kg/m^2/mm thickness 20 mm = 48 kg/m^2 40 mm = 96 kg/m^2
Sizes Generally 300 × 300 × 12 mm with rounded edges and camber for drainage. Coves and verge tiles may be available	Flags to BS 368: 1971 (nominal): 600 × 450, 600 × 600, 600 × 750, 600 × 900—50 and 63 mm thick. Other types in hexagons, circular with infill sections. Comprehensive ranges with tree grilles channels and so on are also made	Facing (nominal inc joints): 225 × 75 on edge, 225 × 112 on flat. Paviors (nominal) 225 × 75, 225 ×112, 225 × 150, 225 × 225. Range of thickness, 20–60 mm. Interlocking paviors in true 2:1 proportions or shaped. Engineering pavers (actual) 219 × 105 × 38, 50 or 73 mm	Rectangular versions normally 200 × 100 × 60, 65 and 80 mm. Interlocking versions to similar effective dimensions or 225 × 112.5. Special edge types also available in some ranges	Continuous membrane only, jointed at movement joints in substrate
Relative cost (approx) as laid* 350	100 BS 368 slabs are base for comparison	270–400	110 (20 mm BS 998 roofing grade)	150 (40 mm BS 1447 paving grade)

*Costs are indicative. Actual costs depend upon the situation, especially the complexity of paving layout. Cost data provided by Davis, Belfield and Everest.

TABLE 19. HARD PAVING MATERIALS: COMPARISON OF PERFORMANCE

Promenade tiles, fibre cement, GRC	Precast concrete flags	Clay paving	Precast concrete paving blocks	Mastic asphalt
Durability A life span of more than 40 years is claimed but appearance is shorter period due to dirt retention. See also strength	To BS 368: 1971, 25 to 30 years, less in some urban situations. Decorative types approx 20 years	Engineering pavers and interlocking paviors have long life, 40+ years. Other paviors should last 25–30 years. Durability of other bricks will vary considerably	Experience in UK is limited. Manufacturers estimate 40 years for pedestrian areas, 25 years in vehicular use. BS 6717: Pt 1: 1986 specifies minimum cement/binder content	Properly specified and laid, mastic asphalt is very durable, up to 40 years. But see resistance to oil and petrol below
Strength Not suitable for heavy loads, so pedestrian use only. Will crack when subjected to sharp impact load. Tiles get more brittle with age	Specified in BS 268: 1971. 63 mm thick slabs 50 per cent stronger than 50 mm. General recommendations: 38–50 mm light pedestrian 50–63 mm heavy pedestrian 75–100 mm vehicular	Strengths of bricks vary: stocks 20 to 30 N/mm^2 paviors 54 to 120 N/mm^2 Engineering: Class A>70 N/mm^2 Class B>50 N/mm^2 General recommendations: 35–38 mm pedestrian 50–65 mm vehicular. Transverse strength of flexible pavers specified in BS 6677: Pt 1: 1986	Minimum average strength 49 N/mm^2 see BS 6717: Pt 1: 1986. General recommendations: 60–65 mm pedestrian and light vehicular 80–100 mm medium to heavy vehicular. But proper bedding not normally possible on roof gardens, pedestrian precincts	'Fully confined' mastic asphalt has a high compressive strength, but in normal situations is susceptible to damage from concentrated loads. It can also be cracked by sharp impact loads. Strength also depends upon temperature

Note—strength in use depends on bedding, roof membrane, insulation (if any) and supporting structure

Promenade tiles, fibre cement, GRC	Precast concrete flags	Clay paving	Precast concrete paving blocks	Mastic asphalt
Frost resistance Not normally affected by frost	Normally excellent, especially those produced to BS 368: 1971	Special paviors and engineering pavers are excellent. Most FL quality facing bricks and stock bricks are good	Careful production ensures excellent frost resistance	Not affected by frost. If water gets under asphalt and then freezes, it can lift the asphalt
Freedom from efflorescence Any slight efflorescence concealed by light grey colour	Normally excellent	Depends upon brick, consult manufacturer for tests to BS 3921: 1985	Normally excellent	Does not effloresce
Freedom from organic growth Fair; dirt can collect in joints and support moss growth. Shaded areas prone to organic growth	Good in most cases. Heavily textured types may support organic growth in damp, shaded situations	Varies with type: pavers and paviors— excellent facing bricks—fair to good stocks—fair, will support growth in shaded situations	Very good	Very good but dimpled surface in shaded situations may collect dirt and lead to organic growth
Resistance to wear Fair; should not be subjected to heavy pedestrian use, no vehicular traffic	BS 368 types good. Some decorative types only fair	Harder types, such as paviors and pavers— very good/excellent, but stocks—fair	Very good	Fair, depends upon grade and amount of aggregate. Becomes 'polished' in areas of heavy wear
Slip resistance Fair; improved in GRC version with chequered surface	Depends upon texture, some very good. Smooth pebble exposed aggregate slippery, especially when damp	Depends upon brick— wirecut production gives good texture. Smooth engineering pavers may be slippery when wet. Interlocking paviors excellent	Very good	Fair, can be improved by 'crimping' surface with roller

179

TABLE 19. HARD PAVING MATERIALS: COMPARISON OF PERFORMANCE (continued)

Promenade tiles, fibre cement, GRC	Precast concrete flags	Clay paving	Precast concrete paving blocks	Mastic asphalt
Resistance to oil, petrol, salts				
Not affected by alkalis but can be stained by oils, etc	Good resistance but lighter colours suffer staining by oils, etc	Good to excellent for paviors, pavers and interlocking paviors. Stocks and facings may suffer staining	Good resistance but lighter colours suffer staining from oil	Poor, can be slightly improved by careful specification (increased aggregate content and additives)
Colour permanence and consistency				
Good permanence; but over the years tend to become stained and dirty. Light colours help to minimise solar gain and ageing in roof membrane. Colour consistency good	Fair permanence; the pigments used to colour concrete are subject to fading. Lighter colours help minimise solar gain and ageing in roof membrane. Some variation in colour between slabs, see samples before selection if an even colour is important	Excellent permanence. Light colours help minimise solar gain and ageing in roof membrane. Colour consistency can be good, but brick paving often chosen for its variation in colours within a given brick specification	Fair permanence, as paving flags. Light colours help to minimise solar gain and ageing in roof membrane. Colour consistency normally good, a few multi-coloured ranges now available	Lightens with age to grey, subject to some marking due to wear and so on. Light protective coatings used for roofing asphalt would quickly wear off with pedestrian or vehicular traffic. Colour consistency good
Fire resistance				
Non-combustible	Non-combustible	Non-combustible	Non-combustible	Partly combustible due to bitumen/asphaltic content

All these paving materials will allow the total system to achieve the highest rating for external fire exposure—P60 to BS 476: Part 3: 1975 (roughly equivalent to previous AA rating)

TABLE 20. BASIC FUNCTIONAL REQUIREMENTS OF TOTAL ROOFING/PAVING SYSTEM

Waterproofing
Will normally be of paramount importance, especially if above shop premises, factories and so on where water penetration could disrupt or even shut down a commercial operation. Type of waterproofing will depend on supporting structures, degree of use, required life, maintenance proposed and, of course, the building cost target. It is risky to skimp on any waterproofing specification. Consider carefully drainage at various levels—surface of paving and at roofing membrane. Keep penetrations through membrane, such as pipes, to minimum.

Durability (including strength/frost resistance)
Most paving materials will actually extend the life of the total system as they protect the membrane from ultra-violet radiation, excessive thermal movement and weathering. In paving of small areas or simply paving for protection, the required durability will not be significantly different from normal roofing situations. Where large areas of paving for public use are involved and replacement would be difficult, consider long term durability of the total system and each individual element.

Thermal insulation
Will depend upon function of space beneath roofing/paving system. Thermal insulation will probably not be required in upper level of a multi-storey car park but is vital on an access balcony with dwellings below. In paving situations, the compressive strength of the insulation may be an important consideration. Check that quoted insulation values can be achieved in practice. Watch cold bridging at columns, pipes and so on.

Sound insulation
As with thermal insulation importance of sound insulation will depend upon use of areas below—this can be a vital consideration in residential accommodation and was a source of problems in access deck blocks of the '60s. Some types of hard paving if properly bedded can make a positive contribution to the sound insulation of the total system although there is little concrete test data.

Allowance for movement
The modern highly engineered building requires careful consideration of movement of various types: thermal, moisture, irreversible material changes and so on. Movement joints in roofing/paving systems are one of the most difficult aspects of building detailing and construction. Many failures have occurred on large structures. Discussion with structural engineers are essential.
Thermal movement varies with the type of structure. Lightweight constructions are subject to relatively greater movement than the heavyweight constructions normally associated with roof gardens, shopping precincts and so on. Shrinkage of concrete is a most important factor.

Fire resistance
The building regulations (England and Wales, Scotland and London) all include fire precautions for roof construction including roof gardens, pedestrian precincts and so on. They are concerned with the ability of the roof covering and deck to act as a fire barrier against fire from a nearby building and the extent of surface ignition. All the hard paving systems described in this article achieve the highest rating when tested to BS 476: Part 3: 1975.

Solar reflectance
As mentioned under durability, pavings help protect the roof membrane. Light coloured pavings reflect a lot of radiant energy and reduce thermal movements in the roof membrane and substructure.

Ease of replacement
Paving systems based on proprietary supports, sand bedding, and so on will allow easier replacement of damaged paving and easier access to the roof membrane to carry out repairs.

TABLE 21. PAVING SPECIFICATIONS FOR MAINTENANCE AND OCCASIONAL PEDESTRIAN ACCESS (FOR EXAMPLE, ACCESS TO MACHINERY ON ROOF, PRIVATE BALCONY)

Fibre cement promenade tiles	*Mastic asphalt*	*Precast concrete slabs*
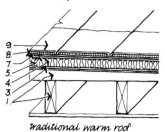	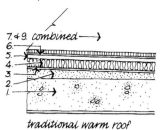	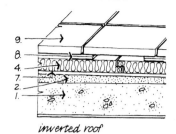
traditional warm roof	*traditional warm roof*	*inverted roof*

Structure
All forms of construction (max suitable roof slope 1 in 40)	Normally concrete, but also timber, woodwool or metal decking in some cases. Latter not recommended by some authorities	Normally concrete, also composite

Insulation
Most slab types of insulation are suitable although some types may require protection from hot bitumen/asphalt when laying waterproof membrane. Some not suitable for certain BS 747 felts

Waterproof membrane
Traditional warm roof. 2 or 3 layer built-up roofs to BS 747, Class 5 top sheet. 2 or 3 layer built-up roofs of modified bitumen and polyester base. Other certified built-up roofs such as bitumen and pitch polymers. 20 mm 2 coat roofing grade mastic asphalt to BS 988: 1973 or 6577: 1985 (R 1162)	Traditional warm roof. Membrane and paving combined— 20 mm 2 coat roofing grade mastic asphalt to BS 988: 1973. Can accept occasional foot traffic for maintenance of machinery, etc, without further protection. It has often been used for private balconies but not recommended as easily punctured by chair feet, etc	Traditional or inverted warm roof. BS 747: 1977, Class 5 top sheet. 3 layer built-up roofs of modified bitumen and polyester base. Other certified built-up roofs, such as bitumen and pitch polymers. 20 mm 2 coat roofing grade asphalt to BS 988: 1973 or 6577: 1985 (R 1162)

Bedding
3 mm thick layer of hot bituminous mastic is laid on roofing. Underside of tiles is coated in bitumen to ensure good bond	Separating membrane of felt to BS 747: 1977 type 4A(i) or glass fibre tissue	Solid mortar bedding not recommended. Mortar blobs at corners separated from waterproof membrane by building paper or similar. Pads at corners and centre made of inorganic felt to give minimum 5 mm clearance. Proprietary supports

Jointing/pointing
Leave 3 mm joint between tiles. Tiles are pressed into mastic so that small amount of bitumen oozes out of joints. Remove excess as soon as it gets cold with a sharp knife. Areas of tiles greater than 9 m^2 may require 25 mm expansion joints sealed with hot bitumen compound. Leave 5 mm joint at edges	Jointless except where movement joints are required in structure underneath	For last three beddings, above, approx 5 mm joint recommended so roof drains at waterproof membrane level. Leave 75 mm gap at edge

Site installation
Store tiles carefully and keep them dry. Lay tiles only in dry weather. Work on small area at a time to provide maximum adhesion	Ensure properly laid in two coats with joints between coats staggered. Kerb fillets to be well tooled into adjacent asphalt	Care necessary in placing flags to avoid damage to roof membrane. Falls in roofing membrane can cause problems in laying flags at ridges, valleys and so on. Careful setting out necessary to ensure minimum cutting

*Other types of paving and specifications of superior performance from Tables 22 and 23 may be used in some situations

TABLE 22. PAVING SPECIFICATIONS FOR FREQUENT PEDESTRIAN USE (SUCH AS ACCESS BALCONY, TERRACE ON PUBLIC BUILDING)

Precast concrete flags	Mastic asphalt	Clay brick paving, paviors, pavers
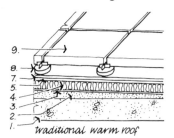	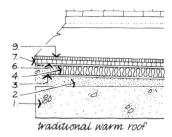	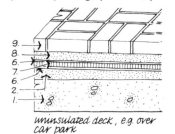
traditional warm roof	*traditional warm roof*	*uninsulated deck, e.g. over car park*

Structure

Normally concrete, also composite	Normally concrete, also composite	Normally concrete, also composite

Insulation

Increased amounts of pedestrian use will require consideration so that a suitably strong insulation is specified. Extruded polystyrene normally used with inverted roof principle

Waterproof membrane

Traditional or inverted warm roof. 3 layer built-up roofs to BS 747: 1977, intermediate and cap sheet Class 5. 3 layer built-up roof of modified bitumen and polyester base. Other certified built-up roofs such as bitumen and pitch polymers 20 or 30 mm (2 or 3 coat) roofing grade mastic asphalt to BS 988: 1973 or 6577: 1985 (R 1162)	Traditional warm roof. Membrane and paving combined— 25 mm 2 coat roofing grade mastic asphalt to BS 988: 1973 with 5–10 per cent grit added to top coat is minimum specification for access balconies. Separate specifications—25 mm 1 coat paving grade mastic asphalt to BS 1446: 1973 or 1447: 1973 on 13 mm one coat roofing grade asphalt to BS 988: 1973 or 6577: 1985 (R 1162)	Traditional cold roof. 3 layer built-up roofs of high performance materials may be suitable; discuss with manufacturer. Normally preferred—20 or 30 mm (2 or 3 coat) roofing grade mastic asphalt to BS 988: 1973 or 6577: 1985 (R 1162). Three coat for extra durability and reliability

Bedding

Proprietary supports are probably the most reliable and give the best looking finish, but, carefully laid mortar blobs can be as successful if separated from waterproof membrane with building paper, pads made of inorganic felt may be subject to some displacement due to heavy foot traffic	Separating membrane of felt to BS 747: 1977 Type 4A(i) or glass fibre tissue	Full, solid mortar bedding is required with small units such as brick. Mortar mix normally 1:3 cement/sand or 1:¼:3 cement/lime/sand. Thickness usually 25 mm for facing bricks and pavers, 35 mm for paviors. A sheet of building paper should be laid as separating membrane. For internal atria, bricks can be laid by semi-dry screed method (CP202) with 40–70 mm thick 1:3½–4 cement/sand. In both cases a slurry of neat cement or 1:1 cement/soft sand just prior to laying will give improved adhesion

Jointing/pointing

Open joints of approx 5 mm are recommended so paving is easily drained on to waterproof membrane level. Leave 75 mm gap at edges, this is often filled with gravel or large pebbles. Some proprietary supports have integral spacers for joints	Jointless except where movement joints are required as structure	Paving bricks, paviors, etc solidly bedded should be pointed in 1:3 cement/sand or 1:½:3 cement/lime/sand mortar with the pointing carried out with the bedding. Pigmented sand or pigmented sand/lime can be used to improve appearance of pointing. If the semi-dry bedded method is used, the joints will have to be very carefully pointed with the mortar, taking care not to smear the face as removal of the mortar is virtually impossible. Grouting of brickwork joints is not recommended

Site installation

Check suitability of supports on specified waterproof membrane. Try to keep falls simple so that supports can be used without extra materials (such as bits of flags) to level the paving surface	With the second, separate, specification above, an additional angle fillet of roofing asphalt is required to seal edge of paving asphalt at kerbs/skirtings. The asphalt surface should be finished by rubbing in sand to break up the bitumen rich surface. The surface can be 'crimped' to increase slip resistance	Good workmanship is required to achieve acceptable results. Try to avoid movement joints under solidly bedded paving as access for maintenance or repair is very difficult. With solid bedding on a rigid base, movement joints are normally required at approx 4.5–5 m intervals in the paving itself

TABLE 23. PAVING SPECIFICATIONS FOR HEAVY PEDESTRIAN USE*

Precast concrete flags	*Clay brick paving, paviors, pavers*	*Precast concrete paving block*
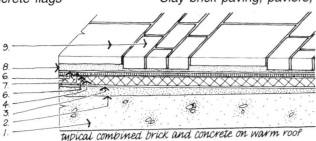 typical combined brick and concrete on warm roof		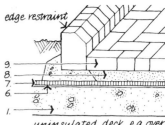 uninsulated deck, e.g. over service access

Structure

Concrete, also composite

Concrete, also composite

Precast concrete

Insulation

Heavy pedestrian use, and possibly electrically powered delivery vehicles, etc. will require stable insulation with some extra loadbearing capability

Waterproof membrane	Traditional warm roof.	Traditional cold roof.
Normally traditional roof, but inverted roofs have been laid on the continent. Ultra High Performance 3 layer built-up roofs have been used in some cases, consult manufacturer, but normally, 30 mm 3 coat mastic asphalt to BS 988: 1973 or 6577: 1985 (R 1162). Five to 10 per cent additional grit to top coat will increase bearing capacity, particularly when new	Difficulty of access for repair and maintenance requires that only the highest possible roofing specification is used, so normally, 30 mm 3 coat mastic asphalt to BS 988: 1973 or 6577: 1985 (R1162) with added grit appears the best possibility. Consult with roofing contractor with experience of this type of specification, also MACEF (see references)	A firm stable waterproof membrane is essential, 3 coat 20 mm mastic asphalt to BS 988: 1973 or 6577: 1985 (R 1162) with added grit appears the best possibility. Consult roofing contractor with experience of this type of specification, also MACEF (see references)

Bedding		
Proprietary supports have been used, particularly on the continent, but normally, 25 mm mortar bed on building paper or other suitable protective layer. Often flags are combined with brick paving so thicker bed and stronger mortar to co-ordinate with brick—see right	Full, solid mortar bedding is required with small units such as brick. Mortar mix normally 1:3 cement/sand or 1:¼:3 cement/lime/sand. Thickness usually 25 mm for facing bricks and pavers, 35 mm for paviors. A sheet of building paper should be laid as separating membrane. For internal atria, bricks can be laid by semi-dry screen method (CP 202) with 40–70 mm thick 1:3½–4 cement/sand. In both cases a slurry of neat cement or 1:1 cement/soft sand just prior to laying improve adhesion. 'Flexible' brick paving may be suitable but it must be considered experimental at this time	Precast concrete paving blocks are normally laid to a 'flexible' specification on a sand bed, into which the bricks are bedded with a plate vibrator. The C&CA cannot see any reason why this type of installation could not work but it must be considered experimental for suspended slabs

Jointing/pointing		
With mortar bedding, joints should be approx 10 mm wide and pointed in 1:3 cement/sand or 1:¼:3 cement/lime/sand mortar. The mortar should be semi-dry and carefully tooled into joints. Alternatively, dry 1:3 cement sand can be brushed into joints but this usually gives a messy finish	Paving bricks, paviors and so on solidly bedded should be pointed in 1:3 cement/sand or 1:¼:3 cement/lime/sand mortar with the pointing carried out with the bedding. Pigmented sand or pigmented sand/lime can be used to improve appearance of pointing. If the semi-dry bedded method is used, the joints will have to be very carefully pointed with the mortar. Grouting of brickwork joints is not recommended	With 'flexible' paving, sand is spread over the blocks and the vibrator ensures sand is forced down into the joints to achieve a good interlock seal. Firm edge restraint is required for flexible paving.

Site installation		
With solid bedding on a rigid base, movement joints are normally required at approx 8 m intervals in paving itself. Flags min 63 mm thickness hydraulically pressed	Good workmanship is required to achieve acceptable results. Try to avoid movement joints under solidly bedded paving as access for maintenance or repair is very difficult. With solid bedding on a rigid base, movement joints are normally required at approx 4.5–5 m intervals in the paving	As with pointed and solidly bedded paving, the tight seal achieved will mean drainage is required at both paving surface and waterproof membrane level. Watch edge restraint and manhole cover details. Including a filter membrane at drainage points

*Specification and detailing are very critical for paving with heavy pedestrian use. Consult manufacturers and trade associations (see references). This table is for preliminary consideration of paving only.

TABLE 24. PAVING SPECIFICATIONS FOR MULTI-STOREY CAR PARKS*

Mastic asphalt	Flexiphalte (Rock Asphalte Ltd)	Salviacim and similar (Tarmac Roadstone Ltd)	Others

insulated case using insulating screed

un-insulated case

un-insulated case

Structure

Concrete	Concrete	Concrete	Concrete

Insulation

Where required, insulation must be able to support the loading of parked vehicles. With defined parking bays there is a tendency for loading to be concentrated in small areas of paving. Insulation materials used include foamed glass, bitumen bonded expanded clay or perlite, cement bonded lightweight aggregate, special extruded polystyrene with topping. Consult manufacturers

Wearing surface			Performance
30 mm one coat paving grade mastic asphalt to BS 1447: 1973 or 1946: 1973. 30–40 per cent aggregate, often with bitumen polymer additive. Where there is no possibility of water, waterproof membrane might be omitted. Concrete surface may be more durable—but watch out for water brought in on cars, washing down and so on. Dense 'tarmacadam' has been used for better resistance to oil, etc.	Normally 32 mm modified paving grade mastic asphalt with roofing grade 'butt straps' at day joints. For lorry parks, service bays, a thicker wearing surface is used. Paving grade is laid on glass fibre tissue to separate it from waterproof membrane	Salviacim is a combination of graded aggregate and bitumen and is laid by traditional road surfacing equipment. The resultant open textured surface is then grouted with a special mixture containing Portland cement, silica sand, plus special binder, plasticiser and water	Various other systems have been developed to overcome the difficult problem of car park deck waterproofing and paving. One system, CDS G. A. Furguson consists of cold applied polyester resins laid in several layers on the specially cleaned concrete deck. Woven glass fibre is used to reinforce critical areas. Aggregates are incorporated into the top coat for skid resistance. Tretol produces: • Tretodek, a fluid applied elastomeric waterproofing and weaving surface combined

Waterproof membrane			
20 mm coat roofing grade mastic asphalt to BS 988: 1973 or 6577: 1985, or 13 mm 1 coat roofing grade mastic asphalt may be sufficient for internal levels. To be laid on glass fibre tissue, *not* felt to BS 747: 1977	Normally recommended one layer polymeric type roof membrane which is bitumen bonded at side and end laps and notionally bonded to substrate. Skirtings are carried out in 2 coat roofing grade mastic asphalt	Salviacim is not normally laid on waterproof membrane as it is usually at ground level. When used on suspended slabs with mastic asphalt waterproof membrane, the manufacturer should be consulted. This specification must be considered experimental	• Tretoflex, a polyurethane resin waterproofing that is applied by spray or roller. This must be protected by paving slabs or similar and has been used for car parks, pedestrian decks and inverted roofs

Ramps

For untreated ramps up to 1:10 slope use 25 mm one coat paving grade mastic asphalt laid *direct* to cross tamped concrete to provide key. Surface to be sanded and crimped	Ramps with a slope greater than 1:20 must be laid with Flexiphalte normally done as traditional mastic asphalt— see left	Consult manufacturer. Salviacim has an Agrément certificate for paving at ground level	

Installation

Consult MACEF for further details	Normally laid by manufacturer or approved subcontractor		

Watch expansion joints in roof level car parks—avoid if possible—do not try a cheap solution. If possible lay structural slab to falls as this saves screed and assists waterproofing

---

*Except for the mastic asphalt specification, car park surfacing is largely based on proprietary systems. Consult manufacturers at an early stage. This table is for preliminary consideration only.

CALCULATING THE EARTH

Reprinted from Landscape Design, September 1992

In most papers on roof gardens, soil amounts are specified in terms of profile depth. Depth specifications have become institutionalised in the landscape architecture literature, for example 150–300 mm for turf, 450 mm for ground cover, 600 mm for shrubs, and 800–1300 mm for trees. In practice these depths are often satisfactory, although they should really be seen as just rules of thumb. A less convenient, but more meaningful way to specify amounts of soil for roof garden planting is cubic metres of unsaturated soil per specified foliage canopy volume of roof garden vegetation. This paper addresses how these soil volumes can be determined for woody plants of a given canopy size.

A basic understanding of the relationship between soil volume and plant growth is fundamental to successful plant development in roof gardens. The soil volumes used to support plant growth on roof gardens perform a number of key functions. These include the provision of:

1. Physical anchorage. As trees and shrubs grow this becomes increasingly important. A subterranean grid of heavy steel mesh suspended across the planting troughs, and other subterranean guying systems allow the anchorage of large shrubs and trees to be largely independent of soil volume.
2. A matrix to supply plant roots with adequate water, oxygen and nutrients to sustain satisfactory canopy growth.

When shrubs and trees are initially planted in a roof garden, the amount of water stored in the soil volume provided (from rainfall alone) generally exceeds their transpiration requirements, and may represent several months supply of water. Assuming the profile drains adequately and contains adequate nutrients, as the plants grow and roots spread, foliage canopy transpiration removes an ever greater percentage of the water that can be stored within the total soil volume. As a result plants begin to experience stress at frequent intervals, reducing photosynthesis. Over time this results in a loss of vigour, a reduction in leaf size and canopy density, and the production of dwarf shoots, as the canopy comes to equilibrium with the moisture regime. In particularly moisture stress-sensitive species, leaf scorch-necrosis and shoot dieback frequently occur.

This all too familiar scenario in roof garden trees can be avoided by:

1. Installing irrigation systems that monitor and respond to increasing demands on soil moisture as transpiration losses from the foliage canopy grow.
2. Using plants whose canopies (and long-term transpiration loads) are relatively small compared to the water stored in the soil volume.
3. Providing a volume of soil large enough to hold sufficient water for the plants, to avoid severe moisture stress and to allow them to grow to the desired dimensions.

These strategies are not mutually exclusive. Where strategy 2) and 3) are not appropriate for either aesthetic or structural engineering reasons respectively, it is possible to support relatively large plant canopies in small soil volumes via strategy 1). This requires a sophisticated irrigation control device, such as the Cuming Moisture Sensor, which automatically irrigates the soil before a critical level of soil moisture stress is reached. With large canopies in small soil volumes this may mean that the soil is irrigated twice a day during the summer. With such systems you can largely ignore the traditional horticultural view that large plants need large pots. Root to canopy ratios are highly flexible in woody plants, and substantially modifiable by manipulating moisture stress in the growing medium. While these high-tech irrigation approaches can be very successful, as the work of Peter Thoday and others has demonstrated, the combination of very low root to canopy ratios and vigorous, relatively stress-free plants may result in the rapid collapse of vegetation if the irrigation falls. With more visually dominant, long-term vegetation such as trees, the consequences of a sudden loss of water supply, which is a problem inherent in low soil volume roof gardens (sooner or later building maintenance staff accidentally turn off the water supply), make these a risky option. Despite the loading problems, it is generally desirable to use large soil volumes to achieve more resilience in the event of irrigation failure. The key question, then, is how much soil is needed to support a tree or large shrubs of given dimensions, within a predetermined irrigation/precipitation regime.

Determining soil volumes

During the past decade there have been a number of methodologies proposed for estimating the volume of soil needed to sustain a given canopy volume. Some of these have attempted to relate soil volume to tree height, to canopy volume, and to trunk diameter. One of the most scientifically valid, and relatively straightforward methodologies is that developed by Lindsey and Bassuk. The steps for calculating the estimated soil volume to support a tree with a mature canopy radius of 4 m are illustrated in Table 25. The tree is growing in London and the assessment is for the period May–July inclusive. It is assumed that the soil volume is brought to field capacity at the end of April and then at fortnightly intervals via a combination of irrigation and rainfall. Table 26 contains examples of roof garden soil volumes required to support woody plants of a given size in various UK cities, using the method in Table 25.

One criticism of the soil volume data in Table 26 is that no real allowance is made for the contribution of precipitation. The methodology used does allow for precipitation to be taken into account, but requires that the interval between significant rainfall events is known. In the UK a significant rainfall event is defined as 'days with more than 0.25 mm of rain'. However, this is not necessarily a significant rainfall

event from the perspective of effective recharge of soil moisture. In the case of Birmingham there are 13 of these significant days in June, corresponding to a mean monthly rainfall of 50 mm. While the actual pattern varies from year to year, on average 3.8 mm of rain falls every 2.3 days in this month. Bearing in mind the potential daily evaporation in June is 3.1 mm, the significance of this rainfall for soil moisture recharge might not be very great. Making meaningful calculations is a problematic exercise. Due to the limited ability of containerised soil to capture precipitation (because of building and tree generated rain shadows, plus the often small surface area of containers enclosing the soil volume) it is probably wise to ignore the contribution of precipitation during the three months of maximum water stress. Clearly the contribution of precipitation during this period will be greatest at planting and increasingly less so as the trees establish and increase in size. Given the structural loadings associated with large soil volumes, which are needed in order to support trees under an infrequent irrigation regime or when relying upon precipitation alone, such volumes are rarely possible in roof garden situations. The use of the smaller volumes shown in Table 26 can be successful, providing irrigation is well managed. Unfortunately in the long term such management is rare. Also, where media choice, profile design, or drainage management result in a high frequency of anaerobic conditions in the soil, the volumes of soil required will be greater than indicated in Table 26.

Plant selection can play an extremely valuable role in adding resilience where you have small root volumes and inadequate irrigation. Tree that have high tolerance of severe moisture stress, such as *Quercus ilex, Pinus* spp. *Platanus orientalis,* and *Ulmus parvifolia* may not grow as large as is desired under a high moisture stress regime but will rarely demonstrate the leaf scorch, premature defoliation, and shoot dieback common in intolerant species. Widely used urban landscape taxa such as many *Acer, Sorbus* and *Tilia* are surprisingly prone to the latter problems when grown in containerised profiles which experience severe moisture stress. To gain a better appreciation of the potential drought tolerance of woody species, it is useful to consult the horticultural literature of the more arid regions of North America. A more in-depth review of this topic can be found in Hitchmough (in press).

TABLE 25. ESTIMATING THE VOLUME OF SOIL NECESSARY TO SUPPORT A ROOF GARDEN TREE (ADAPTED FROM LINDSEY BASSUK 1991).[5]

Stage 1: Estimate whole tree daily water use:
Example: tree growing in London with a canopy 8 m in diameter (400 cm radius).
Calculate tree canopy projection in cm^2 (surface area of ground enclosed by canopy periphery) = $\pi \times 400^2$ (where π = 3.14).
Estimate typical leaf area index (actual leaf surface area relative to area of tree canopy projection) = 4.0 (range for trees = 1.0–12.0, most deciduous trees are 4.0).
Establish mean daily evaporation rate for the period in question in cm (see Table 26) for London it is 0.33.
Assign evaporation ratio (water lost per unit area of leaf tissue as a percentage of water lost per unit area of evaporation pan) = 0.25 (typical value for temperate trees, Lindsey 1990).

$$\text{Water lost per day from trace canopy} = \frac{400^2 \times 3.14 \times 4.0 \times 0.33 \times 0.25}{1000}$$

$$= 165.8 \text{ litres}$$

Stage 2: Determine adequate soil volume to support this canopy volume:
Water lost by tree canopy per day is 165.8 litres.
Assign value for available water holding capacity of the soil = 0.71. Figure given is for a amended silt loam compost. Values for mineral soils typically vary from 0.10–0.25 (10 to 25 per cent).
Identify the number of days between significant rainfall or irrigation events for the period in question that return the soil to field capacity = 14. (In this example it is assumed the soil is returned to field capacity via irrigation on a fortnightly basis.)

$$\text{Total volume of soil required} = \frac{165.8}{0.17 \times 14.0}$$

$$= 13.6 \text{ m}^3$$

Stage 3: Configure soil volume:
Assuming a maximum effective rooting depth of 1.0 m (soil deeper than this is often too poorly oxygenated for effective root growth), suitable configurations are: 3.7 × 3.7 × 1.0 m, 3.0 × 4.5 × 1.0 m.

TABLE 26. CALCULATION OF ROOF GARDEN SOIL VOLUMES FOR WOODY PLANTS, USING THE METHODOLOGY OF LINDSEY AND BASSUK (1991)[5]

Plant type and mature canopy diameter	City	Mean daily evaporation for 3 months of greatest moisture stress: (mm)†			Calculated soil volume (in m³) required when soil returned to field capacity at the following intervals‡			
		May	June	July	weekly	fortnightly	monthly	3 monthly
Large tree, 16 m*	Birmingham	2.7	3.3	3.0	24.8	49.6	109.6	326.3
	Glasgow	2.5	3.1	2.7	23.1	46.3	102.5	304.2
	London	2.9	3.6	3.3	27.3	54.6	120.9	358.8
Medium* tree, 8 m	Birmingham	2.7	3.3	3.0	6.2	12.4	27.5	81.6
	Glasgow	2.5	3.1	2.7	5.9	11.9	26.3	78.2
	London	2.9	3.6	3.3	6.8	13.6	30.1	89.4
Small tree, 4 m*	Birmingham	2.7	3.3	3.0	1.5	3.1	6.9	20.4
	Glasgow	2.5	3.1	2.7	1.4	2.9	6.4	19.0
	London	2.9	3.6	3.3	1.7	3.4	7.5	22.3
Medium§ shrub, 2 m	Birmingham	2.7	3.3	3.0	0.3	0.6	1.3	3.8
	Glasgow	2.5	3.1	2.7	0.2	0.5	1.1	3.3
	London	2.9	3.6	3.3	0.3	0.6	1.4	4.2
Small§ shrub, 1 m	Birmingham	2.7	3.3	3.0	0.05	0.1	0.2	0.7
	Glasgow	2.5	3.1	2.7	0.05	0.1	0.2	0.7
	London	2.9	3.6	3.3	0.07	0.2	0.4	1.0

* = assumes a leaf area index of 4.0.
§ = assumes a leaf area index of 3.0.
† = where the deficit between evaporation and precipitation is maximal.
‡ calculated using the mean of daily evaporation for the three above months.
Note: 0.1m³ = 100 litres.

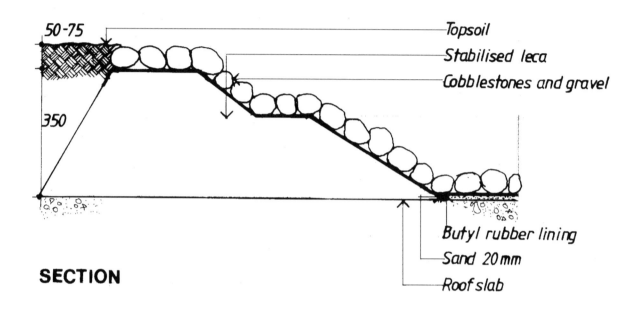

50-75   Topsoil

Stabilised leca

Cobblestones and gravel

350

Butyl rubber lining

Sand 20 mm

SECTION

Roof slab

ROOF GARDEN
pool edge

Scale 1:10

191

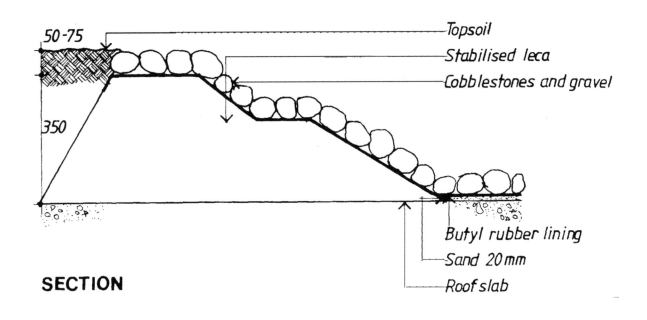

50-75   Topsoil

Stabilised leca

Cobblestones and gravel

350

SECTION

Butyl rubber lining

Sand 20 mm

Roof slab

ROOF GARDEN
cobblestones

Scale 1:10

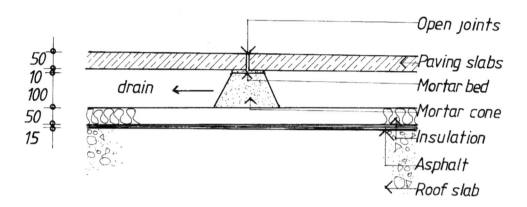

SECTION

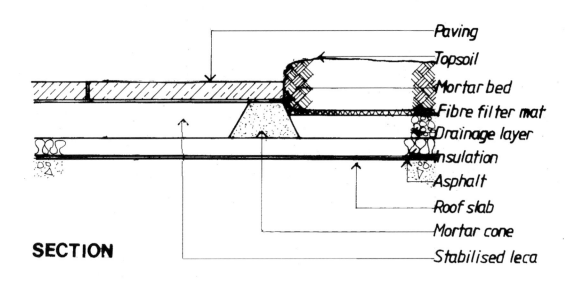

SECTION

Paving
Topsoil
Mortar bed
Fibre filter mat
Drainage layer
Insulation
Asphalt
Roof slab
Mortar cone
Stabilised leca

ROOF GARDEN
paving edge

Scale 1:10

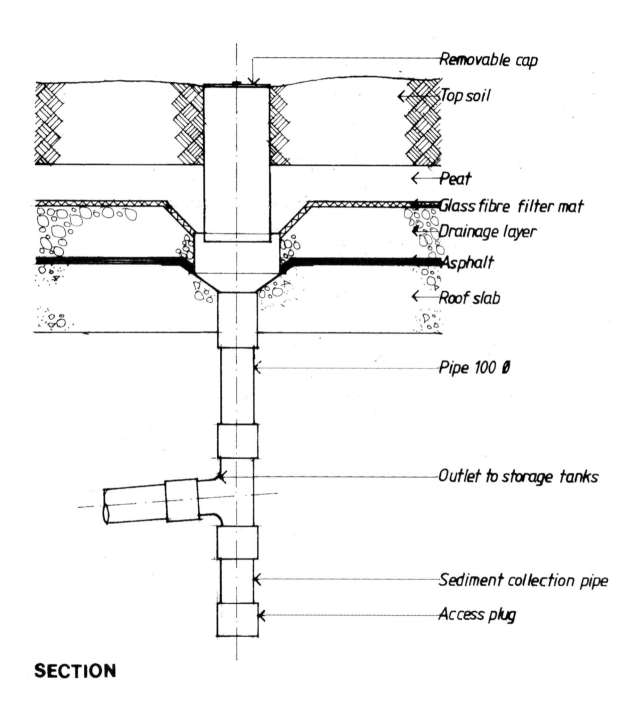

- Removable cap
- Top soil
- Peat
- Glass fibre filter mat
- Drainage layer
- Asphalt
- Roof slab
- Pipe 100 Ø
- Outlet to storage tanks
- Sediment collection pipe
- Access plug

SECTION

Scale 1:10

ROOF GARDEN
drainage outlet

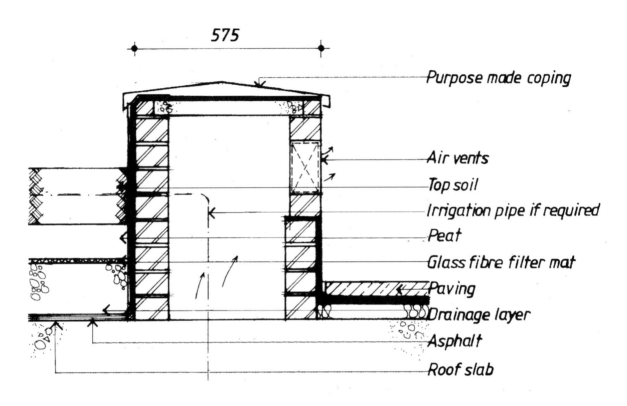

575

Purpose made coping

Air vents

Top soil

Irrigation pipe if required

Peat

Glass fibre filter mat

Paving

Drainage layer

Asphalt

Roof slab

SECTION

ROOF GARDEN
ventilation unit

Scale 1:10

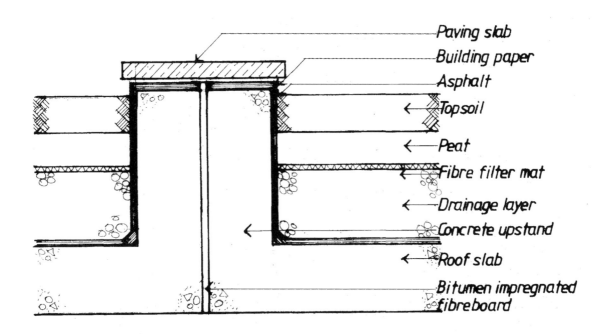

- Paving slab
- Building paper
- Asphalt
- Topsoil
- Peat
- Fibre filter mat
- Drainage layer
- Concrete upstand
- Roof slab
- Bitumen impregnated fibreboard

SECTION

ROOF GARDEN
expansion joint covering

Scale 1:10

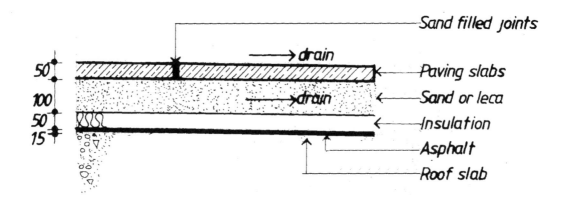

SECTION

ROOF GARDEN

paving drainage

Scale 1:10

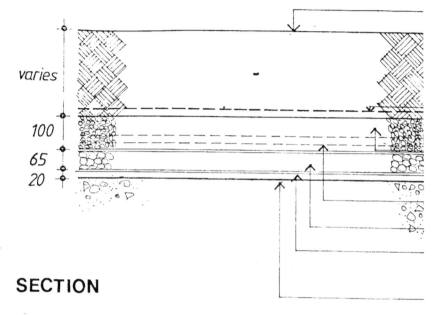

Topsoil 1·1 mixture, loam :
hygrodor 73 in depths
according to planting

Polypropylene mesh for
additional stability

Hygromultas filter and
water store

Irrigation pipes

Styroper drainage slabs

Polyisobutylene or PVC
as sealer

Roof slab

SECTION

varies

100

65

20

Scale 1:10

ROOF GARDEN
BASF method

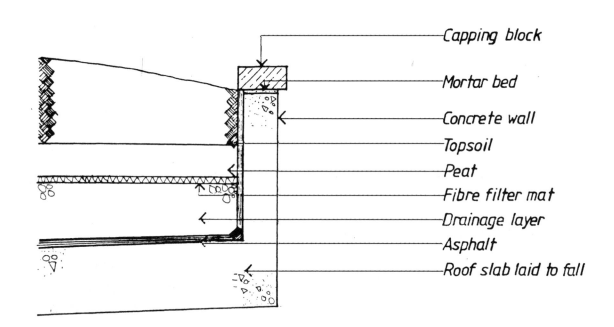

— Capping block

— Mortar bed

— Concrete wall

— Topsoil

— Peat

— Fibre filter mat

— Drainage layer

— Asphalt

— Roof slab laid to fall

SECTION

ROOF GARDEN
raised planter

Scale 1:10

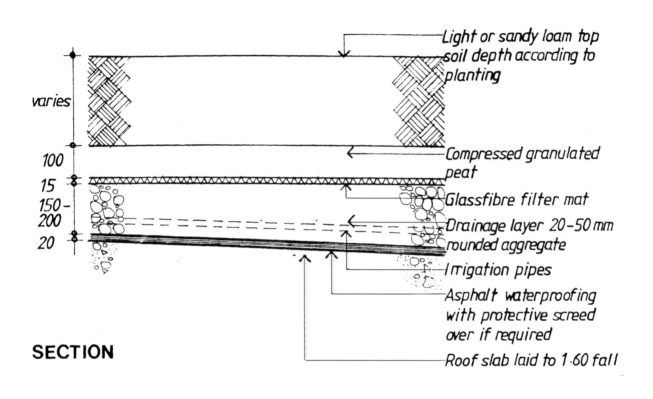

SECTION

varies

100

15

150 –
200

20

Light or sandy loam top soil depth according to planting

Compressed granulated peat

Glassfibre filter mat

Drainage layer 20–50 mm rounded aggregate

Irrigation pipes

Asphalt waterproofing with protective screed over if required

Roof slab laid to 1·60 fall

ROOF GARDEN

Scale 1:10

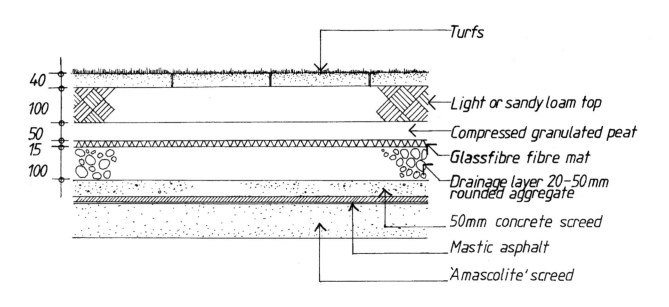

Turfs

40
100 — Light or sandy loam top
50 — Compressed granulated peat
15 — Glassfibre fibre mat
100 — Drainage layer 20–50 mm rounded aggregate

50mm concrete screed

Mastic asphalt

'Amascolite' screed

SECTION

NOTE:–
to be read in conjunction
with architects' drawing
no. 629/337

Scale 1:10

LAWN-ROOF

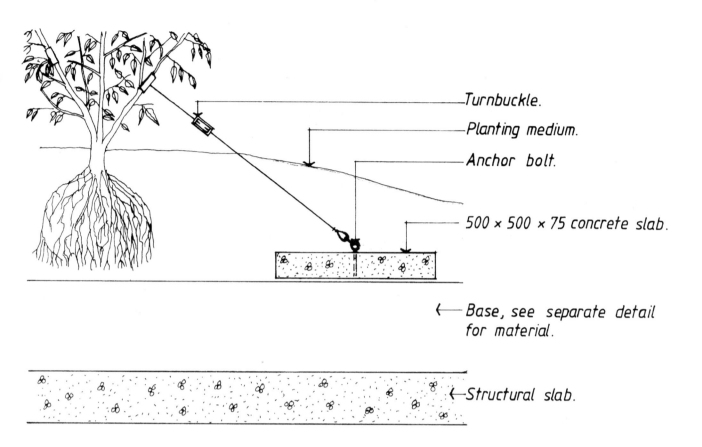

Turnbuckle.

Planting medium.

Anchor bolt.

500 × 500 × 75 concrete slab.

←— Base, see separate detail for material.

←Structural slab.

SECTION

Scale 1 : 10

ROOF GARDEN
anchor detail

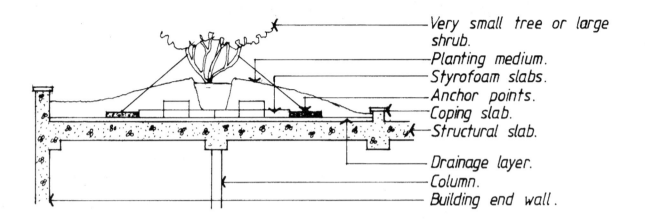

Very small tree or large shrub.
Planting medium.
Styrofoam slabs.
Anchor points.
Coping slab.
Structural slab.

Drainage layer.
Column.
Building end wall.

SECTION

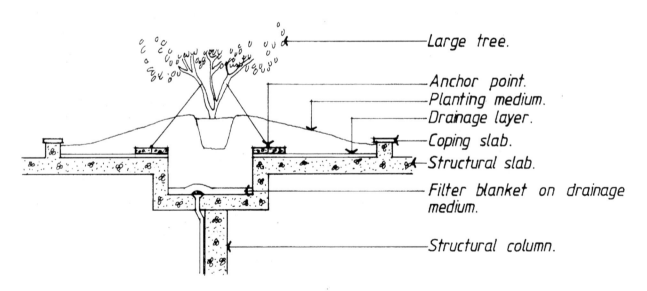

Large tree.

Anchor point.
Planting medium.
Drainage layer.
Coping slab.
Structural slab.

Filter blanket on drainage medium.

Structural column.

SECTION

Scale 1:50

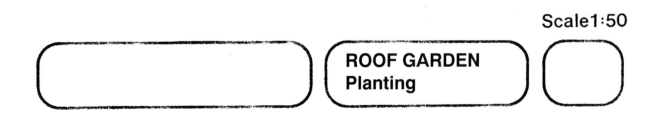

ROOF GARDEN
Planting

204

BIBLIOGRAPHY & REFERENCES

APPENDIX A

Bibliography

AJ Technical Studies, Landscape Brickwork. *Architects' Journal*

AJ Technical Studies, Hard Landscape in Stone. *Architects' Journal*, 19.5.76, p. 1005

AJ Technical Studies, Products in Practice. Supplement 30.11.83, p. 3

AJ Technical Studies, Designing with Plants. *Architects' Journal*, 1984

AJ Technical Studies, Consultants: Landscape Architect. *Architects' Journal*, 18.4.84, p. 65

AJ Technical Studies, Landscape Contracts. *Architects' Journal*, 20.6.84, p. 87

J. Ashurst and F.G. Dimes. *Stone in Building*, Architectural Press, 1984

BTCV, *Footpaths*, 3rd edition, June 1992

E. Beazley, *Design and Detail of the Space between Buildings*, 1960

R.M. Cartwright, *Design of Urban Space*, 1980

Countryside Commission for Scotland, *Footbridges in the Countryside*, 2nd edition, 1989

M.F. Downing, *Landscape Construction*, 1977

M. Gage and T. Kirkbride, *Design in Blockwork*, 2nd edition, Architectural Press, 1976

M. Gage and M. Vandenberg, *Hard Landscape in Concrete*, Architectural Press, 1975

Floyd Giles, *Landscape Construction – Procedures, Techniques & Design*, Stipes, USA, 1992

C.C. Handisyde, *Hard Landscape in Brick*, Architectural Press, 1976

Charles W. Harris and Nicholas T. Dines, *Time Saver Standards for Landscape Architecture*, McGraw-Hill, 1988

How to Build Small Barns & Outbuildings, Monte Barch, Storey, USA, 1992

G. John and H. Heard, *Handbook of Sports and Recreational Building Design*, Architectural Press, 1981

Michael Littlewood, *Tree Detailing*, 1984, Butterworth

D. Lovejoy & Partners, *Spon's Landscape Handbook*, E & F N Spon, 1983

A. Pinder and A. Pinder, *Beazley's Design and Detail of the Space between Buildings*, E & F N Spon, 1990

C. Tandy, *Handbook of Urban Landscape*, Architectural Press, 1972

A.E. Weddle, *Landscape Techniques*, William Heinemann, 1979

J. Ashhurst and F.G. Dimes, *Stone in Building*, Architectural Press, 1984

Building Research Establishment (BRE), *The selection of natural building stone*, BRE Digest 269

Natural Stone Directory, 7th Edition, Ealing Publications, April 1987

The following trade associations will answer technical queries, and publish technical guidance:

Bituminous Roofing Council (BRC) 01444 16881

Brick Development Association (BDA) 01344 885651

Cement and Concrete Association (C&CA) 0171-395 2727

Mastic Asphalt Council and Employers Federation (MACEF) 01444 457786

Specifications

NBS specifications

Woodland Gardening, G. Rose
Willoughby P (1985) 'Automatic
irrigation in a peach orchard'
HortScience 20, pp. 445–446.
Hellwell DR (1986) 'The extent of
tree roots'. Arboriculture Journal,
10, pp. 341–347
Moll G and Urban J (1989) 'Giving
trees more to grow'. American
Forests, May/June, pp. 61–64.
Lindsey PA and Bassuk N (1991)
'Specifying soil volumes to meet
the needs of mature urban street
trees and trees in containers',
Journal of Arboriculture, 17, 6, pp.
141–148.
Lindsey PA (1990) *Differences in
water use rates between four
woody tree species*. Unpublished
Masters Thesis, Cornell University.
Roofing membranes
For a general review of flat roof
membranes see 'Roof coverings'.
AJ products in practice supplement,
28.1.87. This includes an excellent
table of classified references.
For roofs generally see *Flat roofing:
a guide to good practice,* F. March.
Tarmac Building Products, 1982.
For traditional roofs see *Flat roofs
technical guide,* PSA. HMSO. 1982.
For inverted roofs see *The inverted
roof technical guide*. PSA. HMSO.
1984.
For asphalt roofing and paving see
Roofing handbook and *Paving
handbook*, both by MACEF, 1980

References

Timber Research & Development
Association Publications

Finish for Outdoor Timbers,
November 1978
Moisture Content in Wood, March,
1980
*Preservative Treatment for Timber
– a Guide to Specification*, January
1982
*Timbers for River and Sea
Constructions*, January, 1982
*Classification of Wood Properties
and Utilisation*, March 1983
Timber Bridges, May 1983
Wood Decorative and Practical,
January 1985 (R)
*Timbers – Their Properties and
Uses*, January 1985
Timber for Landscape Architecture,
October 1986
Timber in Playground Equipment,
March 1988

California Redwood Association
Publications

Garden Shelters, Data Sheet 3C2-
3, 1966
Garden Work Centres, Data Sheet
3C2-4, 1966
Deck Construction, Data Sheet
3C2-5
Garden Shelters & Work Centres,
Data Sheet 3C3-1, 1968
Nails & Nailing, Data Sheet – 4A1-
1, 1968
Timber Fastenings, 4A1-2, 1968

ORTHO BOOKS 1985

Deck Plans
Garden Construction
Wood Projects for the Garden

INSTITUTIONS AND ASSOCIATIONS

Trade

Aggregate Concrete Block Association (ACBA)
60 Charles Street
Leicester LE1 1FB
Tel: (01533) 536161

Aluminium Coaters Association
c/o British Standards Institution
Quality Assurance Section
PO Box 375
Milton Keynes
Bucks MK14 6LO
Tel: (01908) 315555

Aluminium Extruders Association
Broadway House
Calthorpe Road
Birmingham B15 1TN
Tel: (0121) 4550311
Telex: Bircom-G-338024ALFED

Architectural Salvage
Hutton & Rostron
Netley House
Gomshall
Surrey GU5 9QA
(0148) 641 3221

Asphalt and Coated Macadam Association
see British Aggregate Construction Materials Industries

The Asphalt Institute
Asphalt Institute Building
College Park
Maryland, USA

Association of British Plywood and Veneer Manufacturers
130 Hackney Road
London E2 7QR
(0171) 739 7654

Association of Lightweight Aggregate Manufacturers
c/o Russlite (Scotland) Ltd
Gartshore Works
Twechar
Kilsyth
Glasgow G65 9TW
(01236) 822461

Association of Swimming Pool Contractors
76 Marylebone High Street
London W1

Brick Development Association (BDA)
Woodside House
Winkfield
Windsor
Berks SL4 20X
Tel: (01344) 885651

British Adhesives and Sealants Association (BASA)
Secretary
33 Fellowes Way
Stevenage
Herts SG2 8BW
Tel: (01438) 358514

British Aggregate Construction Materials Industries (BACMI)
156 Buckingham Palace Road
London SW1W 9TR
Tel: (0171) 730 8194
Fax: (0171) 730 4355

British Agricultural and Horticultural Plastics Association
5 Belgrave Square
London SW1X 8PH
Tel: (0171) 235 9483

British Cement Association (BCA)
Wexham Springs
Slough
Berks SL3 6PL
Tel: (02816) 2727
Telex: 848352
Fax: (02816) 2251/3727

British Chemical Dampcourse Association
PO Box 105
Reading
Berks RG3 6NG
(01734) 24911

British Commercial Glasshouse Manufacturers' Association
c/o Cambridge Glasshouse Co. Ltd
Comberton
Cambridge CB3 7BY
Tel: (01223) 262 395

British Decorators Association
6 Haywra Street
Harrogate
N. Yorks HG1 5BL
Tel: (01423) 67292/3

British Precast Concrete Federation Ltd (BPCF)
60 Charles Street
Leicester LE1 1FB
Tel: (01533) 536161
Fax: (01533) 51468

British Quarrying and Slag Federation Ltd
Carolyn House
Dingwall Road
Croydon CR0 9XF
(0181) 680 7850

British Ready Mixed Concrete Association
1 Bramber Court
2 Bramber Road
London W14 9PB
Tel: (0171) 381 6582

British Tar Industry Association
132–5 Sloane Street
London SW1X 9BB
(0171) 730 5212

British Water and Effluent Treatment Association
51 Castle Street
High Wycombe
Bucks HP13 4RN
(01494) 444544

British Wood Preserving Association (BWPA)
Premier House
150 Southampton Row
London WC1B 5AL
Tel: (0171) 837 8217

Calcium Silicate Brick Association (CSBA)
24 Fearnley Road
Welwyn Garden City
Herts AL8 6HW
Tel: (07073) 24538

Cement Admixtures Association (CAA)
2A High Street
Hythe
Southampton
Hants SO4 6YW
Tel: (01703) 842765

Cement and Concrete Association
see British Cement Association

Chartered Land Agents' Society
21 Lincoln's Inn Fields
London WC2

Clay Roofing Tile Council (CRTC)
Federation House
Station Road
Stoke-on-Trent
Staffs ST4 2SA
Tel: (01782) 747256
Telex: 367446
Fax: (01782) 744102

Concrete Block Paving Association (Interpave)
60 Charles Street
Leicester LE1 1FB
Tel: (01533) 536161
Fax: (01533) 514568

Concrete Brick Manufacturer's Association (CBMA)
60 Charles Street
Leicester LE1 1FB
Tel: (01533) 536161
Fax: (01533) 514568

Copper Development Association (CDA)
Orchard House
Mutton Lane
Potters Bar
Herts EN6 3AP
Tel: (01707) 50711
Telex: 265451 MONREF (quote 72:MAG 30836)

Decorative Paving and Walling Association
60 Charles Street
Leicester LE1 1FB
Tel: (01533) 536161
Fax: (01533) 514568

Fencing Contractors Association (FCA)
St John's House
23 St John's Road
Watford
Herts WD1 1PY
Tel: (01923) 248895

Forestry Authority
231 Corstorphine Road
Edinburgh EH12 7AT
Tel: (0131) 334 2576

Glass Reinforced Cement Association
Farthings End
Dukes Ride
Gerrards Cross
Bucks SL9 7LD
(01753) 82606

Guild of Architectural Ironmongers (GAI)
8 Stepney Green
London E1 3JU
Tel: (0171) 790 3431
Telex: 94012229 GAII G
Fax: (0171) 790 8517

Her Majesty's Stationery Office (HMSO)
St Crispin's
Duke Street
Norwich
Norfolk NR3 1PD
Tel: (01603) 22211
Telex: 97301
Fax: (01603) 695582

Horticultural Traders Association
6th Floor, Cereal House
Mark Lane
London EC3

Interpave:
The Concrete Block Paving Association
60 Charles Street
Leicester LE1 1FB
Tel: (01533) 536161

Lead Development Association (LDA)
34 Berkeley Square
London W1X 6AJ
Tel: (0171) 499 8422
Telex: 261286

The Mastic Asphalt Council and Employers Federation
Construction House
Paddockhall Road
Haywards Heath
West Sussex RH16 1HE
Tel: (01444) 457786

Mortar Producers Association Ltd (MPA)
Holly House
74 Holly Walk
Leamington Spa
Warwicks CV32 4JD
Tel: (01926) 38611

National Association of Master Masons
Admin House
Market Square
Leighton Buzzard
Beds LU7 7EU
(01525) 375252

National Federation of Clay Industries Ltd (NFCI)
Federation House
Station Road
Stoke-on-Trent
Staffs ST4 2TJ
Tel: (01782) 416256
Telex: 367446
Fax: (01782) 744102

National Association of Agricultural Contractors (Garden Section)
140 Bensham Lane
Thornton Heath, Surrey

National Federation of Painting and Decorating Contractors
82 New Cavendish Street
London W1M 1AD
Tel: (0171) 580 5588

National Paving and Kerb Association (NPKA)
60 Charles Street
Leicester LE1 1FB
Tel: (01533) 536161
Fax: (01533) 514568

Natural Slate Quarries Association
Bryn, Llanllechid
Bangor
Gwynedd LL57 3LG
Tel: (01248) 600476

Paintmakers Association of Great Britain (PA)
Alembic House
93 Albert Embankment
London SE1 7TY
Tel: (0171) 582 1185

Paint Research Association
8 Waldegrave Road
Teddington
Middlesex TW11 8LD
Tel: (0181) 977 4427
Telex: 928720
Fax: (0181) 943 4705

Refined Bitumen Association
165 Queen Victoria Street
London EC4V 4DD

Sand and Gravel Association Ltd (SAGA)
1 Bramber Court
2 Bramber Road
London W14 9PB
Tel: (0171) 381 1443

Society of Chain Link Fencing Manufacturers
16 Montcrieffe Road
Sheffield S7 1HR
Tel: (01742) 500350

Stone Federation
82 New Cavendish Street
London W1M 8AD
Tel: (0171) 580 5588
Telex: 265763

Timber Growers' Association
35 Belgrave Square
London SW1

Timber Research and Development Association (TRADA)
Stocking Lane
Hughenden Valley
High Wycombe
Bucks HP14 4ND
Tel: (0124024) 2771/3091/3956
Telex: 83292 TRADA G
Prestel: 3511615
Fax: (0124024) 5487

Town Planning Institute
26 Portland Square
London W1

Trade Association of the United Kingdom
Cereal House
Mark Lane
London EC3

Zinc Development Association
24 Berkeley Square
London W1

Professional

Agricultural Engineers Association
6 Buckingham Gate
London SW1

Arboricultural Association
The Secretary
38 Blythwood Gardens
Stanstead, Essex

British Standards Institution (BSI)
Head Office:
2 Park Street
London W1A 2BS
Tel: (0171) 629 9000
Telex: 266933
Fax: (Group 2/3) (0171) 629 0506

British Waterways Board
Melbury House
Melbury Terrace
London NW1

Building Research Station
Bucknalls Lane
Garston, Watford, Herts

Civic Trust
17 Carlton House Terrace
London SW1Y 5AW
(0171) 930 0914

Council for the Preservation of Rural England
4 Hobart Place
London SW1

Council for the Preservation of Rural Wales
Y Plas
Machynlleth
Montgomeryshire

Country Landowners' Association
7 Swallow Street
London W1

Country Naturalists Trusts
(Headquarters in each county)

Countryside Commission
John Dower House
Crescent Place
Cheltenham
Glos GL50 3RA
(01242) 21381

Countryside Commission for Scotland
Battleby
Redgorton
Perth PH1 3EW
Tel: (0738) 27921

Crafts Council
12 Waterloo Place
London SW1Y 4AU
Tel: (071) 930 4811

Crown Estate Commissioners
Crown Estate Office
Whitehall
London SW1

Farm Buildings Information Centre
National Agricultural Centre
Stoneleigh
Kenilworth
Warwicks CV8 3JN
(01203) 22345/6

Horticultural Education Association
65 Tilehurst Road
Reading, Berks

Institute of Civil Engineers
25 Eccleston Square
London SW1V 1NX
Tel: (0171) 630 0726

Institute of Highways and Transportation
3 Lygon Place
Ebury Street
London SW1W 0JS
Tel: (0171) 730 5245

Institute of Park and Recreation Administration
The Grotto
Lower Basildon
Nr Reading, Berks

Institute of Quantity Surveyors
98 Gloucester Place
London W1H 4AT
(0171) 935 5577

Institution of Municipal Engineers
25 Eccleston Square
London SW1V 1NX
(0171) 834 5082

Institution of Structural Engineers
11 Upper Belgrave Street
London SW1
(0171) 235 4535

The Landscape Institute
6–7 Barnard Mews
London SW11 1QU
Tel: (0171) 738 9166

Ministry of Agriculture Fisheries and Food
Great Westminster House
Horseferry Road
London SW1P 2AE
(0171) 216 6311

National Association of Groundsmen
108 Chessington Road
Ewell, Surrey

National Farmers' Union
Agricultural House
Knightsbridge
London SW1

National Farmers' Union for Scotland
17 Grosvenor Crescent
Edinburgh 12
(see Trade Association of the United Kingdom)

National Parks Commission
8 St Andrew's Place
London SW1

National Playing Fields Association
57b Catherine Place
London NW1

National Trust
36 Queen Anne's Gate
London SW1H 9AS
Tel: (0171) 222 9251

National Trust Committee for Northern Ireland
82 Dublin Road
Belfast 2

National Trust for Scotland
5 Charlotte Square
Edinburgh 2

NBS Services Ltd
Mansion House Chambers
The Close
Newcastle upon Tyne NE1 3RE
Tel: (0191) 232 9594
Fax: (0191) 232 5714

Royal Forestry Society of England & Wales
49 Russell Square
London WC1

Royal Horticultural Society
Vincent Square
London SW1

Royal Institute of British Architects
66 Portland Place
London W1N 4AD
(0171) 580 5533

Royal Institution of Chartered Surveyors
12 Great George Street
London SW1 3AD
(0171) 222 7000

Royal Scottish Forestry Society
7 Albyn Place
Edinburgh 2

Sports Council, Technical Unit for Sport
16 Upper Woburn Place
London WC1H 0QP
Tel: (071) 388 1277

Town and Country Planning Association
28 King Street
Covent Garden
London WC2

Tree Council
35 Belgrave Square
London SW1X 8QN
(0171) 235 8854

Water Research Centre
Henley Road
Medmenham
PO Box 16
Marlow
Bucks SL7 2HD
(0149) 166531

CONVERSION TABLES

APPENDIX C

LENGTH
Approximate equivalents

Millimetres to inches		Inches to millimetres	
1	1/32	1/32	1
2	1/16	1/16	2
3	1/8	1/8	3
4	5/32	3/16	5
5	3/16	1/4	6
6	1/4	5/16	8
7	9/32	3/8	10
8	5/16	7/16	11
9	11/32	1/2	13
10 (1cm)	3/8	9/16	14
11	7/16	5/8	16
12	15/32	11/16	17
13	1/2	3/4	19
14	9/16	13/16	21
15	19/32	7/8	22
16	5/8	15/16	24
17	11/16	1	25
18	23/32	2	51
19	3/4	3	76
20	25/32	4	102
25	1	5	127
30	1 3/16	6	152
40	1 9/16	7	178
50	1 31/32	8	203
60	2 3/8	9	229
70	2 3/4	10	254
80	3 5/32	11	279
90	3 9/16	12 (1 ft)	305
100	3 15/16	13	330
200	7 7/8	14	356
300	11 13/16	15	381
400	15 3/4	16	406
500	19 11/16	17	432
600	23 5/8	18	457
700	27 9/16	19	483
800	31 1/2	20	508
900	35 7/16	24 (2ft)	610
1000 (1m)	39 3/8		

Metres to feet/inches		Yards to metres	
1	3' 3"	1	0.914
2	6' 7"	2	1.83
3	9' 10"	3	2.74
4	13' 1"	4	3.66
5	16' 5"	5	4.57
6	19' 8"	6	5.49
7	23' 0"	7	6.40
8	26' 3"	8	7.32
9	29' 6"	9	8.23
10	32' 10"	10	9.14
20	65' 7"	20	18.29
50	164' 0"	50	45.72
100	328' 1"	100	91.44

Length	1 millimetre (mm)	= 0.0394 in
	1 centimetre (cm)/10 mm	= 0.3937 in
	1 metre/100 cm	= 39.37 in/3.281 ft/1.094 yd
	1 kilometre (km)/1000 metres	= 1093.6 yd/0.6214 mile
	1 inch (in)	= 25.4 mm/2.54 cm
	1 foot (ft)/12 in	= 304.8 mm/30.48 cm/0.3048 metre
	1 yard (yd)/3 ft	= 914.4 mm/91.44 cm/0.9144 metre
	1 mile/1760 yd	= 1609.344 metres/1.609 km
Area	1 square centimetre (sq cm)/ 100 square millimetres (sq mm)	= 0.155 sq in
	1 square metre (sq metre)/10,000 sq cm	= 10.764 sq ft/1.196 sq yd
	1 are/100 sq metres	= 119.60 sq yd/0.0247 acre
	1 hectare (ha)/100 ares	= 2.471 acres/0.00386 sq mile
	1 square inch (sq in)	= 645.16 sq mm/6.4516 sq cm
	1 square foot (sq ft)/144 sq in	= 929.03 sq cm
	1 square yard (sq yd)/9 sq ft	= 8361.3 sq cm/0.8361 sq metre
	1 acre/4840 sq yd	= 4046.9 sq metres/0.4047 ha
	1 square mile/640 acres	= 259 ha/2.59 sq km
Volume	1 cubic centimetre (cu cm)/ 1000 cubic millimetres (cu mm)	= 0.0610 cu in
	1 cubic decimetre (cu dm)/1000 cu cm	= 61.024 cu in/0.0353 cu ft
	1 cubic metre/1000 cu dm	= 35.3147 cu ft/1.308 cu yd
	1 cu cm	= 1 millilitre (ml)
	1 cu dm	= 1 litre see **Capacity**
	1 cubic inch (cu in)	= 16.3871 cu cm
	1 cubic foot (cu ft)/1728 cu in	= 28,316.8 cu cm/0.0283 cu metre
	1 cubic yard (cu yd)/27 cu ft	= 0.7646 cu metre
Capacity	1 litre	= 1.7598 pt/0.8799 qt/0.22 gal
	1 pint (pt)	= 0.568 litre
	1 quart (qt)	= 1.137 litres
	1 gallon (gal)	= 4.546 litres
Weight	1 gram (g)	= 0.035 oz
	1 kilogram (kg)/1000 g	= 2.20 lb/35.2 oz
	1 tonne/1000 kg	= 2204.6 lb/0.9842 ton
	1 ounce (oz)	= 28.35 g
	1 pound (lb)	= 0.4536 kg
	1 ton	= 1016 kg
Pressure	1 gram per square metre (g/metre^2)	= 0.0295 oz/sq yd
	1 gram per square centimetre (g/cm 2)	= 0.228 oz/sq in
	1 kilogram per square centimetre (kg/cm^2)	= 14.223 lb/sq in
	1 kilogram per square metre (kg/metre^2)	= 0.205 lb/sq ft
	1 pound per square foot (lb/ft^2)	= 4.882 kg/metre^2
	1 pound per square inch (lb/in^2)	= 703.07 kg/metre^2
	1 ounce per square yard (oz/yd^2)	= 305.91 g/metre^2
	1 ounce per square foot (oz/ft^2)	= 305.15 g/metre^2
Temperature	To convert °F to °C, subtract 32, then divide by 9 and multiply by 5	
	To convert °C to °F, divide by 5 and multiply by 9, then add 32	
Force	1 Newton	Force exerted by 0.225 lbs
	1 KN or 1000 Newtons	Force exerted by 1/10 ton
Stress	1 N/mm^2	147 lbs/sq. inch
	15.2 N/mm^2	1 ton/sq. inch
	1 KN/m^2	0.009 tons/sq. ft.
	107 KN/m^2	1 ton/sq. ft.
	1 KN/M	68.5 lbs/ft.
Speed	1 Metre/Sec.	2.2 m.p.h.

STANDARD GRAPHIC SYMBOLS

APPENDIX D

FLEXIBLE MATERIALS

 Gravel

 Hardcore

 Hoggin

 Rock

 Rubble

 Sand

 Topsoil

 Water

UNIT MATERIALS

 Brick paving

 Brickwork

 Cobbles

 Concrete – p.c. blockwork

Unit Materials contd.

 Concrete – pc paving units

 Metal

 Setts

 Stone – natural, cut

 Stone – reconstituted

 Rubble stone – random

 Rubble stone – coursed

 Timber – dressed (wrot)

 Timber – rough (unwrot)

IN-SITU MATERIALS

 Asphalt

 Concrete – in-situ

 Mortar

LEGEND

section

213

FLEXIBLE MATERIALS

Grass

Gravel

Hoggin

Sand

Soil

Rock

Rubble

Water

UNIT MATERIALS

Brick – stretcher bond

Brick – basket weave

Brick – stack bond

Brick – herringbone

Cobbles – random laid

Cobbles – coursed

Cobbles – flat, parallel laid

Unit Materials contd.

Concrete – p.c. paving slabs

Concrete – p.c blocks

Concrete – p.c hexagonal slabs

Setts – stack bond

Setts – stretcher bond

Stone – natural

Stone – reconstituted

Stone – random paving

Tiled paving

Timber

IN·SITU MATERIALS

Asphalt

Concrete – i.s. broom finish

Concrete – i.s. exposed aggregate

Concrete – i.s. trowelled finish

Concrete – i.s. marked finish

LEGEND

plan